REIMAGINING THE HUMAN
IN CONTEMPORARY
FRENCH SCIENCE FICTION

Liverpool Science Fiction Texts and Studies, 78

Liverpool Science Fiction Texts and Studies

Editors
David Seed, *University of Liverpool*
Sherryl Vint, *University of California Riverside*

Editorial Board
Stacey Abbott, *University of Roehampton*
Mark Bould, *University of the West of England*
Veronica Hollinger, *Trent University*
Roger Luckhurst, *Birkbeck College, University of London*
Andrew Milner, *Monash University*
Andy Sawyer, *University of Liverpool*

Recent titles in the series

62. Gavin Miller, *Science Fiction and Psychology*
63. Andrew Milner and J.R. Burgmann, *Science Fiction and Climate Change: A Sociological Approach*
64. Regina Yung Lee and Una McCormack (eds), *Biology and Manners: Essays on the Worlds and Works of Lois McMaster Bujold*
65. Joseph Norman, *The Culture of "The Culture": Utopian Processes in Iain M. Banks's Space Opera Series*
66. Jeremy Withers, *Futuristic Cars and Space Bicycles: Contesting the Road in American Science Fiction*
67. Sabrina Mittermeier and Mareike Spychala, *Fighting for the Future: Essays on Star Trek: Discovery*
68. Richard Howard, *Space for Peace: Fragments of the Irish Troubles in the Science Fiction of Bob Shaw and James White*
69. Thomas Connolly, *After Human: A Critical History of the Human in Science Fiction from Shelley to Le Guin*
70. John Rieder, *Speculative Epistemologies: An Eccentric Account of SF from the 1960s to the Present*
71. Sarah Annes Brown, *Shakespeare and Science Fiction*
72. Christopher Palmer, *Apocalypse in Crisis: Fiction from 'The War of the Worlds' to 'Dead Astronauts'*
73. Mike Ashley, *The Rise of the Cyberzines: The Story of the Science-Fiction Magazines from 1991 to 2020: The History of the Science-Fiction Magazine Volume V*
74. J. Jesse Ramírez, *Un-American Dreams: Apocalyptic Science Fiction, Disimagined Community, and Bad Hope in the American Century*
75. Istvan Csicsery-Ronay, Jr., *Mutopia: Science Fiction and Fantastic Knowledge*
76. Tobi Evans, *Reimagining Masculinity and Violence in Game of Thrones and A Song of Ice and Fire*
77. Harry Warwick, *Dystopia and Dispossession in the Hollywood Science-Fiction Film, 1979–2017: The Aesthetics of Enclosure*

REIMAGINING THE HUMAN IN CONTEMPORARY FRENCH SCIENCE FICTION

CHRISTINA LORD

LIVERPOOL UNIVERSITY PRESS

First published 2023 by
Liverpool University Press
4 Cambridge Street
Liverpool
L69 7ZU

This paperback edition published 2025

Copyright © 2025 Christina Lord

Christina Lord has asserted the right to be identified as the author of this book in accordance with the Copyright, Designs and Patents Act 1988.

All rights reserved. No part of this book may be reproduced, stored in a retrieval system, or transmitted, in any form or by any means, electronic, mechanical, photocopying, recording, or otherwise, without the prior written permission of the publisher.

British Library Cataloguing-in-Publication data
A British Library CIP record is available

ISBN 978-1-80207-849-7 (hardback)
ISBN 978-1-83624-507-0 (paperback)

Typeset by Carnegie Book Production, Lancaster

Contents

Acknowledgments   vii

   Introduction   1

Part One: Evolutionary and Ecological Shifts

1   From Spears to Spaceships: Alien Encounters in the SF of J.H. Rosny aîné   23

2   Becoming Orangutan: Animal Encounters in the Fiction of Éric Chevillard   65

Part Two: Posthuman Bodies, Posthuman Minds

3   Cyborg Encounters in the Fiction of Jean-Claude Dunyach and Ayerdhal   93

4   Encounters with Posthuman Women in the Films of Luc Besson   123

Conclusion   151

Bibliography   161

Index   189

Acknowledgments

It's hard to believe that I began research for this book in 2016 during my doctoral work at the University of Kansas. Since then, the project has gone through many phases of rethinking and revision as I developed my writing. I have many people, institutions, and awards for which to be grateful as I went down the writing wormhole. This project, in its dissertation phase, would not have been possible without the financial support of the KU Department of French, Francophone & Italian Studies, the KU Graduate Studies' Summer Research Scholarships, or the KU Hall Center for the Humanities' Richard and Jeannette Sias Graduate Fellowship. I am especially indebted to the Hall Center for granting me a private, quiet office space (and with a window, no less) for my entire final year as a PhD candidate, which contributed immensely to my writing progress and successful defense.

My KU mentors and committee members always supported my work and gave me constructive feedback to push me to become a better researcher and cultivate my scholarly voice: Van Kelly, Paul Scott, Diane Fourny, Bruce Hayes, Antje Ziethen. Van and Paul continued to be there for me in the book proposal stage. I can't thank them enough for their feedback and advice via Zoom and email. I am also indebted to my science fiction colleagues and teachers at the KU Gunn Center for the Study of Science Fiction/Ad Astra Center for Science Fiction and the Speculative Imagination, Kij Johnson and Chris McKitterick; I learned so much working with them during independent studies or courses.

Thank you to my colleagues and mentors at the University of North Carolina Wilmington. I started working at UNCW right before the COVID-19 pandemic shut everything down. Preparing a book proposal and manuscript during this time was challenging, so I'm especially grateful to folks who were still able to support me in different ways when much more important things were going on in the world. Brian Chandler deserves a special shoutout here for being an amazing mentor.

I'm also lucky to have a thoughtful and incredibly thorough writing partner at UNCW, Blevin Shelnutt, who read and exchanged ideas with me on my second chapter. Thank you, Diana Pasulka, for your advice and book proposal model. Thank you to my chair, Derrick Miller, for supporting my research endeavors and advocating for faculty in the Department of World Languages and Cultures.

A massive thank you to Katelyn Knox for her invaluable dissertation-to-book summer bootcamp and resources as well as the J.H. Rosny aîné archive in Bayeux, France and the Bibliothèque nationale de France. I am indebted to the French SF specialist who thoughtfully reviewed my manuscript and helped me improve it. Writing and revising can be an isolating and frustrating process, but I found myself in good company with my reviewer (not something I imagine many authors would say) as I reread my manuscript alongside comments that were occasionally peppered with several exclamation marks of excitement or even an encouraging smiley face. It was nice to know that this scholar was on my side and wanted my work to be the best it could be.

Most importantly, I would not have made it through this process without my family. I would like to thank my awesome husband, Ben, who miraculously withstood the chasms of writing despair (and equally celebrated the peaks of triumph, to stick with the metaphor) since I started writing in 2016. Thank you, Mom and Dad, for your love, encouragement, and support in everything I do.

Introduction

In his polemical treatise of author interviews and fictional musings, *Pourquoi j'ai tué Jules Verne* (1978) [Why I Killed Jules Verne], Bernard Blanc begins with a story where the narrator goes back in time with the help of H.G. Wells's time machine in order to commit an act of French science-fictional patricide: Jules Verne must be killed. Finished with Verne's legacy of "scientific junk" ["pacotille scientifique"], Blanc's book is a call to arms evoking the countercultural revolt of May '68, that is, an explosive time of civil unrest in France that can be oversimplified as a generational clash of epic proportions. In Blanc's view, it is time for a French science fiction (SF) that "breaks myths and blows up rockets, that talks about cops and the military today and explains that they are on the wrong side of exploiters or tyrants" (qtd. in Curval 1978).[1] Blanc's narrator accuses the "father of SF" of tainting a generation and spreading an ethos of techno-optimism that fueled capitalist and exploitative imaginaries: "For fifty years, because of you, Jules, we went off and trashed planets! You're going to pay for that. And, still, if only you had been a socialist like your friend Wells! Not even, eh! Typical. Rockets belong to the rich! You need some dough to mount an atomic engine" (1978, 16).[2] This accusation strikes a particular chord in 2021 as Amazon CEO and richest man on Earth Jeff Bezos blasted into low-Earth orbit, thus seeming to bring to life Verne's American Gun Club members who went to the moon and back in *De la Terre à la Lune* (1867) [*From the Earth to the Moon*] – humankind's ultimate mastering of (and

---

[1] "casse les mythes et incendie les fusées, qui parle aujourd'hui des flics et de l'armée et explique qu'ils sont du mauvais côté des exploiteurs et des tyrans." All translations are mine unless otherwise noted.

[2] "Pendant cinquante ans, à cause de toi, Jules, on est allé saccager les planètes! Tu vas payer pour ça. Et si encore t'avais été socialiste comme ton copain Wells! Normal: les fusées appartiennent aux riches! Faut du pognon pour enfourcher un moteur atomique."

escape from) its environment. Instead of prolonging Verne's positivist, redemptive visions of technology's capacity to explore the depths of the Earth or the chalky surface of the Moon, Blanc believed that the cultural and sociopolitical shifts of post-1968 meant bringing SF to the here and now rather than "somewhere else and tomorrow" ["ailleurs et demain"]. To be more impactful, for Blanc, SF needed to shift gears and focus on what was affecting human beings at that moment with the powerful tools of the imagination expressed through SF.

Even though Blanc wished for SF to become more sociopolitical and come back down to Earth, so to speak, the irony is that Verne's brand of techno-optimism – which wreaked havoc on other (fictional) planets – was already wreaking havoc on the ground beneath our feet. Due to human activity and technology, such as deforestation, urbanization, nuclear testing, and the burning of fossil fuels, geologists agree that we have entered a new geological epoch, the Anthropocene.[3] Coined by atmospheric chemist and Nobel laureate Paul Crutzen in 2000, the Anthropocene marks an approximate end to the Holocene era, which began 11,700 years ago after the last glacial period. The Anthropocene signals that humankind has become such a global force that it has made a significant impact on the entire planet, resulting in an accelerating rate of biodiversity loss, mass extinctions, and climate change. Socio-economic, geopolitical, environmental, and energy crises (e.g. climate refugees, food and petroleum shortages) feed off of such ecological shifts (Servigne and Stevens 2015, 3). The Anthropocene, then, creates an ecological imperative to view the interconnected nature of various biological, socio-economic, and even information systems across both time and space.

From the perspective of a scholar trained in the humanities, the physical dangers posed by the Anthropocene – that is, the risk that the planet will potentially become an uninhabitable environment for humans and nonhumans – require a reworking of human imagination and knowledge. As Timothy Clark argues, we can trace "environmental degradation to mistaken knowledge," such as the supposed superiority of the (male) human over the nonhuman world or the notion that resources can be extracted from the planet without impacting the biosphere (2015, 18). Indeed, although geologically speaking the Anthropocene began in 1945, for some humanists and social scientists, this gigantic force of Anthropos could be traced back to nineteenth-century industrialization, European discoveries of the New World, or even the Neolithic era. All

---

[3] See the international Anthropocene Working Group's 2019 report: http://quaternary.stratigraphy.org/working-groups/anthropocene/.

of these potential markers of a new geological epoch imply wielding new technologies in an attempt to master the environment. What's more, scholarship has also investigated who is largely responsible (the West? Capitalism? Rich anglophone countries?) for the existential crisis in which we find ourselves (Haraway 2016; Bonneuil and Fressoz 2016; Moore 2016). There is an impetus to reconfigure the human, previously considered the center of all things, as independent of other complex systems of life on Earth and throughout the cosmos.

Because of its capacity to engage in thought experiments while remaining anchored to our empirical reality, science fiction is a mechanism through which we can reconsider humanity's role and responsibility on the planet – to other humans, to nonhumans, and to future posthumans (who have survived the technological singularity). In the SF works that I analyze in this book, cognitively estranging referents (to use Darko Suvin's famous terms for defining SF) include intelligent aliens, cyborgs, posthuman women, and orangutan extinction as an ecological event that triggers human and environmental degradation. In the case of aliens, for example, the notion that such a foreign entity could exist given that humans have never encountered any represents a cognitive estrangement; yet the representation of said aliens is grounded in cognitive reality with scientific explanation (or extrapolation) with astronauts and space travel, or the implementation of a scientific method in prehistoric times as a way to study the "alien" creatures. The speculative nature of science fiction allows for an exploration of hypothetical boundary crossings and hybridities between human and nonhuman. As Elaine Graham argues, to interrogate representations of the human and posthuman "is to draw out the implicit desires, anxieties and interests that are fueling humanity's continuing relationship with its tools and technologies" (2002, 1). Science-fictional representations are "just as revealing, in their own way, of the ethical and political dimensions of the digital and biotechnological age as are the material artefacts of humanity's technological endeavors," such as CRISPR biotechnology, a gene-editing tool based on sequences in bacteria DNA that could not only fight viral attacks but could prevent future ones (Graham 2002, 1).[4]

[4] In 2011, Jennifer Doudna, an American biochemist, and Emmanuelle Charpentier, a French scientist in genetics and microbiology, were able to use a gene-editing tool based on sequences in bacterial DNA. This technology, called Clustered Regularly Interspaced Short Palindromic Repeats (CRISPR) is "faster, cheaper, more accurate, and more efficient than other existing genome editing methods"; research is already underway to treat single-gene disease like cystic fibrosis and more complex diseases like cancer and

The French have had a lot to say about the malleable and vulnerable status of the human in their stories. My aim in this book is to show how contemporary French science fiction imagines two broad philosophical inquiries into this powerful yet terrifying Age of Anthropos: posthumanism and transhumanism. While the posthumanist perspective calls attention to the interdependence and co-evolution of humans and nonhumans within a complex ecosystem of life, the transhumanist perspective of coping with the Anthropocene offers more pragmatic, tool-based solutions, rather than a reworking of the human imagination. Given the French tradition of interrelations between philosophical thought and storytelling, French science fiction is particularly suited to an ethical and metaphysical analysis surrounding reimaginings of the human. To be clear, my chosen works in this study are not "responding to" or "anticipating" the Anthropocene because, as British author China Miéville puts it, "the idea [that] the text has to be 'about it' on a narrative level is an extraordinarily crude way of looking at things" (qtd. in Miéville 23). In this sense, I follow the same logic proposed by Stephanie Posthumus (2017) or Timothy Clark (2015) whereby any text can be read ecologically, yet I extend it the Anthropocene, as other scholars of speculative fiction have equally done (Carroll and Sperling 2020; Heise 2016; Beau and Larrère 2018). Indeed, the Anthropocene forces the human to confront the geologically and cosmically ineffable expanses of time and space, and as a result, the finitude of human existence. The dawn of this geological epoch ultimately reveals Anthropos to be simultaneously powerful and powerless. As such, I frame my works within Anthropocene themes, such as issues of timescale, evolution, survival, adaptation, and extinction.

This book consists of a corpus of exemplary works within contemporary French fiction and film from the 1990s to the 2010s with a preliminary look at an early twentieth-century author who is a founding father of contemporary French SF, as I define it in this study. The representative works that I have chosen interrogate crucial areas of posthumanist and transhumanist thought, that is, the false

---

HIV ("What are"). However, this poses ethical problems regarding future germline versus somatic gene editing. While somatic gene editing allows changes to be made to the genome of a single person, germline editing makes changes that pass on to future generations. Germline editing delves into questions regarding human enhancement of traits like height or intelligence, even though this level of precision is still far from being technologically feasible. Germline editing also raises questions of which disorders should be considered "defects" and eradicated, which recalls the lasting cultural effects of Nazi and other state-sponsored programs in eugenics.

dichotomies between humans and nonhumans, a major trope in science fiction narratives: Belgian author J.H. Rosny aîné's SF novellas of alien encounters, *Les Xipéhuz* (1887) [*The Xipehuz*], *Les Navigateurs de l'infini* (1925) [*The Navigators of Space*], and *La Mort de la Terre* (1910) [*The Death of the Earth*]; French author Éric Chevillard's ecological novel reminiscent of slipstream and New Weird anglophone fiction, *Sans l'orang-outan* (2007) [*Without the Orangutan*]; French co-authors Jean-Claude Dunyach and Ayerdhal's space opera of diverse cyborg populations, *Étoiles mourantes* (1999) [*Dying Stars*]; French filmmaker Luc Besson's space opera *The Fifth Element* (1997) and posthuman film, *Lucy* (2014). I argue that in their complex blend of transhumanist and posthumanist approaches to living in the Age of Anthropos these works problematize the stories we tell about human technologies and the degrees to which they do or do not allow us to coexist and co-evolve with nonhumans.

The Malleable Human in Posthumanism and Transhumanism

It was during initial discussions in an interdisciplinary seminar on "The Posthuman?" hosted by my doctoral institution's humanities center when I came to the realization that posthumanism, the posthuman, and transhumanism are all terms understood in vastly different ways based on whether one is a trained philosopher, literary scholar, or science fiction author. To make matters more confusing, these terms are used interchangeably in writings by contemporary French philosophers interested in this web of humans and posthumans, such as Luc Ferry and Frédéric Neyrat. What I saw during this interdisciplinary seminar was, in fact, two seemingly opposing ideologies for understanding the legacy of Renaissance and Enlightenment humanism. Moreover, as I read more about the Anthropocene as both a scientific and cultural term, it became clearer that posthumanism and transhumanism could be viewed as broad ideological perspectives to coping with this new age of the Human, helping us navigate the effects of human activity and technology and reimagine what it means to be human during a pivotal time in our species's history.

Transhumanists believe that anything – from the limitations of the human body to the effects of climate change – can be overcome by technology. Both an international movement and an ideology, its principal aims are to physically, mentally, and emotionally enhance humans to reach our full biological potential as individuals. Take the ideas of computer scientist Ray Kurzweil, a famed futurist often cited for his techno-fantasies of becoming one with computers. In an imaginary, didactic dialogue in *The Age of Spiritual Machines* (1999), he writes that computers were once extensions of our minds but "will end up extending our minds" themselves (95). For Kurzweil, language, art, and computers are technologies that are not only extensions of ourselves but important markers of our evolving intelligence and adaptability. Philosopher Nick Bostrom also proselytizes overcoming our bodily limitations, and he defends the morality and rationality of doing so. He notes that biological enhancements could reveal greater cultural values than "low-tech means" of personal enhancement, such as education and moral self-scrutiny (2003, 496). Bostrom's and Kurzweil's ideas showcase how transhumanism engages in a liberatory politics of technology, thus freeing the human body "from bondage to nature, finitude, and the vagaries of disease, decay, and death" (Graham 2002, 9).

With roots in secular, rational humanism from the Renaissance and the Enlightenment, transhumanism amplifies the notions of individualism and personal choice to self-improve. The humanist logic of Michel de Montaigne's skepticism ("Que sais-je?" or "What do I know?") and René Descartes's rationalism (the cogito) illustrate a connection between the idea of the human individual endowed with the freedom of autonomous knowledge and the transhumanist notion of the human individual endowed with the freedom of choice to self-augment. Nevertheless, transhumanism is more often linked to Enlightenment humanism, particularly to that of Jean-Jacques Rousseau. For Rousseau, the human is a "free agent" ["agent libre"], capable of either acquiescing to its instinct, like nonhuman animals, or repressing it (1992, 182–183).[5] As Tzvetan Todorov astutely notes: "Man is distinguished from the beasts, says [Rousseau's] *Discourse on the Origins of Inequality*, as we have seen, by perfectibility, that is, his capacity to become other than he was, by the fact that he can escape from pure necessity and enter the realm of freedom" (2002, 69).[6] Transhumanists exploit "Rousseau's potentially

---

[5] "il se reconnaît libre d'acquiescer, ou de résister; et c'est surtout dans la conscience de cette liberté que se montre la spiritualité de son âme" ("he at the same time perceives that he is free to resist or to acquiesce; and it is in the consciousness of this liberty, that the spirituality of his soul chiefly appears," Rousseaul 2009, 26).

[6] Rousseau 1992, 183: "c'est la faculté de se perfectionner; faculté qui, à l'aide des circonstances, développe successivement toutes les autres, et réside parmi nous tant dans l'espèce que dans l'individu" ("this is the faculty of improvement; a faculty which, as circumstances offer, successively unfolds all the other faculties, and resides among us not only in the species, but in the individuals that compose it," Rousseau 2009, 26–27).

infinite notion of human 'perfectibility',"[7] thus becoming something greater (Ferry 2016, 48). Transhumanism, then, prolongs the legacy of the Enlightenment into the twentieth and twenty-first centuries by literalizing these notions of perfectibility, thus engaging in a larger, aspirational project to "bring about progress through the employment of technology (as knowledge)" (Miah 2008, 89).

Posthumanism takes a markedly different path in its relationship to Enlightenment humanism by bringing together French anti-humanist thought from between the 1930s and 1950s and political animal rights movements from the 1960s. Intellectuals such as Alexandre Kojève, Georges Bataille, and Jean-Paul Sartre saw the division, destruction, and devaluation of human life that stemmed from the world wars as a reason for proposing an atheist anti-humanism that was "not bound by humanism, rejecting Man's prominence as founder and guarantor of knowledge, thought, and ethics, and seeking to offer alternatives to the political and historical impasse they diagnosed" (Geroulanos 2010, 3). The perception of a world philosophically and politically centralized by the figure of "Man," that is, "a conception dating to Descartes and proceeding through the tradition of natural law, the Enlightenment, the French Revolution, and nineteenth-century liberalism and Marxism," was no longer sufficient to explain the denigration of human life in the early twentieth century (Geroulanos 2010, 2). Drawing from the same critiques launched by French anti-humanists, Anglo-American animal rights movements served as a precursor to what would become posthumanism. Indeed, because the animal was always "frightfully nearby," it easily became an antithetical figure for defining the human (Wolfe 2009, 6). This fledgling posthumanism not only signaled a renewed kinship and interest in the biological world but rejected the humanist model of Anthropos as autonomous agent of absolute knowledge (Feder 2014, 226).

French anti-humanist thought gave way to that of the poststructuralists during the 1960s, which continued to heavily influence Anglo-American intellectual life both within and outside of posthumanism studies. In fact, what became known as "French Theory" – that is, the American importation of French deconstructionist thought of Gilles Deleuze, Michel Foucault, Jacques Derrida, and Hélène Cixous in the 1960s and 1970s – served as a foundation for postcolonial, queer, and feminist work by the likes of Judith Butler, Donna Haraway, Homi Bhabha, and Edward Said. It was shortly after this time that identity-based studies and departments in Anglo-American universities began to take shape in the 1980s. Such

---

[7] "notion rousseauiste d'une 'perfectibilité' potentiellement infinie de l'être humain."

studies implicitly rejected the same foundational logic of superiority that the anti-humanist and animal rights activists battled, ultimately reframing posthumanism into what it is widely conceived as today, that is, an "ongoing re-definition of an 'ethics of bodies that matter'" (Miah 2008, 88). Posthumanism argued that the foundational logic of superiority over nonhuman creatures was the same one that fueled discrimination against marginalized human communities, thus "marking them as animal" (Wolfe 2014, 6). Recent research in English literature, critical race studies, and African-American studies utilizes posthumanism and the posthuman as frameworks for examining the dehumanization of black bodies in the antebellum era (Ellis 2018) and the speculative futures that could change the lived experience and status of black bodies (Lillvis 2017). Thus, within Anglo-American scholarship, contemporary posthumanism is a poststructuralist framework in cultural and literary studies for addressing different manifestations of human and nonhuman Otherness.

The irony here is that while "French Theory" heavily informed anglophone posthumanists and transformed American intellectual life, when it returned to France in regurgitated form – both in the 1990s and as recently as 2021 – it was not reassimilated into French criticism for two interrelated reasons. For one, literary scholars in France follow a different scholarly tradition than those in the North American and British academies. Interdisciplinary work – especially with such a traditional French discipline as philosophy – does not typically take place within literary criticism of French and francophone works. Texts published in France by leading SF scholars such as Simon Bréan (2012), Natacha Vas-Deyres (2013; 2018), Irène Langlet (2006), and Amaury Dehoux (2020) have focused on literary history, genre formation, the place of SF in the university institution, and the SF genre's textual function. As a result, these philosophical questions have been prevalent among contemporary francophone philosophers and social scientists like Bruno Latour, Catherine Larrère, Isabelle Stenghers, and Catherine Malabou, but they have not been a part of discussions among literary scholars in France. Second, some French thinkers view posthumanism – despite its substantial ideological support from French poststructuralism – as part of a larger threat from American cultural and intellectual imperialism. Given the posthumanist investment in bodies that matter (both human and nonhuman), French philosophers such as Luc Ferry interpret posthumanism as nothing more than Anglo-American identity politics in a repackaged form,[8] that is "a sensitivity entirely in line with the ideology

---

[8] Similarly, the idea of *le wokisme* or "wokeness," critiqued by those on both the left and the right in France, has now entered the daily lexicon of

INTRODUCTION 9

of 'deconstruction' exported to the United States by 1968 ideologies ['la "Pensée 68"'], this French antihumanism which brought its intellectual legitimacy to the political correctness of American universities because of its criticisms of classical humanism in all its forms" (Ferry 1992, 60).[9] Given the lineage of French humanist thinkers such as Montaigne, Descartes, and Rousseau, this lack of engagement with or outright rejection of posthumanist thought is unsurprising.

Ferry's disinterest in, or even disdain for, the poststructuralist, anti-dualistic thought of thinkers like Derrida and Foucault explains why he and several other francophone scholars interpret the term *posthumanism* very differently than what I have described thus far, or, in some cases, do not use it at all.[10] In fact, some francophone scholars may focus exclusively on transhumanist thought, even when they address scholars who operate within posthumanism. In their *Encyclopédie du transhumanisme et du posthumanisme*, Belgian authors Gilbert Hottois, Jean-Noel Missa, and Laurence Perbal, basing their approach in biology, medicine, and philosophy, offer definitions of "transhumain," "transhumanisme," and "posthumain"; ironically, they have no definition for "posthumanisme." Their definition of transhumanism is that professed by Kurzweil and Bostrom: "a philosophical movement of transition to a later stage in the evolution of the human species, deliberately pursued" (Hottois et al. 2015, 163).[11] Other French scholars use contradictory terms to those used by their anglophone counterparts.[12] Ferry defines transhumanism as the *process* of human augmentation. He argues that

---

French newspapers and politicians who fear another American imposition on French universalism, not only in French universities but in the public sphere in general. For an overview of what led the French government to target Anglo-American "ideas" as a threat to national values in 2020 and 2021, see Traisnel (2021) and Cusset (2008).

[9] "une sensibilité tout à fait en phase avec l'idéologie de la 'déconstruction' exportée aux États-Unis par la 'Pensée 68,' cet antihumanisme à la française qui apporta sa légitimation intellectuelle au politiquement correct des universités américaines en raison de ses critiques de l'humanisme classique sous toutes ses formes."

[10] Cf. Thierry Hoquet's *Cyborg philosophie: penser contre les dualismes* (2011) as an example of non-dualistic, posthumanist thought from France.

[11] "un mouvement philosophique de transition vers un stade postérieur d'évolution de l'espèce humaine, délibérément poursuivi."

[12] Cf. Mattei's *Questions de conscience: de la génétique au posthumanisme* (2017), Ferone and Vincent's *Bienvenue en transhumanie: Sur l'homme de demain* (2011), and Lecourt's *Humain, posthumain: la technique et la vie* (2011), which either ignore the term posthumanism or use it to designate a branch of thought associated with Kurzweil's and Bostrom's transhumanism, which promotes

this strand of thought dreams of "a humanity that is more reasonable, more fraternal, more united, and, frankly, more loveable because more loving – therefore both identical and different from that which has so far bloodied the world with wars as absurd as they are incessant" (2016, 53).[13] This description recalls the ethics of posthumanism that Ferry otherwise ignores. He continues to define posthumanism as the end goal for the biotechnological augmentation of the human and transhumanism as the trajectory toward that goal. Posthumanism, then, results in a completely new species that has nothing to do with the current biological *Homo sapiens* (Ferry 2016, 50).

This question of bodily modification addressed by Ferry as well as by transhumanist advocates is a significant point of contention between posthumanism and transhumanism. For posthumanism, the body physically grounds us to the Earth and to other organisms as part of our evolutionary biology. In other words, the body is an expression of the lived experience of marginalized human Others. For transhumanism, the body's evolution allowed humans to overcome the battle with Nature and increase our longevity. Yet the body remains a hindrance to the path of self-mastery. For instance, the scientists and pioneers in robotics and artificial intelligence Hans Moravec and Norbert Wiener once proposed the transhumanist idea of being able to upload one's mind onto a computer. But leaving the body behind, in the posthumanist view, problematizes the human experience. Although "posthumanism and transhumanism [seem to] stand in stark opposition to each other," the body is in fact a potential point of reconciliation (Posthumus 2017, 129). Posthumanists such as Katherine Hayles and Donna Haraway see the questions surrounding technological enhancement of the human as an opportunity to move past the humanist values that have ironically led to dehumanization and marginalization of the Other, while *keeping* elements of humanism that could lead to a better understanding of Otherness. In this sense, posthumanism "names the embodiment and embeddedness of the human being in not just its biological but also its technological world," which is impossible to ignore, especially in this age of Anthropos (Wolfe 2009, xv–xvi). While in some instances, my texts reveal that transhumanist ideology lacks empathy with the

human–machine integration to the point of the creation of an entirely new species.

[13] "une humanité plus raisonnable, plus fraternelle, plus solidaire et, pour tout dire, plus aimable parce que plus aimante – donc à la fois identique et différente de celle qui a jusqu'à présent ensanglanté le monde par des guerres aussi absurdes qu'incessantes."

(nonhuman, posthuman, human) Other, in others they "relegitimize" the transhumanist dream of disembodiment, instead portraying it as a posthumanist gesture.

Contemporary French Science Fiction: A Paradox

Given the history of philosophical thought's entanglement with literature in France, French science fiction can tell us a lot about this existential crisis of Anthropos as both destroyer and savior of other worlds and bodies alike. As Stephanie Posthumus (2017, 25) observes, French philosophy has a long history of being intertwined with literature, from Voltaire's *contes philosophiques* to Jean-Paul Sartre's existentialist novels *La Nausée* and *Les Chemins de la liberté* [*The Roads to Freedom*], to which I would add the Theatre of the Absurd and Surrealist literature and film. Alain Badiou writes that philosophy draws from literary language and has long preserved a tradition of accessibility for the general public as well as the academic community, which dates to Descartes's *Discours de la méthode* [*Discourse on Method*]. Descartes wrote his 1637 treatise in French rather than in Latin, which was "everyone's language" ["la langue de 'tout le monde'"], Badiou writes. This gesture to make philosophical thought more accessible demonstrates "an originally democratic determination of the formation and destination of thought" (Badiou 2004, 466).[14] Citing Sartre, Rousseau, Gilles Deleuze, Blaise Pascal, and Denis Diderot, Badiou further argues that the French language is a *"material place"* ["*lieu matériel*"] through which philosophical thought flows to "order one's Idea" ["ordonne son Idée"] (2004, 472; emphasis original). Given its longstanding tradition within popular culture, isn't science fiction the *genre de tout le monde* [everyone's genre]? Any contemporary French filmmaker or writer would have been exposed to such important national literary and philosophical traditions during their high school education, where exams on both subjects are required. This fact may explain why longstanding author and editor Gérard Klein differentiates French SF by its "control of philosophy with the important support of psychology" (qtd. in Ledit 2018).[15] That is not to say that French SF

---

[14] "une détermination originairement démocratique de la formation et de la destination de la pensée."
[15] "prise en main plus philosophique, avec un apport psychologique important." Bradford Lyau (2011) argues that novelists of the 1950s were writing within the tradition of the *conte philosophique*, the philosophical tale of the eighteenth century (Voltaire's *Micromégas* and *Candide* being

artists are all working necessarily within philosophical traditions or that all French SF is, at its core, philosophical by nature. Rather, the works I have chosen to examine closely in this book are particularly well-suited to a posthumanist and transhumanist analysis.

Scholars from many disciplines often look preponderantly to modern anglophone science fiction to speculate from either posthumanist or transhumanist approaches on the possible consequences of modifying our minds, bodies, societies, and relationships with other beings (Bostrom 2005; Gomel 2014; Graham 2002; Hayles 1999). Given "the stubborn imperial fact [...] that English is the lingua franca," any written SF not translated into English has risked remaining in the shadows (Csicsery-Ronay 2012, 482). As a result, science fiction "remains bound up with the hegemony of Anglophone culture" (Csicsery-Ronay 2012, 493). Beyond issues of translation, there is also the problem of the common classification of SF as an American genre, as James Gunn argues:

> To consider science fiction in countries other than the United States, one must start from these shores. American science fiction is the base line against which all the other fantastic literatures in languages other than English must be measured. That is because science fiction, as informed readers recognize it today, began in New York City in 1926 [when Luxembourg expatriate Hugo Gernsback coined the term "scientifiction" in the first issue of his SF magazine, *Amazing Stories*]. (2010, 27)

Gernsback's *Amazing Stories* indeed established a way of coherently categorizing SF in the United States (Bréan 2012, 33). I certainly do not dispute the significance of this brand of American SF, a genre in its own right that has influenced twentieth-century SF in France and across the globe. However, claiming that Anglo-American SF is the post-1926 epicenter of the genre not only promotes an Anglo-centric worldview but also suggests that other cultures do not have their own speculative traditions either before or after 1926, as Bréan cogently states: "The birth of science fiction in pulps [like Gernsback's magazine], these inexpensive pamphlets, at the end of the twenties, marks the culmination of an Anglo-Saxon process, the perfected form of which is mostly American. The history of science fiction merges here with

prime examples), rather than within the tradition of literary realism or the scientific romance.

the history of science fiction in the English language" (2012, 34).¹⁶ Of course, given the proliferation of scholarship over the past ten to 15 years highlighting national SF traditions outside of the Anglo-American sphere, many scholars contest this notion of SF as solely an American or British product. Interestingly, some SF scholars have taken this notion further and renamed the tradition "Anglo-French," perhaps in an effort to recognize the importance of French-language SF in formulating the genre in the late nineteenth and early twentieth centuries (Milner 2012).¹⁷ Nevertheless, in my mind, because of the hegemony of Anglo-American SF, it is necessary to examine French SF as a genre paradoxically both apart from and within Anglo-American science fiction. As Elisabeth Vonarburg, a highly accomplished French SF author who emigrated to Québec early in her career, observes: "If, as a writer, I ask myself about the influence of anglophone SF on my own SF, I first and foremost see that, like all non-native English-speaking authors, I am writing both with *and* against it" (qtd. in Mather and Rheault 2015, 128).

Part of the issue faced by most French SF authors like Vonarburg stems from Jules Verne, an author ironically deemed both French and American. Verne was first appropriated into an American canon by Gernsback and then influenced Golden Age American writers. Gunn writes that the

> American character of science fiction occurred in spite of the fact that its major influences were European, first Jules Verne, who may have been the greatest force toward an acceptance of this new kind of literature, with his *voyages extraordinaires*, because he focused his writings almost entirely on the way technology would change humanity's exploration of the earth and the solar system. (2010, 27)

---

[16] "La naissance de la *science fiction* dans les *pulps*, ces fascicules à bon marché, à la fin des années vingt, marque l'aboutissement d'un processus anglo-saxon et dont la forme achevée est surtout américaine. L'histoire de la science-fiction se confond ici avec l'histoire de la science-fiction en langue anglaise."

[17] Andrew Milner writes that science fiction has a "selective tradition" that "goes back only to Wells, Verne and Shelley," whose "particular national contexts occupied a peculiarly central location within the general nineteenth-century literary economy. SF begins, then, as a literary genre located in England and France, which is subsequently exported to other media and other regions" (2012, 155–156). The call for papers for the International Association for the Fantastic in the Arts's online conference in October 2022 sought discussions of the global fantastic "in countries beyond the Anglo-French axis," which not only shows recognition of Milner's observations but seeks to go beyond it ("International Association," 2022).

Jules Verne's absorption into a majority anglophone, yet global literary heritage of SF (e.g. Cyrano de Bergerac, Jonathan Swift, Mary Shelley) is a paradox for two reasons. The first may seem clear enough, yet reading Verne in translation – especially a work like *From the Earth to the Moon* which features the American Gun Club blasting off into the stratosphere – could easily convince an anglophone reader with no prior knowledge that Verne was also anglophone. Second, the French author has had a problematic paternal status for French SF that left a sour taste in the mouth of many French creatives in the mid-twentieth century, as Blanc wrote in his treatise cited at the beginning of this Introduction. When Verne's work returned to France as part of an American influx of SF around 1950, articles began to appear in the quest to find a French SF figurehead and tradition among this literary invasion, with the obvious example being Verne (Slusser 2005, 62). The question of Verne's illegitimate reign ultimately revealed contradictory opinions on the author: he may have been viewed as the French father of SF by default but, ultimately, his (American-tinged) techno-optimism and longtime designation as an author for adolescents (unlike Wells, who wrote "for adults") could not be ignored (Slusser 2005, 62). Tainted by the driving factors behind this dispute, "SF in the Hexagon is perceived as an element of American folklore, devoid of any literary or scientific ingenuity, and whose unyielding icon of SF is the flying saucer" (Lehman 1999).[18]

Yet what the French have mostly viewed as an American genre is, in fact, something more hybridized. While I am not making claims for degrees of "Frenchness" or "Americanness" within my corpus, my intent is to show how the complicated history and origins of French science fiction – including the cultural conditions during which my authors and filmmaker worked – inform the stories they create. Indeed, these artists have all engaged with anglophone culture and SF production to varying degrees: Rosny spent a significant amount of time in London during the height of the Darwinian evolution debate; Chevillard has an elite literary status yet engages with both SF themes and an SF mode of storytelling (much like Raymond Queneau and Boris Vian, prominent literary writers from the mid-twentieth century who were heavily influenced by both Surrealism and SF); Dunyach and Ayerdhal's engagement with hard SF, which is less common in France and more often associated with American writers of space operas and cyberpunk; finally, Besson works

---

[18] "la SF, dans l'Hexagone, est perçue comme un élément du folklore américain, dépourvu de génie littéraire ou scientifique, et dont l'icône indéboulonnable demeure la soucoupe volante."

in Hollywood (usually perceived as a threat to French cinema) and reworks genre expectations and tropes of superheroes and nonhuman female characters. These authors and filmmaker demonstrate the chimeric nature of French SF and its capacity to investigate both the immaterial (the psychological state of the mind) and material (the body) stakes of posthumanist or transhumanist thinking.

Corpus and Chronology

Rather than being quite anti-Verne like Bernard Blanc, the work of the authors and filmmaker I study are *post*-Verne in their utilization of science fiction in our contemporary understanding of the term. Editorially speaking, French science fiction begins in 1950 with the arrival of large collections such as Le Rayon fantastique and Présence du futur, and the magazine *Fiction*. The year 1950 also marks the first use of the word *science-fiction* in French. My choice of *contemporary* science fiction is conceptual and narratological rather than strictly chronological, thus building on the important distinction made by Arthur Evans between the didactic nature of scientific fiction and cognitively estranging science fiction in France. Rather than using science in the same instructive manner as Verne, the works in my corpus use science "primarily as a catalyst for plot progression and special effects, as a verisimilitude builder, and as a means for creating a kind of Brechtian 'estrangement' in the reader" (Evans 2014, 83). I emphasize this narratological difference because it permits a richer posthumanist and transhumanist analysis throughout my project.

Although my focus is on tracing human–nonhuman archetypes in select works from the 1990s to the 2010s, I begin with a preliminary chapter on a critical figure from the French Golden Age of the *merveilleux-scientifique* [scientific-marvelous], Belgian author J.H. Rosny aîné. Rosny's reimagining of the Human on an epic, ontological scale was a thematic difference in a new branch of philosophically inclined science fiction that emerged in France in the 1880s and flourished between 1900 and 1930, *le merveilleux-scientifique*. This corpus of works followed a schema similar to that of British author H.G. Wells's first novels, as Bréan notes (2015, 196). Coined by Maurice Renard, writer and friend of Rosny, in 1909, *le merveilleux-scientifique* is "all about extending science fully into the unknown, and not simply imagining that science has finally accomplished such and such a feat currently in the process of coming to be" (Renard 1994, 400). Referencing celebrated novels by Wells (*The Time Machine*) and Verne (*20,000 Leagues Under the Sea*), Renard distinguishes the British novelist for his ability to use both science and the scientific method to propel the reader into the unknown; *le merveilleux-scientifique* consists of "having the idea of a time machine to explore time, and not about a fictional protagonist who has managed to construct a submarine at a time when real engineers are hot on the trail of such an invention" (1994, 400). Rosny's science fiction, beginning with his *merveilleux-scientifique* precursor, *Les Xipéhuz* in 1887, arguably contributes to a shift from nineteenth-century *scientific* fiction in France to twentieth-century *science* fiction.

I frame the following two chapters, which analyze the works of Chevillard and Ayerdhal/Dunyach as distant literary cousins of the French Golden Age of the *merveilleux-scientifique*; my reasoning for the chronological gap is twofold. All of my texts engage with both techno-scientific change and the *merveilleux* (which could be best translated as the SF term "sense of wonder") in a way that impacts how human–nonhuman encounters unfold within the narrative. This kind of SF wanes in the mid-twentieth century due to both cultural and publishing fluctuations. After witnessing the horrors of modern technology over the course of two world wars, many French authors were uninterested in pursuing the profound possibilities of science that Verne, Rosny, Renard, or postwar American authors showcase in their SF (Bréan 2012, 413; Lehman 1999). Moreover, Bréan (2012) and Lehman (1999) note that this specific tradition of the *merveilleux-scientifique* disappears in the mid-twentieth century due to the post-1950 editorial shift in SF. Lehman even asserts that this long-forgotten subgenre manages to exert its influence from beyond the grave. He writes that *merveilleux-scientifique* authors such as Rosny, Jacques Spitz, Maurice Renard, and José Moselli were the only ones from the period 1880–1940 to be regularly republished in special collections in the second half of the twentieth century, thus suggesting that their creative energy permeated the minds of later SF generations (Lehman 1999, n. 7). Nevertheless, I should clarify that I am not suggesting a direct filiation between Rosny and these later artists in terms of authorial influence. My project is not a literary history nor is it a study of editorial and publishing developments in French science fiction, although I do draw from French scholars' work on the subject. My corpus of exemplary works of contemporary science fiction, rather than *scientific* fiction, allows for an exploration of archetypal human–nonhuman encounters within the context of posthumanism and transhumanism. Given the literary trends and changes in French SF explained above, it is not surprising that these archetypes are dormant at times and active at others.

Visual representations of archetypal nonhuman–human encounters further serve as vehicles of posthumanist and transhumanist thought via both a literary approach to characterization as well as an attention to cinematic form. Luc Besson subverts Hollywood SF genre expectations and tropes, particularly superheroes and nonhuman female characters in film, and is thus representative of the "hybrid" nature of SF produced in France. I examine not only the gendered human and posthuman relationships in Luc Besson's films but also the ways in which Besson uses cinematic techniques to express these relationships; in other words, I interpret his techniques from both posthumanist and transhumanist perspectives. While it is tempting to diversify by also considering francophone *bandes dessinées* or BD (comics and graphic novels), a chapter dedicated to both cinematic and BD traditions would become an unwieldy monster that could not do justice to either genre, as they are both profoundly rich. Furthermore, Besson's films are both able to bridge the chronological jump in my corpus and nod to this major artistic medium of BD in France. Besson pays tribute to the post-1968 *bande dessinée* tradition both in style and content. The films I discuss – *The Fifth Element* and *Lucy* – draw from *Valérian and Laureline* (1967–2010), *The Incal* (1981–1988), and other SF comics from the 1960s–1980s that Besson grew up reading.

Human–Nonhuman–Posthuman Encounters

Rather than attempt to give an exhaustive overview of modern French science fiction works that examine the physical and philosophical crisis of the human, I have chosen works that explore four categories of archetypal, nonhuman Otherness often found in SF, because as Graham observes, "definitive accounts of human nature may be better arrived at not through a description of essences but via the delineation of boundaries" (2002, 11). Each of my chapters is primarily dedicated to a false ontological human/nonhuman dichotomy. The categories of human/alien and human/animal examined in Part One concentrate on ecological evolutions and shifts, thus taking a sweeping look at Anthropocene questions of time, survival, and adaptation. In Part Two, my attention shifts to the Cartesian dance of bodies and minds within a cybernetic, posthuman context of human/machine and man/woman dualisms. J.H. Rosny aîné (1856–1940), Éric Chevillard (1964–), Jean-Claude Dunyach (1957–), Ayerdhal (1959–2015), and Luc Besson (1959–) are all noteworthy francophone producers of SF who "creat[e] fictional worlds in which ontological alterity is literal and not metaphorical," thus "enabl[ing] us to confront the political and ethical crisis of humanism" (Gomel 2014, 26).

Using evolution as a loose guide, Rosny's Anthropocene saga calls into question humanity's own reign from prehistoric times (*Les Xipéhuz*, 1887) to the space-faring age of the near future (*Les Navigateurs de l'infini*, 1925), to the far future of a dried-up Earth (*La Mort de la Terre*, 1910). In the first chapter, I demonstrate that for Rosny, the technological tools of humanity are critical for the species's survival yet engage in a posthumanist approach to the alien Other. Clashes between human and alien species illustrate transhumanist impulses to master biology, including both successes (such as the discovery and implementation of the scientific method) and failures (such as the inability to adapt to environmental changes due to climate change). I examine Rosny's portrayal of empathetic alien encounters through Emmanuel Levinas's ethics of the "face" of the Other (*Humanisme de l'autre homme*, 1972 [*Humanism of the Other*]), where seeing the face elicits a shock and challenge to the Self, thus providing a theoretical, posthumanist framework for examining contact with the alien Other, who may not even possess a face. Indeed, Rosny's human protagonists "see the face" of the alien Other (i.e. they can relate to human-like qualities in the Other while simultaneously accepting completely alien mental and physical characteristics) and recognize the necessary evolutionary shift between species that does not always favor humans, eventually accepting the inability to adapt to a changing environment.

Whereas Rosny's final human protagonist ultimately fails to adapt to changing conditions on Earth and cedes human superiority to the alien Ferromagnetics in *La Mort de la Terre*, Éric Chevillard's human protagonist Albert strives to reverse ecological and evolutionary shifts provoked by the extinction of our simian relative in his 2007 novel *Sans l'orang-outan* [*Without the Orangutan*]. In the novel, where the death of the last two orangutans inexplicably triggers seismic shifts in the environment, Albert, their caretaker, attempts to revive the extinct species by means of behavioral modification and biotechnological experiments. Via Albert's posthumanist efforts to rebalance the ecosystem, Chevillard reverts to an anthropocentric impulse, a heroic, transhumanist endeavor to use technology (in vitro fertilization) to master nature (animal extinction and environmental degradation). In the second chapter, I use the language of ecocritical theory to show how Chevillard positions humanity as irrationally attempting to adapt to a disaster of its own making. While not categorized as an SF author per se, Éric Chevillard is a major contemporary writer who often integrates the techniques of science fiction in his absurdist novels of ambiguous characters that challenge both narrative and human–animal boundaries. Paying tribute to the French literary heritage of Theater of the Absurd writers like Samuel Beckett and Eugène Ionesco, Chevillard relies on the comically strange to propel his hypothetical orangutan extinction to extreme conclusions.

As science and technology become more implicated in the human identities, constructions, and contact with various nonhuman and posthuman Others investigated in my book, the tension and even, at times, synergy between transhumanist and posthumanist thinking becomes more apparent. In my third chapter, I examine human-machine encounters in *Étoiles mourantes* (1999) [Dying Stars], where French co-authors Jean-Claude Dunyach and Yal Ayerdhal (who simply goes by Ayerdhal) envision a diversified population of four cyborg societies. The novel's climax takes place at a dying star, where one cyborg society threatens to unravel space-time itself – a macrocosm of the terrestrial climate crisis of the Anthropocene – by harnessing the power of the star at the expense of three other societies. Ultimately, the protagonists from each cyborg faction must look past their mutual xenophobic repulsion and work together to save the universe; Levinas's terminology of seeing the face of the Other becomes critical here. Using theoretical foundations in Katherine Hayles's critique of the transhumanist goal of disembodiment, I show that a more symbiotic mind-body interface in the novel results in a better capacity for posthumanist understanding of Otherness and interconnectedness. A more divided human–machine interface translates to a transhumanist worldview, where the quest for human perfectibility and using technology to master one's environment leads to a negligent and even aggressive attitude toward human and nonhuman others. Not necessarily part of the literary "mainstream," Dunyach and Ayerdhal are nevertheless highly literary writers whose world-building skills and intellectual engagement with questions of death, memory, and art come together to investigate posthumanist and transhumanist stakes of the cyborg body.

In my fourth chapter, I examine how gender raises new questions about the interconnected body in posthumanist and transhumanist discourse. Luc Besson, a "transnational filmmaker," investigates Anthropos as the male-constructed, posthuman female body within the framework of gendered archetypes in cinema, such as the man-made female robot, the femme fatale, or the hypermasculine cyborg. In *The Fifth Element* (1997), Leeloo is a revered bioengineered being reanimated by humans to save the world of men from destruction. In *Lucy* (2014), Lucy starts as an average human but becomes posthuman in both her physical strengths and intellect when drug dealers surgically place a strange drug into her abdomen. These characters use their biologically enhanced powers to reject male objectification (e.g. their bodies are created or manipulated by men, positioning them as tools), master their male-constructed bodies, and thereby redeem an androcentric humanity in peril in Besson's two films. Using the theories of Simone de Beauvoir, Laura Mulvey, and Donna Haraway, I show how these posthuman women both reclaim their identities and symbolize a female-coded heroism rooted in love. Lucy and Leeloo thus problematize the transhumanist idea that technology is primarily a masculine-coded tool for mastering the body and the environment.

Part One
Evolutionary and Ecological Shifts

Chapter One

From Spears to Spaceships: Alien Encounters in the SF of J.H. Rosny aîné

In 1891, Jules Huret compiled a series of interviews in *Enquête sur l'évolution littéraire* [Survey of Literary Evolution], mostly conducted by correspondence, with young authors recently hailed as *psychologues* or *symbolistes*. The interviews revolved around the emerging question of whether Naturalism was dead. A French literary movement that flourished between the 1870s and 1890s, Naturalism insisted on a scientific approach to the novel by examining the deterministic relationship between characters and their environmental milieu. Naturalists rejected any form of idealism and insisted on materialist, rather than theological, reasons for the tragic fall of their contemptible, listless protagonists (White 2011, 522). J.H. Rosny aîné (1856–1940), a French-speaking Belgian and relatively new author, believed that Naturalism's demise had been on the horizon for quite some time due to what he understood to be an excess of materialism within the movement (Huret 1891, 231).[1] Rosny's first novel *Nell Horn* (1886), which documented life in the slums of London, had been dismissed by Émile Zola, a major figure in the Naturalist movement. In a letter to Rosny in 1886, Zola expressed his disinterest in reading his work: "Eh! My dear colleague, what would I write if I read your work? Truth be told, what's the point? Why waste both your time and mine?" (Zola 1886).[2] Yet, after sending a copy to Edmond de Goncourt, Zola's literary rival,

---

[1] J.H. Rosny aîné is the pseudonym of Joseph-Henri Böex. He shared it with his brother, Séraphin-Justin François, until their official collaboration ended in 1908, at which time they split the pseudonym into J.H. Rosny aîné and J.H. Rosny jeune. Scholars have attributed the most talent, and all of their works of science fiction, to Joseph-Henri (Ransom 2013, 292; Stableford, "Introduction" 2010, 11). This is not surprising, given the themes of his nonfiction publications. I will refer to Rosny aîné simply as Rosny.

[2] "Eh! Mon cher confrère, que vous écrirais-je, si je vous lisais? La vérité ne peut se dire: puis, à quoi sert-elle? Pourquoi perdre votre temps et me faire

Rosny became a well-established writer, a protégé of Goncourt, and later president of the Académie Goncourt, which continues to award the most prestigious literary prize in France today. Rosny and other disciples of Goncourt went as far as publishing a new Naturalist credo in the form of an open letter, *Le Manifeste des cinq*, following the publication of Zola's *La Terre* in 1887 (Rosny 1921, 219). In Rosny's own words, this gesture was not only "a general revolt against the depressing nature of contemporary literature" but also a revolt "against a Master [...] powerful because of his talent but with such narrow, petty ideas [that] endlessly irritated me with their trivial, impoverished theories" (1921, 222).[3]

Rosny proposed instead "a higher, more complex literature ... a step towards broadening the human mind, a deeper understanding, more analytical and more faithful to *the whole* universe of humble individuals, informed by both the science and philosophy of the modern era" (Huret 1891, 232–233; emphasis original).[4] Rather than remaining within what he viewed as Zola's limited scope of humanity's devolution, Rosny insisted on a different kind of evolution of humanity and various other life forms – one that would be neither progressive nor regressive but would explore the unseen forces at work in the cosmic picture of life at all stages of existence (1921, 222). This, then, was the framework in which Rosny wrote his science fiction, the first work of which, *Les Xipéhuz* (1887), appeared shortly after *Nell Horn* and told the story of a prehistoric human–alien encounter. This novella not only shifted away from Naturalism but also from the legacy of Jules Verne in two distinct ways: the purpose and use of contemporary scientific theories and the portrayal of alien creatures.

Rosny believed in the awesome potential of scientific discoveries to reveal hidden stories about the imperceptible. His proto-hard SF heavily emphasizes scientific extrapolation or extending the application of scientific methods to posit a scenario of what *could happen* today

---

le mien?" All translations in this chapter are my own unless otherwise stated.

[3] "une révolte générale contre les tendances dépressives de la littérature contemporaine," "contre un Maître [...] puissant par le talent, mais si étroit d'idées, si mesquin de goûts, m'agaçait à l'infini par l'indigence et la trivialité de ses théories." See Notes and drafts of *Le Manifeste des cinq*. Box number 6: "Œuvre littéraire: manuscrits autographes." Legs Borel-Rosny, La Médiathèque Municipale de Bayeux, Bayeux, France.

[4] "une littérature plus complexe, plus haute ... c'est une marche vers l'élargissement de l'esprit humain, par la compréhension plus profonde, plus analytique et plus juste de l'univers *tout entier* et des humbles individus, acquise par la science et par la philosophie des temps modernes."

or in the future or what *could have happened* in the past.⁵ As Danièle Chatelain and George Slusser have cogently argued throughout their dense translators' introduction to Rosny's work in *Three Science Fiction Novellas: From Prehistory to the End of Mankind* (2012, ix–xiv), contemporary evolutionary science based on both the theories of English naturalist Charles Darwin (1809–1882) and French biologist Jean-Baptiste Lamarck (1744–1829) influenced Rosny's worldview and how he approached SF writing.⁶ Unlike Verne, however, Rosny professed no allegiance to one specific scientific theory, whether evolutionary science or other fields: "I go beyond it, I reform it, I don't allow myself to be influenced by any theories. It's the possibilities of science that I take advantage of. They nourish my dreams" (1921, 12).⁷ His self-professed "extreme taste for metaphysics and science" ["goût extrême pour la métaphysique et pour la science"] ultimately allowed him to reimagine the human and the nonhuman on an epic, ontological scale (Rosny 1921, 11).

Given their similar methods of extrapolating science into unknown territory, literary critics often compared Rosny to H.G. Wells. In his preface to the 1912 publication of his novella, *La Mort de la Terre* [*The Death of the Earth*], Rosny reacts to English critics' claims that Wells was partially inspired by his works, including *Les Xipéhuz*:

> I don't believe that's quite right. I'm even inclined to believe that Wells hasn't read a single one of my works [...] In any case, there's a fundamental difference between Wells and me in the way in which we create new beings. Wells prefers living beings that are analogous to what we already know, while I imagine mineral-based creatures, like in *The Xipéhuz*, creatures made of something else other than

---

⁵ Definitions of hard SF and its genealogy are too complex to go into detail here, but hard SF, as exemplified by the American Golden Age (1938–1946), "should respect the scientific spirit; it should seek to provide natural rather than supernatural or transcendental explanations for the events and phenomena it describes" (Nicholls 2019).

⁶ Rosny was an active member of both literary and scientific circles in Paris. He published three articles in *La Revue du mois*, a scientific journal edited by mathematician Émile Borel: "Les Principes de l'énergétique" (1912), "La Contingence et la détermination" (1914), and "Les Milieux interstellaires et interatomiques" (1920). Rosny was also close friends with Jean Perrin, who won the Nobel prize for physics in 1926.

⁷ "je la dépasse, je la réforme, je ne me laisse influencer par aucune théorie. Ce sont les possibles de la science qui me saisissent et sont la pâture de mes chimères."

what *we're* made of. Or even creatures that exist in a world governed by different forces than ours.[8] (i–ii; emphasis original)

Indeed, Rosny was intrigued by alternative beings and forces that resisted our terrestrial classification of various forms of life. His "poétique de l'altérité," that is, his imagining of genuinely alien creatures distinguished Rosny not only from Wells but also from his French predecessor, Verne, whose fiction does not tend to explore figures of alterity (Clermont 2011, 90; Gouanvic 1994, 47).

Rosny's alien characters are indeed truly strange beings whose contact with humans is meant to examine human nature on a metaphysical and ontological scale, and thus encourages a sympathetic attitude toward the alien Other. This factor makes Rosny unique among early science fiction authors, whose literary portrayals of aliens can range from faceless monsters lacking any dynamic qualities with which humans could possibly identify to benevolent divine beings, to allegorical figures whose outside perspective reveals a specific culture's foolish mores. Rosny's work thus takes a step beyond the aliens of his French predecessors such as Cyrano de Bergerac, Voltaire, or perhaps even his English contemporary, Wells, simply due to "the systematic dimension of an *œuvre* centered on the description of 'different lifeforms,' an expression of a speculative, biological otherness that was quite varied, thematizing often unfortunate encounters between human and nonhuman others" (Clermont 90, 2011).[9] In Rosny's novellas, *Les Xipéhuz* (1887), *Les Navigateurs de l'infini* (1925) [*The Navigators of Space*], and *La Mort de la Terre* (1910) [*The Death of the Earth*], he utilizes the alien encounter trope to reimagine the human as a fallible species, vulnerable to evolutionary processes out of our control. In portraying what French SF writer and editor Serge Lehman calls a "Guerre des règnes" (2011, 7), that is,

---

[8] "Je crois que cela n'est pas juste, je suis même enclin à croire que Wells n'a lu aucune des mes œuvres […] D'ailleurs, il y a une différence fondamentale entre Wells et moi dans la manière de construire des êtres inédits. Wells préfère des vivants qui offrent encore une grande analogie avec ceux que nous connaissons, tandis que j'imagine volontiers des créatures ou minérales, comme dans les Xipéhuz, ou faites d'une autre matière que *notre* matière, ou encore existant dans un monde régi par d'autres énergies que les nôtres."

[9] "la dimension systématique de son œuvre centrée sur la mise en scène et la description de 'vies différentes', expression d'une altérité biologique spéculative très variée, thématisant des rencontres souvent malheureuses entre l'homme et les autres."

an existential clash between different species, Rosny's fiction already operates on the grandiose scale of the Anthropocene.

Despite being a prolific writer, president of the prestigious Académie Goncourt, and having an SF award named after him (le Prix Rosny aîné), Rosny did not receive much critical attention until the 2010s. In the anglophone sphere, Brian Stableford ("Introduction" 2010) and Danièle Chatelain and George Slusser (2012) have done the diligent work of translating and offering critical introductions of Rosny's major works. In French-language scholarship, science fiction (especially French) has been denied academic legitimacy for most of the genre's history, persistently relegated to the margins both as a "paralittérature" and a fan subculture separate from scholarship (Langlet 2012, para. 1). However, as Irène Langlet wrote in the 2012 inaugural issue of *ReS Futurae*, the first journal in French dedicated to French – and some anglophone – SF in various media, things are certainly evolving within the French academy (2012, para. 2).[10] As work on French science fiction on both sides of the Atlantic has increased over the past decade, more specific scholarship on Rosny has appeared, ranging from analyses of the Belgian author's pluralistic, scientific philosophy and prehistoric fiction (Diaz and Hummel 2019; Robles 2014; Clermont 2011; Clermont et al. 2010) to his portrayal of alien–human relations (Scott 2021; Slusser 2011; Gaudreault 2019). The scholarship on Rosny – of which a large portion is in French – tends to take a broader view on his work as part of a larger academic project of making up for lost time, so to speak, by examining broader bodies of French SF texts. As a result, analyses do not tend to offer close readings as I do in this chapter.

This chapter tracks such themes observed by recent scholarship but primarily builds on the significant work done by Chatelain and Slusser (2012) in their detailed, critical introduction, cited above. They argue that Rosny, rather than Jules Verne or H.G. Wells, was the first author to use science in a neutral, "ahumanistic" way in his fiction, which they name "evolutionary ecology." My analysis broadens the theoretical scope of this insight by examining the posthumanist and transhumanist tension across three of Rosny's novellas (two of which Chatelain and Slusser have translated) at different points in humanity's evolution within the Anthropocene. Moreover, I propose a broader historization by

---

[10] Of course, North American and British science fiction has faced similar struggles for "legitimacy" within the academy, but some might say that this battle has been mostly won; for French academics, the study of SF – especially French SF – is a more recent "victory."

1) situating Rosny's approach to the alien contact narrative within French and Anglo-American SF and 2) establishing a literary link between this father of French SF and contemporary French authors.

Rosny's Anthropocene saga puts into question humanity's own reign from prehistoric times (*Les Xipéhuz*), to the space-faring age of the near future (*Les Navigateurs de l'infini*), to the far future of a dried-up Earth (*La Mort de la Terre*). In this chapter, I trace the impact of human–alien contact events on Rosny's human protagonists via Levinas's ethics of the "face" of the Other. These protagonists all come to understand the tragic beauty of a dynamic universe, where humanity is not guaranteed a permanent position as the dominant species. Indeed, this Anthropocene saga ends with humankind's inability to adapt to a changing environment. Ultimately, Rosny's narratives reveal a strange paradox between transhumanist and posthumanist thinking because one species' triumphant survival is another's annihilation. In order to understand why Rosny's depiction of extraterrestrials is so innovative for his time, it is important to briefly look at critical examples of various alien contact narratives within French and Anglo-American literary tradition.

Human–Alien Contact in French and Anglo-American SF

Since Rosny's fiction and nonfiction were based on pluralism and evolution, it is not surprising that he believed in the possible existence of extraterrestrials and incorporated them into his science fiction. He was interested in "alternative evolutions" which could certainly posit scenarios like a crucial moment in humanity's evolutionary beginnings or the evolutionary intertwining of different species.[11] Elana Gomel

---

[11] Rosny's ideas on pluralism and his version of the multiverse (multiple universes), or "le quatrième univers" as he called it, became quite prevalent in his nonfiction essays, most notably "La Légende sceptique" (1889), "Vers le quatrième univers" (1931), and *Compagnons de l'univers* (1934). In the *Encyclopedia of Science Fiction*, the entry on "Parallel Worlds" cites one of Rosny's stories, *Un autre monde* (1895), as a notable example of early SF utilizing a variation of this concept by depicting life forms on Earth that are hidden from human perception. The notion of multiple universes, parallel worlds, or parallel dimensions is "one of the oldest speculative ideas in literature and legend" which appears in many literary traditions around the world (Stableford and Langton 2016). The idea of an alternate reality extends as far back as Plato's *Timaeus* and his reflections on earthly and heavenly realities. Within the French tradition, writers such as Bernard Le Bovier de Fontenelle, Voltaire, and Camille Flammarion explored the concept of many worlds. Fontenelle wrote *Entretiens sur la pluralité des mondes*

contends that alien contact narratives tend to fall into three major categories: confrontation, assimilation, and transformation, which "mark the degrees of engagement with the Other" (2014, 7–8). I propose a modified taxonomy that frames Rosny's novellas within the French literary history of alien encounters before him: 1) communicative and observational; 2) quasi-divine; and 3) confrontational (apocalyptic, imperialistic, or territorial).

Before the birth of modern SF, canonical French authors like Cyrano de Bergerac (1619–1655), a pioneer, and Voltaire (1694–1778), an influencer, used human–alien communication and observation as a template for examining and satirizing social mores. Cyrano and Voltaire used the contemporary literary device of criticizing their own society from an outsider's perspective, which is an invaluable tool that science fiction can provide on a much greater scale by utilizing a nonhuman Other. However, these are simply narratives where humanity holds up a mirror to itself. In this case, the alien encounter trope is only meant for societal self-reflection. Voltaire's and Cyrano de Bergerac's goals were not necessarily to portray a true nonhuman, alien Other. Rather, their alien figures are representative of a radically different human culture to that of France.

In Cyrano de Bergerac's *L'Histoire comique des États et Émpires de la Lune* (1650) [*Other Worlds: The Comical History of the States and Empires of the Moon and Sun*], the narrator, also named Cyrano, manages to make a machine that travels to the Moon, where he meets four-legged creatures called Selenites, whose ways of life and moral values greatly differ from those of Western European culture on Earth. Cyrano, the author, uses science fiction as a framework to examine the relativity of cultures. Any critique of common practice in seventeenth-century Europe can be investigated under the guise of human–alien contact; how would an extraterrestrial view a human being's society? Cyrano's Selenites express strong criticisms of the Church, traditional Aristotelian physics, and Ptolemaic cosmology. Toward the end, the narrator and one of the Selenite philosophers discuss the existence of God. The narrator insists that believing in God does no harm. Why not cover your bases to avoid potential damnation for not believing in God, he asks (Bergerac 2012, 125). The Selenite argues that if God wanted His existence to be known, He would not have hidden Himself from

---

(1686), which focused on explaining contemporary scientific theories to the general public and is presented as a dialogue between a philosopher and a marquise who discuss the heliocentric model of Copernicus and the possibility of life on other planets.

some and showed Himself to others: "Because to believe that he'd play hide-and-seek with humans [...] that sets up a God that's either stupid or mischievous" (Bergerac 2012, 125).[12] By using the trope of alien–human contact, Cyrano is not only able to examine various moral and cultural "truths" from the perspective of the Other, but he can take a step further by questioning anthropocentric thinking through the eyes of the alien Other.

Voltaire's *Micromégas* (1752) is a *conte philosophique* [philosophical tale] that recounts the earthly visit of a gigantic being from a planet circling the star Sirius and his companion from the planet Saturn. While Cyrano builds a rocket-like contraption to fly himself to the Moon, there is no scientific precision to *Micromégas*. As René Pomeau notes, Voltaire is not concerned about scientific rigor. He certainly does not mention a vessel that would allow his characters to travel through space (1966, 125). Micromégas and his Saturnian companion jump on the rings of Saturn and launch themselves onto a comet (Voltaire 1966, 136). While Voltaire was very interested in science and read Isaac Newton's work on gravitational forces, he was less interested in using plausible scientific methods for the basis of his extrapolation (Pomeau 1966, 124).

Micromégas's journey across the universe is the result of his exile; he publishes a scientific study on insects, but it is deemed heresy on his home planet. His travels with the Saturnian eventually lead him to Earth and contact with human philosophers. As with Cyrano, humans are small creatures with big egos: "The Sirian [...] talked to them with much kindness even though, deep down, he was a little angry to see that the infinitely small had a sense of pride that was almost infinitely huge" (Voltaire 1966, 147).[13] Topics such as the meaning of the human soul are argued by Lockian, Cartesian, and Aristotelian philosophers who are simply not able to explain themselves effectively to Micromégas. When an Aristotelian cites something in Greek, and Micromégas admits that he does not understand this language, the philosopher says, "Me neither" ["Ni moi non plus"] (Voltaire 1966, 146). It eventually becomes clear to the reader that Micromégas is a giant next to the Saturnian, but miniscule compared to inhabitants of other worlds. Humans are equally *des micromégas* who can find truth in their reasoning but also make many mistakes (Pomeau 1966, 128–129).

---

[12] "Car de croire qu'il ait voulu jouer avec les hommes à cache-cache [...] c'est se forger un Dieu sot ou malicieux."
[13] "Le Sirien [...] leur parla encore avec beaucoup de bonté quoiqu'il fût un peu fâché dans le fond du cœur de voir que les infiniment petits eussent un orgueil presque infiniment grand."

In order to go beyond this figure of the human Other in alien disguise, the author must try to conceive of physical and mental characteristics that are outside a human framework, which is a challenging task. The writings of Camille Flammarion (1842–1925), both a fiction writer and astronomer, anticipated the major transition from communication with and observation of the metaphorical alien to a "hard SF" alien in French science fiction – in other words, an alien creature based on conjectural science. His first publication portrayed the alien figure as "a distinct being" rather than a caricature of human characteristics (Stableford and Clute, 2015). *La Pluralité des mondes habités* (1862) [The Plurality of Inhabited Worlds] investigated the condition of habitability of other worlds based on astronomy, physiology, and natural philosophy. Flammarion's belief in extraterrestrials was deeply rooted in both science and mysticism, especially the thought of Emmanuel Swedenborg (1688–1772) and Franz Mesmer (1734–1815), whose ideas permeated the nineteenth century. Mesmer postulated the existence of a subtle, universal fluid that permeates the universe, which causes the mutual influence of celestial bodies and living bodies (Baron 2012, 41). This *magnetism*, or *mesmerism*, is both a psychic and physical force (Bays 1954, 85). While its applications are intended to be both medicinal and spiritual, magnetism is most of all a cosmological theory that explains the relationships between visible entities like humans, plants, animals, and even celestial objects, an early permutation of posthumanism. Swedenborg, whose pseudoscience was not dissimilar to Mesmer's, believed in the possibility of clairvoyance into the world of angels and the deceased. This world would manifest in the unseen parallels between our material world and that of spirits. Flammarion saw psychic research and the scientific method as two ways to progress to universal Truth. For example, in his novella *Lumen* (1887) a human being meets the soul of an alien that has been reincarnated on different planets and can travel at the speed of light. Empirical observations are mixed with reflections on the ecospheres of alien planets and how human perception can change with time travel – a prescient understanding of time dilation within Einstein's 1905 theory of special relativity.

Flammarion's work anticipates Rosny's brand of hard science appreciation mixed with a sense of admiration and wonder for the unknown. As an astronomer, Flammarion believed in the importance of this scientific field because he thought that one day humans could live elsewhere in the universe through reincarnation. While Rosny equally understood the importance of astronomy, among many other sciences, it was for different reasons. For him, astronomy could provide "a measuring-device by virtue of which humans could appreciate the true magnitude of creation – a magnitude that inspired [him] to a kind of metaphysical extrapolation very different from Flammarion's, and allowed him to develop an even more distinctive view of humankind's place in Cosmic nature" (Stableford 2002, 20). Rosny was, perhaps paradoxically, able to blend metaphysical extrapolation with a hard SF utilization of the alien trope.

Rosny's SF work, like Flammarion's, is representative of the cognitive shift in the nineteenth century that was brought about by discoveries in natural history. The medieval Christian notion of time, for instance, which conceived of a biblical history of 6,000 years, operated on a distinctly human scale (Rose 1981, 96). Yet, thanks to discovery of the Neanderthal and Darwin's formulation of the human as part of a natural history of evolution, humanity could no longer escape the notion that it was embedded in natural processes on a time scale that seemed unfathomable. If we could synthesize the early nineteenth century into a single concept, it would be a "redefined reality as the historical process of becoming," that is, a period of social, technological, and spiritual progress (Rose 1981, 98). The "revolution in natural history" in the latter part of the century established a sense of ironic alienation from nature, despite the undeniable link with the natural environment, as new discoveries had demonstrated; this provoked a sense of malaise that humanity would perhaps share the same fate as other species that had gone extinct (Rose 1981, 98–99).[14]

An existential malaise about the human species as a whole gave rise to narratives of human–alien conflict in Anglo-American science fiction as well, with H.G. Wells's *War of the Worlds* (1897) a prime example. *War of the Worlds* set a precedent for the utilization of the alien Other in Anglo-American SF as a violent, monstrous being that was representative of the enemy human Other (Gomel 2014, 28). In other words, this creature was an allegory for all perceived enemies in real-world, human conflicts. War between aliens and humans is ultimately a portrayal of good versus evil, which only exacerbates the boundaries of identity between the two. A further example would be *The Puppet Masters* (1951) by American author Robert Heinlein, where parasitic aliens invade Earth and control the minds of humans. This situation is explicitly symbolic of the Red Scare during the Cold War between the United States and the Soviet Union in the 1940s and 1950s. Wells and Heinlein thus use the

---

[14] While interested in the vast expanses of time and space, including our possible telepathic and spiritual connections with alien beings, Flammarion also shared this concern for the future of humankind, as in *La Fin du monde* (1894).

trope to portray the more monstrous qualities of humans, as opposed to a demonstration of the relativity of cultural mores that we see in early French literary history of human–alien contact. This dialectic between good and evil within the human/alien opposition continued to be utilized in the Golden Age of American science fiction (1938–1946), where SF became more widespread and of interest to the general public. Ultimately, Rosny's stories touch on this sense of conflict between humans and aliens evoked from the time of Wells to the American Golden Age. At the same time, Rosny pays tribute to the French SF traditions of communication and observation while blending metaphysical experiences that transcend the daily terrestrial life of his protagonists.

Les Xipéhuz

In Rosny's Anthropocene saga, the Xipéhuz symbolize the nascent human ingenuity of the scientific method. After countless humans are inexplicably slaughtered by intelligent, inorganic life forms in the novella, the prehistoric tribe of Pjehou turns to the protagonist, Bakhoûn. As a modern, rational man before his time, Bakhoûn uses the scientific method to study the Xipéhuz in order to find their weakness and save humanity from extinction. In other words, he utilizes the "tool" of human reason to observe, hypothesize, and experiment when studying the alien creatures. By anachronistically attributing the scientific method to a prehistoric period, Rosny emphasizes the importance of the notion of human reason, instead of divine providence, as a defining factor in human exceptionalism. Two thousand years of Platonic-Christian thought emphasized the human as a "rational animal," yet still physically weak (Fromm 1996, 30). The genealogy of the Scientific Revolution and the Industrial Revolution continued this narrative of positivist science and reason as contributing factors to human exceptionalism and human dominance over Nature, previously an entity that reminded humanity of its own fallibility and eventual mortality. As mentioned above, the discoveries in natural history and geology in the nineteenth century complicated such notions of human dominance over nonhuman creatures. The human was then implicated in the natural progression of life on the planet. How, then, could we deny our tentacular connections with nonhuman life?

Bakhoûn's study represents this paradoxical situation, establishing human superiority and the ability to adapt to a life-threatening situation. His method allows for a rational inquiry into the life of the nonhuman Other instead of its vilification or deification. Unlike other members of his tribe, Bakhoûn is able to accept both the relatable, anthropomorphic qualities of the Xipéhuz and those that he cannot understand. Bakhoûn's posthumanist understanding of the alien Other quickly reveals itself to be incompatible with the overarching conflict of the narrative because only one species can survive in *Les Xipéhuz*. Bakhoûn organizes the attack on the alien forms after discovering how to kill them, but his post-battle lament questions a universe where he cannot coexist with an alien creature. Bakhoûn ultimately becomes a vehicle for posthumanist thought, the recognition that the nonhuman Xipéhuz are neither more nor less worthy of survival than humans. While humanity is victorious in this battle of two kingdoms, in the ecological and evolutionary framework of Rosny's universe, humanity is never guaranteed a permanent, superior position.

The Tribe's Encounter: Fear of the Alien Other

Although the novella gradually favors a rational view of the alien Other that emphasizes empirical evidence based on observation, *Les Xipéhuz* begins with a similar binary to that seen in Wells's *War of the Worlds*. Rosny evokes a similar irrational fear of the Other, and his heterodiegetic narrator even satirizes the alien encounter trope by noting what is clearly, for an informed late nineteenth-century reader, an irrational reaction by the Pjehou tribe. The unfamiliarity of the aliens' shape stuns the prehistoric humans, practically immobilizing them. Rosny uses the language of superstition ("superstitieuse" and "ensorcellement") to underline the tribe's perception of the Xipéhuz, which are originally called "les Formes":

> The tribe looked on, awestruck. A superstitious fear paralyzed the bravest among them. It grew even more as the Forms began to undulate in the grayish shadows of the clearing [...] The tribe, spellbound by this spectacle, moved not at all, continued to look on. The Forms hit them. The shock was tremendous. Whole clusters of warriors, women, children collapsed to the floor of the forest, mysteriously struck down as if by the sword of lightning. (2012, 4)[15]

---

[15] Translated from the French by George Slusser and Danièle Chatelain. "La tribu regardait, ébahie. Une superstitieuse crainte figeait les plus braves, grossissante encore quand les Formes se prirent à onduler dans les ombres grises de la clairière [...] Toute la tribu, dans l'ensorcellement de ce prodige,

Fear and superstition then transition to the attribution of magical and divine powers. For an ancient civilization such as the Pjehou tribe, the alien evokes Freud's description of an animistic view of the universe, including "the attribution of carefully graded magical powers (*mana*) to alien persons and things" (2003, 147). The Great Priest of the Pjehou tribe quickly attributes divine powers to the Xipéhuz (Rosny 1973, 14–15). When he orders the sacrifice of various animals to assuage the murderous Xipéhuz, he cries out: "Are you appeased, O Gods?" ["Êtes-vous apaisés, ô dieux?"] (2012, 7; 1973, 17). Rosny depicts this rite as unsuccessful and resulting in only more human deaths, thus mimicking a scenario of colonial conquest. Indeed, encounters between different societies, such as between Europeans and indigenous peoples in the Americas, have led to disease, religious conversions, and massacres. For instance, the leader of the Aztecs in the sixteenth century, Montezuma, "mistook the explorer Hernando Cortez for the lost god Quetzalcoatl and delivered his civilization to the Spanish conquistadors" (Harrison 2011, 661).

Believing an unknown, alien figure to be a divinity is a common science fiction trope that appears in Anglo-American novels in the twentieth century, such as Arthur C. Clarke's *Childhood's End* (1953), James Gunn's *The Listeners* (1972), and Carl Sagan's *Contact* (1985). In *Childhood's End*, multiple visits to Earth by an ostensibly benevolent extraterrestrial race with red horns, wings, and a tail reveal a cogent explanation for humanity's primal fears of what it thought to be a demonic creature. Both *The Listeners* and *Contact* have religious undertones when an astronomer receives a complex radio signal from outer space, and Christian leaders interpret it as a message from God. These twentieth-century works encourage us to speculate on human loneliness and our place in the universe by evoking voices in the sky in the form of radio waves. The Xipéhuz, however, do not possess this ethereal otherworldliness; their threatening existence takes on a terrestrial reality. Misinterpreting them as gods in a prehistoric, prescientific context anticipates this divine alien paradigm set in twentieth-century high-tech culture, where science and technology have alienated humanity instead of saving it from extinction.

Humanity's endangerment in *Les Xipéhuz* becomes a sobering reality as territorial invasions affect other neighboring tribes. There is finally a collective realization that humanity is in danger of complete annihilation

---

ne bougeait point, continuait à regarder, et les Formes l'abordèrent. Le choc fut épouvantable. Guerriers, femmes, enfants, par grappes, croulaient sur le sol de la forêt, mystérieusement frappés comme du glaive de la foudre" (Rosny 1973, 7–8).

and, furthermore, that its fallibility is exposed: "From that day on a sinister tale, corrosive, mysterious, spread from tribe to tribe, whispered from ear to ear, at night, beneath the vast star-filled Mesopotamian sky. Mankind was *going to perish*! The *Other*, ever growing larger, in the forest, on the plains, indestructible, day by day would devour the fallen race!" (Rosny 2012, 8; emphasis original).[16] This threat establishes a very clear divide between humans and the Xipéhuz, explicitly distinguishing them as the indestructible "other" who "devour" the human race. As "the subtle enemy" ["le subtil ennemi"] (Rosny 2012, 7; 1973, 18) they are visible, Wellsian monsters.

Bakhoûn's Encounter: Scientific Observation of the Alien Other

Although Rosny's prehistoric tribe believes the alien (whether terrestrial or extraterrestrial) invaders to be hostile, Bakhoûn represents a more nuanced, scientific approach to the us-versus-them scenario typical of an alien encounter in SF of this period. His character encourages reflection on how the Other can be understood by the human Self. After the devastation of the Pjehou tribe, its members are forced to turn to Bakhoûn, who is exceptional because of his modern beliefs. When he is first introduced, he is described as "an extraordinary man" ["un homme extraordinaire"], very distinct from the rest of the tribe. He lives "the life of Eden" ["la vie d'Eden"] in "pleasant solitude" ["belle solitude"] with his family, harvesting crops instead of living a nomadic lifestyle like that of his peers (Rosny 2012, 9). Bakhoûn's modern ideas represent a new era of human civilization and the development of curiosity as opposed to the animism of the Great Priest:

> First, he espoused the idea that sedentary existence was preferable to nomadic life, allowing man to channel vital forces toward the development of the mind. Second, he thought that the Sun, the Moon and the Stars were not gods but luminous bodies. Third, he taught that man should only believe in things that can be proven by Measurement. (Rosny 2012, 9)[17]

---

[16] "De ce jour une histoire sinistre, dissolvante, mystérieuse, alla de tribu en tribu, murmurée à l'oreille, le soir, aux larges nuits astrales de la Mésopotamie. L'homme allait périr. L'autre, toujours élargi, dans les forêts, sur les plaines, indestructible, jour par jour dévorerait la race déchue" (Rosny 1973, 20).

[17] "Premièrement, il croyait que la vie sédentaire, la vie à place fixe, était préférable à la vie nomade, ménageait les forces de l'homme au profit de l'esprit. Secondement, il pensait que le Soleil, la Lune et les Étoiles n'étaient

The third tenet of Bakhoûn's belief system is what anticipates his development of a scientific method to observe the Forms, the name he gives the Xipéhuz in his study. His "inquiring rational mind" is the reason why humans can master their environment. At the same time, "Rosny also invokes the dynamics of evolution in order to imagine new life forms that will change humankind's sense of its unique destiny" (Chatelain and Slusser 2012, 39).

Bakhoûn's scientific study is an anthropological illumination of the differences and similarities between humans and the Xipéhuz, including the limitations he encounters in his endeavor to fully understand them. This eventually reveals an internal conflict in Bakhoûn between a sensibility to the alien Other and a struggle to survive. In "The Book of Bakhoûn," he speaks of the Xipéhuz's movement, what they eat, their emotions, their reproduction, their physical senses, form of communication, and how they educate their young. Despite the Xipéhuz's ability to change shape, he distinguishes them after a period of observation and notes their different, human-like personalities:

> My prolonged sojourn among them led me, despite their metamorphoses (the laws governing which vary for each individual, to a minor degree perhaps, but with characteristics sufficiently different to be noticed by a determined observer), to get to know several Xipéhuz with a certain intimacy, and to reveal to me particularities that indicate differences about their persons ... or should I say about their "characters"? (Rosny 2012, 15)[18]

While Bakhoûn hesitates to call them characteristics per se, humanity is his only frame of reference for explaining the different "personalities" of the Xipéhuz. Ironically, in order to better understand them, Bakhoûn must anthropomorphize certain aspects of Xipéhuz life. Yet this is due to the veritable alienness of their community and physiology. Projecting human characteristics onto the Xipéhuz allows Bakhoûn to traverse the boundary between human/alien and locate his own cognitive limits of interspecies understanding.

pas des dieux, mais des masses lumineuses; Troisièmement, il disait que l'homme ne doit réellement croire qu'aux choses prouvées par l'expérience" (Rosny 1973, 21–22).

[18] "Mon long séjour près d'eux avait fini, malgré les métamorphoses (dont les lois varient pour chacun, faiblement sans doute, mais avec des caractéristiques suffisantes pour un épieur opiniâtre), par me faire connaître plusieurs Xipéhuz d'une façon assez intime, par me révéler des particularités sur les différences individuelles ... Dirais-je sur leurs caractères?" (Rosny 1973, 36).

Bakhoûn no longer comprehends the Xipéhuz when he observes certain aspects of their life for which there is no human reference. When he sees an older Xipéhuz sitting among younger ones and flashing various symbols with its rays of light, the young ones imitate the symbols perfectly (Rosny 1973, 37). Bakhoûn anthropomorphizes the Xipéhuz, assuming that these are educational lessons, but he fails to interpret them. His observations indicate a veritable desire to understand the Xipéhuz's education; he marvels at the mystery of the lessons, thus appreciating something completely beyond his human capabilities:

> To me these lessons were marvelous, and of everything the Xipéhuz did, there is nothing that held my attention more, nothing that occupied more my sleepless nights. It seemed to me that it was here, in this dawning of the race, that the veil of mystery might part, here that some simple, primitive idea would perhaps issue forth, would illuminate for me a small corner of this deep dark abyss. No, nothing held me back; for years, I was witness to this education, I hazarded innumerable hypotheses. How many times did I feel myself at that moment on the verge of grasping some fleeting glimpse of the Xipéhuz's essential nature, an extrasensory glimpse, a pure abstraction, and which, alas, my poor senses buried in flesh were never able to pursue. (Rosny 2012, 15)[19]

This remarkably posthumanist maneuver on the part of Rosny emphasizes the limitations of the human body. By characterizing his bodily senses as frail and incapable of fathoming what he sees, Bakhoûn briefly positions the human as an inferior creature. The Xipéhuz's physiological and sociological structures are too abstract and fleeting to be fully grasped by humans, even for the clever and scientifically methodical Bakhoûn. Instead of fearing the unknown or figuring it to be divine and infallible like the rest of his tribe, Bakhoûn's intimate observation of their daily

---

[19] "Ces leçons étaient bien merveilleuses à mes yeux, et de tout ce qui concerne les Xipéhuz, il n'est rien qui m'ait si souvent tenu attentif, rien qui ait plus préoccupé mes soirs d'insomnie. Il me semblait que c'était là, dans cette aube de la race, que le voile du mystère pouvait s'entr'ouvrir, là que quelque idée simple, primitive, jaillirait peut-être, éclairerait pour moi un recoin de ces profondes ténèbres. Non, rien ne m'a rebuté; j'ai, des années durant, assisté à cette éducation, j'ai essayé des interprétations innombrables. Que de fois j'ai cru y saisir comme une fugitive lueur de la nature essentielle des Xipéhuz, une lueur extra-sensible, une pure abstraction, et que, hélas! mes pauvres facultés noyées de chair ne sont jamais parvenues à poursuivre!" (Rosny 1973, 37).

lives transforms his perception of the alien Other. As Gomel states, anthropomorphizing differences in an alien form may allow us to transcend the boundary between human Self and alien Other:

> In the encounter with an alien agency, humanity is confronted with the deceptive nature of Theory of Mind [or understanding someone else's beliefs, desires, emotions], which forces us to see similarity in difference. But the very failure to understand the Other may create the conditions for transcending the self. (2014, 27–28)

Bakhoûn thinks he is able to interpret what he observes as educational lessons (Theory of Mind), yet he reaches an impasse, dampened by his weak, human senses, at which point he can no longer speculate about the Xipéhuz. Rather than exhibiting a sense of frustration or perhaps human superiority, Bakhoûn instead shows a profound respect and awe for the Xipéhuz in the education scene, thus recognizing their "essential alterity" that "cannot be assimilated into the discourse of the Same [or Self] by being humanized" (Gomel 2014, 25).

Within this paradox of anthropomorphizing the alien Other while accepting its strange qualities enters Levinas's ethics of the face, which seeks similar qualities of the Self in the Other. Levinas's ethics of the face-to-face encounter is situated in his approach to the Self that is invested in itself and turns to the world for nourishment and enjoyment (Morgan, 2011, 38; Levinas 1979, 45–46). The Self is not alone because confrontation with the radically different Other, whose experience and perspective the Self is unable to know, beseeches a sense of moral responsibility. The Other exists outside of the Self and depends on the latter (Morgan 2011, 40; Levinas 1968, 174–175). Levinas calls the appearance of the Other the "face" ["visage"] (1972, 51). The realization of the existence of the Other's face is "la visitation," which blurs the boundary between Self and Other. In other words, the Self must see itself within the Other; in fact, it is the face of the Other that brings out intersubjective responsibility, or a sense of fraternity (Hayat 1999, xiv).

Even though, as inorganic beings, the Xipéhuz do not have actual faces, it is important to keep in mind that in a science-fictional context, the Other may not be human, nor would it necessarily have a face. Bakhoûn does not need to perceive emotion in the eyes of the Other's face ("the complete nakedness of their eyes" ["la nudité totale de ses yeux"]), for instance, in order to understand its personhood and thus its inherent value as a living organism (Levinas 1968, 173). Indeed, as Morgan underscores within Levinas's logic, the face is "characteristic of a living thing, an animal or person, and its bodily presence. The face is the most expressive physical manifestation of such a living being's inner self, its feelings and thoughts and attitudes" (2011, 66). Bakhoûn's observation of their educational lessons allows him to envisage a metaphorical face and locate a sense of fraternity with an alien species during his moment of awe at their incomprehensible complexity. It is the combination of a failure to understand truly alien characteristics and an anthropomorphization of those alien characteristics that ultimately leads to Bakhoûn's final regret.

Nevertheless, it is arguably the lack of an anthropomorphic face, as well as an overall aggression towards humans, that makes Bakhoûn's mission of finding a weakness in the Xipéhuz ethically easier to accomplish; for Levinas, it is the Other's gaze that implores the Self not to kill the Other. The gaze forces the Self to see that the Other is not a thing, which highlights an underlying Darwinian struggle for life within Levinas's ethics that echoes the evolutionary confrontation in *Les Xipéhuz* (Morgan 2011, 63). Yet Bakhoûn's core mission does not change: "From the fact that the Xipéhuz were in no way immortal, I was able to deduce that it would be possible to fight and defeat them, and since then I have begun a series of experiments in combat techniques about which I will say more later" (Rosny 2012, 12).[20] Bakhoûn tells the reader that during his study he must be constantly vigilant because the Xipéhuz "did all they could to exterminate us, my brave [horse] Kouath and me" (Rosny 2012, 14).[21] Thus, when Bakhoûn discovers how to finally kill them after a series of experiments of throwing rocks and shooting arrows at them, he is initially elated: "And so, after all, the dreadful Xipéhuz were vulnerable to man's weapons! We could hope to destroy them!" (Rosny 2012, 19).[22] This climactic discovery characterizes Darwinian evolution at work as a large step in humanity's successful struggle for survival. However, Bakhoûn becomes acutely aware of the cruelty of life and the impossibility of interspecies coexistence with the Xipéhuz; he knows that he cannot reach a cooperative position based on science. He immediately expresses "the sorrowful realization that mankind and Xipéhuz could not coexist, that the total destruction of one must be

---

[20] "J'ai dit plus haut que j'avais cru longtemps les Xipéhuz immortels. Cette croyance ayant été détruite à la vue des morts violentes qui suivirent quelques rencontres entre Xipéhuz, je fus naturellement amené à chercher leur point vulnérable et m'appliquait chaque jour, depuis lors, à trouver des moyen destructifs" (Rosny 1973, 37–38).

[21] "ont tout fait pour nous exterminer, mon brave Kouath et moi" (Rosny 1973, 34).

[22] "Ainsi donc ils étaient vulnérables à l'arme humaine, ces épouvantables Xipéhuz! Ainsi donc on pouvait espérer les détruire!" (Rosny 1973, 46).

the terrible condition of life for the other" (Rosny 2012, 19).[23] While this moment does not stop Bakhoûn from carrying out his mission, it prompts a new sense of ethical movement within his conscience that does not fully manifest itself until the Xipéhuz are gone.

Bakhoûn's Regret

After organizing the battles against the Xipéhuz, Bakhoûn finally drops his scientific guise to pose an ethical question. Bakhoûn asks Unique, whom we might assume to be a predecessor of a deity in a monotheistic religion, why life must be destroyed in order to live. For Levinas, religious terminology plays a role in the vocative, intersubjective relationship between Self and Other. He calls the face-to-face encounter "religion," which he associates with imploring, prayer, and *speaking* to the Other (Levinas 1953, 272). In the science-fictional context of a faceless alien, this notion of religion shifts from the Other beseeching the Self not to kill them to Bakhoûn imploring the higher power, Unique, for the answer as to why the universe would place him in such a position: "And I bury my face in my hands and a cry of sorrow arises in my heart. For now that the Xipéhuz have perished, my soul misses them, and I ask of the Unique One what Fatality has ordained that the splendor of Life be soiled by the Blackness of Murder?" (Rosny 2012, 28).[24] By choosing the word "murder," not "death," to describe what happens to the Xipéhuz, Bakhoûn is amplifying his ethical guilt as a result of seeing the "face" of the alien Other. His final reflection addressed to Unique is, in Levinas's terms, a manifestation of a transcendence of the *Moi* or Ego, that is "not able to shirk responsibility" [ne pas pouvoir se dérober à la responsabilité] (Levinas 1972, 54). Even though Bakhoûn's ethical reflection takes place after humanity's victory, his questioning of Unique demonstrates a longing for coexistence and fraternity with a nonhuman species, which moves past the limitations of Levinas's anthropocentric and anthropomorphic face. This marks the beginning of a posthumanist "ethics of ontological transformation as an alternative to [...] humanist

---

[23] "le chagrin que l'homme et les Xipéhuz ne puissent pas coexister, que la vie de l'un dût être la farouche condition de l'anéantissement de l'autre" (Rosny 1973, 46).

[24] "Et j'ai enterré mon front dans mes mains, et une plainte est montée de mon cœur. Car, maintenant que les Xipéhuz ont succombé, mon âme les regrette, et je demande à l'Unique quelle Fatalité a voulu que la splendeur de la Vie soit souillée par les ténèbres du Meurtre!" (Rosny 1973, 66–67).

ethics," which reconfigures the notion of the alien as the unequivocal Other (Gomel 2014, 27).

While emotively Bakhoûn moves beyond his human Self and occupies a position between Self and Other, it is difficult for him to completely reconcile this with the pragmatic need for human survival. In Rosny's universe, both the Xipéhuz and humans are organisms that must struggle to survive. Bakhoûn's painful awareness that complex evolutionary forces are out of his control manifests in his final elegiac reflections typical of Rosny's "lyrisme funèbre," which translates such a melancholic realization into poetic expression (Ledzinski 2019, 105). The protagonist ponders: "Now I am alone, at the edge of Kzour, in the pale night. A half moon of copper color stands fixed above the Setting Sun. Lions roar at the stars. The river wanders on its peaceful course through the willows; its neverending voice speaks of times that pass, the melancholy of things that perish" (Rosny 2012, 27–28).[25] Bakhoûn's sorrow serves as a reminder of Darwinian evolution where, for instance, "the birds idly singing round us mostly live on insects or seeds, and are thus constantly destroying life" (Darwin 1859, 62). As Bakhoûn's final actions indicate, the Darwinian concept of the struggle for life requires "destruction as a necessary check to natural selection" (Robles 2014, 473).

Life prevails, but only for humanity. Paradoxically, a peaceful existence cannot be achieved through interspecies integration. Once Bakhoûn realized this, he knew conflict could not be avoided, despite his desire to do so. He questions the fatality of such a universe where a single entity or an entire species is powerless against its evolutionary forces. By asking "the Unique One" how the splendor of Life could be soiled by the darkness of Murder, Bakhoûn is contemplating the struggle for life, questioning the mysterious forces that propel evolutionary transitions. The Unique One must represent a mysterious higher power, or perhaps it is a divine manifestation of Rosny's fourth universe, a dimension of space-time imperceptible to the human eye. Bakhoûn rejects the animism of his fellow humans in a way that signals the eventual ascent of monotheism. While he does not believe that various terrestrial and celestial objects are divine, he does appreciate them in the modern ecological sense. Instead, he holds a belief in a single higher power that must control evolutionary processes beyond human comprehension. Already sensitive to a larger cosmic system of life, this particular aspect of Bakhoûn's mentality instills in him a sense

---

[25] "Et me voici seul, au bord de Kzour, dans la nuit pâle. Une demi-lune de cuivre se tient sur le Couchant. Les lions rugissent aux étoiles. Le fleuve erre lentement parmi les saules, et sa voix éternelle raconte le temps qui passe, la mélancolie des choses périssables" (Rosny 1973, 66).

of greater humility and openness to posthumanist coexistence between human and alien.

Les Navigateurs de l'infini

Rosny's 1925 novella *Les Navigateurs de l'infini* builds on the posthumanist understanding introduced in *Les Xipéhuz* by sending three human astronauts to Mars, thus blending an anthropological approach to new creatures through careful, scientific observation with an appreciation of both the strange and familiar characteristics of alien lifeforms. As Marc Ross Gaudreault (2019, 141) underscores, the fact that Rosny sends scientists to the red planet rather than the "pugnacious American heroes" ["des héros bagarreurs américains"] of the much-imitated planetary romance of Edgar Rice Burroughs, *A Princess of Mars* (1912), further demonstrates Rosny's vision of the scientific method as antithetical to xenophobia. While the blatant male bravado and imperial ethos of Burroughs's novel – the protagonist battles monsters and villains to win beautiful Martian princesses – is mostly absent from *Les Navigateurs*, Rosny is nonetheless aware of the possible implications of human exploration of a new planet. By situating the novella in a near future where humanity is a space-faring species with the capacity to change the new environments it encounters, Rosny positions humans as potential territorial invaders, or at least disruptors. In other words, humans are now the alien Others. The story recounts three human astronauts' mission to study Mars in the hope of finding intelligent life. They quickly learn that the Martian environment is home to three lifeforms: 1) the flat, spongy, invertebrate species of the Zoomorphs; 2) the phosphorescent Ethereals, which resemble terrestrial aurora borealis; and 3) the six-eyed, three-legged Tripeds. In a state of evolutionary decline, the resigned Tripeds suddenly find hope in the humans' arrival; they ask the humans for help in holding off the territorial invasions of the Zoomorphs in order to ensure their species's survival. While in *Les Xipéhuz,* the alien–human conflict presents the impossibility of interspecies coexistence in humanity's ancient past, *Les Navigateurs de l'infini* situates humanity's near future as a delicate balancing act between interventionism and interspecies collaboration.

Furthermore, *Les Navigateurs* anticipates ruminations on the body – its excesses, its perversions, its connections – manifested in late twentieth-century French SF, as my analyses in later chapters reveal. For Bakhoûn's prehistoric society, the human body was extremely vulnerable to the mortal heat strikes of the Xipéhuz. Yet the bodies of the astronauts of *Les Navigateurs* defy gravity through the transhumanist feat of space exploration; at the same time, the immaterial, sublime connection between one astronaut Jacques, and a Triped named Grace illustrates the dialectic between transhumanism and posthumanism. The astronauts have mastered their bodies, projecting them into the zero gravity environment of space. The human body even functions without protective respiratory equipment in the Martian atmosphere. This transhumanist mastery of the environment transforms into a blend of fascination, repulsion, and wonder in the face of both the human and Triped bodies via the special relationship that develops between Jacques and Grace. Humbled by his interactions with Grace, Jacques recognizes the strangeness within himself and of the human body. Ultimately, the body is no longer something mastered but rather an impediment to an otherworldly experience with the alien Other, which subverts the transhumanist notion that the body must be manipulated or left behind in a project of self-mastery. Indeed, Jacques does not need the materiality of his body to build a posthumanist connection with the alien Other or, ultimately, for the birth of a human-alien child.

Human as Cosmic Force

While the Anthropocene indicates the age of Anthropos, humanity actually working like a geological force on planet Earth, the influence of Anthropos can certainly extend to the cosmos.[26] As representatives of Anthropos, the three astronauts in *Les Navigateurs* are perceived by the Tripeds to be a cosmic force that defies gravity and flies to the stars: "[Grace] judged [humanity] to be much more superior to the Tripeds since we had been able to cross the dreadful interstellar abyss" (1927, 162).[27] Indeed, Rosny's astronauts of the near future are, by definition, transhumanist masters of biology; their physical propulsion through the interstitial space between Earth and Mars demonstrates the emancipatory power of spaceflight. The Tripeds also see the astronauts as capable of changing the course of evolution on a different planet, which extends the terraforming power of Anthropos to another world. For George Slusser, *Les Navigateurs* is a turning point in Rosny's SF because the Tripeds' decline on our sister planet could indicate humanity's future; Rosny's astronauts "now exploit a freedom of movement that allows

---

[26] Cf. Michael J. Gormley's literary exploration of the "Astropocene," a term he coined to examine humanity's role in the universal ecosystem in *The End of the Anthropocene* (2021).

[27] "jugeait très supérieure aux Tripèdes puisque nous avions pu franchir l'effroyable abîme interstellaire."

humanity to put evolution in their favor" (Slusser 2011, 43). Rosny situates humans as saviors of another species, which "mark[s] a turn toward the aggressive anthropocentrism of the coming American Golden Age," such as "Asimov's and Heinlein's visions of mankind imposing its evolutionary destiny on other species" (Slusser 2011, 45–46). In other words, the astronauts are cosmic interventionists. Yet, in *Les Navigateurs*, the Tripeds solicit the astronauts' evolutionary intervention. So while *Les Navigateurs* certainly departs from Rosny's previous work, the author purposefully avoids an easy delineation of portraying the Tripeds as the colonized and the astronauts Jean, Jacques, and Antoine as the colonizers under the guise of a French *mission civilisatrice* [civilizing mission], a French paternalist attitude that emphasized assimilation of colonized peoples. Such a view positioned colonized peoples as children who needed to be educated, modernized, and, most importantly, molded into French-speaking citizens of France.[28]

Once a thriving, complex society with industry and agriculture, the Tripeds have become endangered due to territorial invasions by the Zoomorphs. After such invasions, "little by little, the soil becomes incapable of producing vegetation … it's toxic. The animals are perishing; life is becoming untenable for the Tripeds" (Rosny 1927, 134–135).[29] This crisis has rendered the Tripeds helpless and resigned to their species' fate, a motif that will reappear among Targ's Last Men in *La Mort de la Terre*. The Triped chief expresses a pessimistic self-degradation that speaks to his waning society:

> "We are nothing!" he said. And a melancholy passed over his magical eyes. How much shorter the life of our planet will be than that of yours! The radiant age has already passed … and our Ancestors were never allowed to cross the abysses of the Expanse … Too small and too far from the sun, our celestial body could not have an evolution comparable to that of yours! (1927, 187–188)[30]

[28] This model contrasted with British colonial expansion, which could be best expressed via Rudyard Kipling's justification in his poem "The White Man's Burden" (1899). For the British empire, it was rather a question of governing supposedly barbaric people by force because they were incapable of becoming "civilized" on their own (Ousselin 2018, 86–87).

[29] "peu à peu le sol devient incapable de produire des végétaux … il est intoxiqué. Les animaux périssent; la vie devient intenable pour les Tripèdes."

[30] "Nous ne sommes rien, fit-il – et une mélancolie passait sur ses yeux magiques. Combien la vie de notre planète sera plus courte que celle de la vôtre! Déjà l'âge rayonnant est passé … et il ne fut jamais permis à nos Ancêtres de franchir les abîmes de l'Étendue … Trop petit et trop éloigné

For the chief, the Tripeds have already reached the height of their evolution and now it is time for another species' dominance: "All living things see their demise!" ["Tous les vivants ont leur fin du monde!"] (Rosny 1927, 140). Because of the Zoomorphs' territorial expansion, the Tripeds have been forced to live underground as their species gradually declines; yet by helping the Tripeds fight off the Zoomorphs' continuous expansion, the human astronauts prolong what the Tripeds see as inevitable: "And since our numbers decrease over the centuries, all we want is for the *Others* to give us time. Maybe you will help us?" (Rosny 1927, 140–141; emphasis original).[31] This request is indicative of the transhumanist power of humans – in other words, the power to change the otherwise "natural" course of organic life.[32] Yet the influence of Anthropos in *Les Navigateurs* is not an obvious example of an anthropocentric humanity that scours the universe, intervening in exo-ecologies as it pleases. Instead of humans having recourse to a transhumanist impulse – a "we can fix it!" attitude – it is, in fact, the Tripeds who believe that technology – human technology, in particular – can spare their species an imminent extinction, as it ultimately does.

Nevertheless, the astronauts' decision to ultimately help the Tripeds stems from anthropic weaknesses. They see themselves in the Tripeds to various degrees, which places them in a similar position to Bakhoûn. In

---

du soleil, notre astre ne pouvait avoir une évolution comparable à celle du vôtre!"

[31] "Et puisque notre nombre diminue de siècle en siècle, tout ce que nous souhaitons, c'est que les *Autres* nous laissent le temps. Peut-être nous aiderez-vous?."

[32] Even the potential scientific and technological power of Anthropos presents itself in a small way in *Les Navigateurs*. Jean, Antoine, and Jacques manipulate the chemistry of Martian water to make it safer for them to drink ["transformer l'eau martienne en eau terrestre et de rendre digestible trois des aliments consommés par les Tripèdes"] (Rosny 1927, 154). As a result, they can indefinitely prolong their stay. To the modern-day science fiction reader, this is not a new concept, of course. Plenty of authors have sent protagonists to Mars and other planets to geoengineer them in order to make them hospitable for human life. Terraforming projects in anglophone SF became more prominent in the mid- to late twentieth century with works such as Arthur C. Clarke's *The Sands of Mars* (1951) and Kim Stanley Robinson's Mars trilogy in the 1990s. However, terraforming appeared as early as 1930 in Olaf Stapledon's *Last and First Men*, where the characters modify the composition of Venusian oceans to allow for more oxygen in the atmosphere (Edwards et al. 2018)]. For Rosny's time of writing in 1925, Martian ecology – let alone other exoplanets – was still shrouded in mystery. Yet scientists knew that it was a cold and sterile planet.

Levinas's ethical terms, Jean, Jacques, and Antoine see the face of the alien Other and sympathize with their plight, but they do so with ulterior motives. When Jacques remarks how captivating the Tripeds are, Antoine accuses him of being an "anthropocentric" ["anthropocentriste"], adding that the "Ethereals, even the Zoomorphs, should seem more exciting to you! They're just an equivalent of organisms on Earth" (Rosny 1927, 111).[33] When prompted by Jacques, Antoine admits that he has "the same weakness" ["la même faiblesse"] (Rosny 1927, 111). The astronauts cannot help but feel connected to the Tripeds, even though they are mesmerized by the beauty and sophistication of the other Martian species, such as the Ethereals. Because of the Tripeds' "vertical nature, especially their mentality, surprisingly close to ours, their emotivity, their charm, and above all the charm of their companions increased a sense of familiarity each day,"[34] the astronauts accede to the Tripeds' pleas for help, ultimately viewing them as "our extraterrestrial family" ["notre famille d'Outre-Terre"] (Rosny 1927, 202).

However, this is not the only reason why the astronauts decide to help the Tripeds. They also see the Tripeds' declining civilization as a presage of their own possible future. As I argue throughout this book, science fiction storytelling gives us insight into the place of Anthropos and the nonhuman Other and proposes different ways of understanding both. As Bill McKibben writes in *Eaarth: Making a Life on a Tough New Planet*, "the world hasn't ended, but the world as we know it has – even if we don't quite know it yet. We imagine we still live on that old planet [...] It's a different place. A different planet. It needs a new name. Eaarth" (2011, 2–3). Ursula Heise poignantly describes this notion as having a "science-fiction twist" (2016, 8). Adventures on an alien planet, such as in Rosny's novella, allow us to imagine similar changes more concretely on Earth. Slusser observes of *Les Navigateurs* that "Earthmen, at a much earlier stage in their development, discover a Martian race dying of the same loss of their water. On Mars, however, this loss is not yet a catastrophe for us; it is more a warning, which could allow humanity to change its ways, and perhaps avoid this fate at least" (2011, 41). Indeed, many aspects of Martian ecology and evolution remind Rosny's astronauts of home (1927, 200).

---

[33] "Ethéreaux, voire les Zoomorphes devraient vous paraître bien plus passionnants! Ceux-ci ne sont qu'une manière d'équivalent des terriens."

[34] "station verticale, leur mentalité surtout, étonnamment proche de la nôtre, leur émotivité, leur charme et surtout le charme de leurs compagnes accroissaient chaque jour une familiarité."

Beyond the Body: Jacques and Grace's Relationship

As I discussed in the Introduction, the body is the critical nexus of posthumanist and transhumanist thought. For the former, it physically grounds us to the Earth and to other organisms as part of our evolutionary biology. For the latter, the body's evolution allowed humans to overcome the battle with Nature and increase our longevity. But the body remains a hindrance to the path of self-mastery. In imagining alien beings, whether on our world or another, Rosny clearly had an interest in questions of the physical body, including the senses. You will recall how Bakhoûn found that his frail, human physical characteristics were incapable of comprehending the language of the Xipéhuz. In *Les Navigateurs*, we see a different permutation of the limits of the physical realm in the notion of love for the alien Other, which elicits the power of Rosny's poetic expression to doubly describe what may be indescribable: passion and mysterious lifeforms (Ledzinski 2019, 104–105). While perhaps perceived at first by the astronauts as strange, there is nothing monstrous about the Tripeds. Jacques calls the birth of a child "a poem" ["un poème"] and proclaims that "there is something divine about the primitive birth and growth of these beings" [la naissance et la croissance primitives de ces êtres ont quelque chose de divin"] (Rosny 1927, 159). Jacques's emotional journey of interspecies love takes him from a grotesque view of these strange alien bodies and his own human body to an appreciation of Grace's sublime alien beauty, as well as the sublime nature of their relationship.

Les Navigateurs continues to dialogue with both the French literary tradition and science fiction tropes by ruminating on the grotesque. As I demonstrated with regard to *Les Xipéhuz*, the Levinasian "face" of the alien Other evoked a posthumanist sympathy in Bakhoûn, thus moving away from monstrous depictions of the alien Other in the late nineteenth- and early twentieth-century alien contact narratives. The notion of the grotesque as an exaggeration and hyperbolism of the human body has a long European tradition that extends to the Rabelaisian body in *Gargantua* (1534): "The grotesque body is a body in the act of becoming. It is never finished, never completed. It is continually built, created, and builds and creates another body" (Bakhtin 1984, 317). In science-fictional terms, the grotesque "brings the sublime to earth, making it material and on our level, forcing attention back to the body. It traps the sublime in the body, partly to subvert it" (Csicsery-Ronay 2008, 182). Because of aliens' different biologies and evolutions, they are "reimaginings of physical form – often in ways more repulsive to us than our own, or in ways that make our own seem repulsive" (Csicsery-Ronay 2008, 190).

When Jacques sees the Tripeds for the first time, he resorts to poetic imagery, comparing physical features to terrestrial objects and landscapes. It is important to note that his bond with the Tripeds falls into Levinas's ethical framework of the face, connecting with the eyes in particular:

> But how to describe these faces? How to conceive of their rhythmic shape, comparable to that of the most beautiful Hellenic vases, the lovely shades of their skin which together evoked flowers, twilight clouds, Egyptian enamels? None of those vulgar appendages of flesh that are our noses, our ears, our lips, but six marvelous eyes, compared to which our most beautiful earthly eyes are no more than beetles' wing cases, eyes through which passed all the gleams of dawn, morning meadows, rivers at sunset, eastern lakes, oceans, thunderstorms, clouds ... (Rosny 1927, 94–95)[35]

Interestingly, he calls human appendages like ears and noses "vulgar" or crude, suggesting a partial recoil at the physical human body, rather than the alien Other's body. Jacques remarks how strangely he has adapted to the bizarre Triped faces and how, little by little, all of their physical characteristics began to appear normal: "Oddity of adaptation! I was getting used to those flat faces, lacking that fragment of flesh, fundamentally so ugly, through which we breathe and smell; I got used to this skin so unlike ours, to these strange twigs that replaced our hands" (Rosny 1927, 141).[36] There is no doubt that the face evokes the sublime for Jacques: "We looked at each other in the night; the eyes of

---

[35] "Mais comment décrire ces visages? Comment faire concevoir leur forme rythmique, comparable à celle des plus beaux vases hellènes, les nuances ravissantes de leur peau qui évoquaient ensemble les fleurs, les nuages crépusculaires, les émaux égyptiens? Aucun de ces grossiers appendices de chair que sont nos nez, nos oreilles, nos lèvres, mais six yeux merveilleux, devant lesquels nos plus beaux yeux terrestres ne sont plus que des élytres de hannetons ou de carabes, des yeux où passaient toutes les lueurs des aurores, des prairies matinales, des fleuves au soleil couchant, des lacs orientaux, des océans, des orages, des nuées ..."

[36] "Bizarrerie de l'adaptation! Je m'habituais à ces visages plans, où manquait ce fragment de chair, au fond si laid, par quoi nous respirons et flairons; je m'habituais à cette peau si peu comparable à la nôtre, à ces étranges rameaux qui remplaçaient nos mains."

Grace shone like the constellation of Orion; her life seemed to subtly spill over my face" (Rosny 1927, 165).[37]

Jacques's turn to observations of the physical human body shows a sense of self-estrangement, because "instead of meeting the alien across a barrier of otherness, man discovers himself to be in some sense the alien" (Rose 1981, 181). Jacques later realizes how he always thought that "the human face, with the soft bump of the nose, producing mucus, with the ridiculous appendages of the ears, with that oven-shaped mouth – in short, disgusting because of its brutal function"[38] was no more interesting or aesthetically pleasing than the features of various animals like the boa, vulture, or toad. As he becomes more habituated to living among the Tripeds, his dislike for certain human characteristics grows stronger, and he perceives the repulsive and even absurd imperfection of the human body, using language such as "ridiculous" ["ridicule"] and "disgusting" ["répugnante"] (Rosny 1927, 144). When Jacques asks Grace if she thinks humans are ugly, her response foreshadows how their compassion for each other will transcend not only the human sense of love, but also the boundaries – physical and mental – of a human–alien relationship:

> "Grace, don't humans look ugly to you?"
> "I thought so, at first," she replied, "though that ugliness never struck me as unpleasant. I now realize that your bodies and your faces have their beauty ... You, I no longer know. I look forward to your arrival ... I find an unknown charm in our meetings, which surprises me." (Rosny 1927, 166–167)[39]

Jacques is overwhelmed by Grace's sentiments and explains how he feels their worlds colliding, a manifestation of a posthumanist encounter that transcends material coexistence: "In the limbo of the subconscious, it seemed as if a world was being built, supernatural beings were rising from the depths, a mysterious light was clarifying legends, possibilities

---

[37] "Nous nous regardions dans la nuit; les yeux de Grâce luisaient la constellation d'Orion; sa vie semblait se répandre subtilement sur mon visage."

[38] "le visage humain, avec la bosse molle du nez, producteur de mucus, avec les appendices ridicules des oreilles, avec cette bouche en forme de four – en somme répugnante par sa fonction brutale."

[39] "'—N'est-ce pas, Grace, les hommes vous paraissent bien laids?' '—Je le croyais, d'abord, répondit-elle, quoique cette laideur ne m'ait jamais semblé désagréable. Je conçois maintenant que vos corps et vos visages peuvent avoir leur beauté ... Vous, je ne sais plus. J'attends votre arrivée avec impatience ... je trouve à nos rencontres un charme inconnu et dont je m'étonne.'"

were springing up from creative eternity – and I felt the world of Grace join the dark world of my ancestors" (Rosny 1927, 167).[40] He realizes how much he is attracted to Grace's presence but does not know how to fully express this: "The feelings that attracted me to her are decidedly indefinable" (Rosny 1927, 163).[41] He cannot name it love nor tenderness, nor friendship; he can only describe his feelings as if they were a poem: "How to describe this emotion which mingled the stars with the beating of a puny human chest, which invaded me as the waves of the equinox invade the estuary" (Rosny 1927, 167).[42]

The transgression of this human/alien boundary reaches its apogee when Grace and Jacques have a telekinetic union that surpasses materiality. This union is an act of grace "as a force that intercedes and co-opts the process of evolution" (Slusser 2011, 44). This is the creation of a posthuman that occupies the intermediary position between human and alien. The final line of the novella leaves the reader to assume the creation of life because of their unique union: "Everything ceased to exist. Everything disappeared in this miracle which seemed the very miracle of Creation" (Rosny 1927, 220).[43] This immaterial, ineffable connection unites Grace and Jacques, thus highlighting a posthumanist interconnectedness between human Self and alien Other.

La Mort de la Terre

La Mort de la Terre (1910) depicts the final installment in Rosny's "Anthropocene saga" of human–alien contact. Hundreds of thousands of years in the future, a combination of a drastically different Earth and the ascent of a mineral species, the *ferromagnétaux*, or Ferromagnetics, ultimately results in human extinction. We follow the story of the *derniers hommes*, the Last Men who live in small communities called oases. While many generally accept that humankind's demise is on the

---

[40] "Dans les limbes de l'inconscient, il semblait qu'un monde fut en train de se construire, des êtres surnaturels montaient des profondeurs, une lumière mystérieuse éclairait les légendes, les possibles jaillissaient de l'éternité créatrice – et je sentais le monde de Grace rejoindre le monde obscur de mes ancêtres."
[41] "Les sentiments qui m'attiraient auprès d'elle sont décidément indéfinissables."
[42] "Comment dépeindre cette émotion qui mêlait les astres aux battement d'une chétive poitrine humaine, qui m'envahissait comme les vagues de l'équinoxe envahissent l'estuaire."
[43] "Rien n'était plus. Tout disparaissait dans ce miracle qui semblait le miracle même de la Création."

horizon, the protagonist, Targ, initially has hope that humanity might survive. However, as earthquakes ravage the oases, water becomes a scarce resource, and the Ferromagnetics continue to dominate the planet, Targ finally accepts his own fate and that of humanity.

This posthumanist novella succeeds in decentering the human in three significant ways. First, it portrays the hubris of the transhumanist attempt to master the environment during the "radioactive era" ["l'ère radioactive"] (Rosny 2011, 699). Second, Rosny portrays the strange species of the Ferromagnetics in a sympathetic light. Like Bakhoûn, Targ knows that the alien Other is neither more nor less worthy of replacing humans. Third, Rosny takes a step further than he did in *Les Xipéhuz* and *Les Navigateurs de l'infini* by utilizing a scaled narrative perspective as a way to depict a symbiotic relationship between humans and other forms of life. Although Rosny's other alien contact novellas examined in this chapter demonstrate his overarching vision of what Chatelain and Slusser (2012) have called his evolutionary ecology, *La Mort de la Terre* is the most ecological and the most effective at conceptualizing the geological era of the Anthropocene itself. It reimagines humanity's place within the deep geological time of the Earth by means of both an "alien" encounter and science-fictional narrative techniques, thus permitting Targ to recognize evolutionary shifts and his ultimate inability to adapt to a changing environment.

Masters No More: Human Inability to Adapt to a Changing Earth

In the novella's account of human history and Targ's personal story, there is a delicate tension between humanity's transhumanist impulse to master its environment and Rosny's posthumanist depiction of humanity's eventual failure to adapt. *La Mort de la Terre* operates on an epic spatial and temporal scale, thus positioning humans as geological, rather than simply biological, agents of change; that is, humans "have reached numbers and invented technologies that are on a scale large enough to have an impact on the planet itself" (Chakrabarty 2009, 206–207). The novella's epigraph demonstrates how human technology – specifically, biological mastery on a micro-level – sparked a chain of events that created massive geological change: "Mankind harnessed everything right down to the mysterious force that bound together the atom. This frenzy heralded the death of the Earth" (Rosny 2012, 59).[44] In one sentence, Rosny elegantly describes

---

[44] "L'homme capta jusqu'à la force mystérieuse qui a assemblé les atomes. Cette frénésie annonçait la mort de la terre" (Rosny 2011, 687).

the transhumanist pretension of humans by juxtaposing the mysterious energy that binds atomic particles together with its macro-impact on the entire planet. It was not until 1942 that physicist Enrico Fermi successfully executed a controlled nuclear chain reaction evocative of Rosny's epigraph. Yet, given Rosny's friendship with future Nobel laureate of physics Jean Perrin, whose research focused on atomic behavior, it is not surprising that he anticipated the devastating power of atomic energy if harnessed incorrectly.

The "frenzy" unleashed through the mastery of atomic energy is starkly apparent in the first pages of the novella, in which Targ reminisces about the "sacred times of Water" ["temps divins de l'Eau"], signaling the preciosity and scarcity of this vital resource (Rosny 2012, 61; 2011, 689). The reader learns that

> During these very distant times, during the first centuries of the radioactive era, it was already noticed that the waters were receding; numerous scientists predicted that Mankind would perish by drought. But what effect could such predictions have on people who saw glaciers covering their mountains, rivers without number flowing through their dwellings, immense seas washing up on their continents? (Rosny 2012, 71)[45]

This passage has an eerie resonance with climate change skepticism today.[46] Furthermore, the hubristic lack of action because of humanity's purported mastery of other areas of life that guarantee survival, such as GMOs and the eradication of disease, is reminiscent of the twenty-first century's lack of urgency and sufficient collective action to address a warming planet:

> This horde of people had at its command unlimited energy. They derived it from protoatoms (as we still do ourselves, however imperfectly), and they barely worried about the retreat of the waters, for they had perfected farming techniques and the science of nutrition to such a great degree. They even flattered themselves

---

[45] "à des époques fort anciennes, aux premiers siècles de l'ère radioactive, on signale déjà la décroissance des eaux: maints savants prédisent que l'Humanité périra par la sécheresse. Mais quel effet ces prédictions pouvaient-elles produire sur des peuples qui voyaient des glaciers couvrir leurs montagnes, des rivières sans nombre arroser leurs sites, d'immenses mers battre leurs continents?" (Rosny 2011, 699)

[46] Cf. Greg Garrard, *Climate Change Scepticism: A Transnational Ecocritical Analysis.* Bloomsbury Academic, 2019.

that they would soon be able to live on organic elements synthesized in the chemist's laboratory. (Rosny 2012, 72)[47]

Yet, eventually, the natural forces that govern climate change, as well as the human actions that possibly triggered those shifts, become too drastic for humans to overcome. Targ's ancestors were confident in their ability to manipulate nature, so they did not see a need to be concerned about the changes in the Earth's ecosystem, nor on a microbiological level, for that matter. Despite the elimination of illnesses following the extinction of most animals,[48] diseases began to develop from within the human body, thus demonstrating Rosny's prescient extrapolation of a war on microbes, whether good or bad:

> They did not live any longer: because many good microbes had disappeared along with the others, maladies proper to the human machine had developed, and new maladies had broken out, maladies that people were able to believe were caused by "mineral microbes." Consequently, men found inside their bodies enemies that were analogous to those that had menaced them from without. (2012, 64–65)[49]

Even the physical body cannot escape the exterior forces of climate change, which fully embraces the Darwinian hypothesis, thus repatriating the human into the history of the Earth (Schaeffer 2007, 63). In fact, Anthropos's physical deficiencies become even more apparent as humans become increasingly dependent on birds which have evolved into more sophisticated and intelligent beings. They have "a language that only allowed for concrete terms and image-phrases"

---

[47] "la population humaine […] ne s'inquiétait guère de la fuite des eaux, tellement elle avait perfectionné les artifices de la culture et de la nutrition. Même, elle se flattait de vivre prochainement de produits organiques élaborés par les chimistes" (Rosny 2011, 699).

[48] Zoonotic diseases are very common. The Centers for Disease Control estimate that "3 out of every 4 new or emerging infectious diseases in people come from animals." See https://www.cdc.gov/onehealth/basics/zoonotic-diseases.html.

[49] "Leur vie n'en était pas plus longue: beaucoup de microbes bienfaisants ayant disparu avec les autres, les infirmités propres à la machine humaine s'étaient développées, et des maladies nouvelles avaient surgi, maladies que l'on eût pu croire causées par 'microbes minéraux'. Par suite, l'homme retrouvait au-dedans des ennemis analogues à ceux qui le menaçaient au-dehors" (Rosny 2011, 692).

(Rosny 2012, 63).⁵⁰ Targ and the Last Men rely on the birds, the only animal species left, because of their ability to predict the near future, which helps them anticipate life-threatening earthquakes: "As mankind had not been able to recover its instincts, lost over the ages of its domination, the present nature of its milieu forced it to grapple with phenomena that its machines, inherited from its ancestors, as sensitive as they were, could barely detect, and that the birds could foresee" (Rosny 2012, 63).⁵¹

Rise of the Ferromagnetics

The rise of the Ferromagnetics demonstrates not only an inability to adapt but also the paradoxes of transhumanist impulses in Rosny's fictional world. In contrast to *Les Xipéhuz*, the reader is informed of the origins of the alien species that puts humanity on the edge of extinction. In fact, the "new kingdom could only have been born, therefore, thanks to a human environment" (Rosny 2012, 75).⁵² Indeed, the narrator notes how violet streaks on human-manipulated iron began to develop (Rosny 2011, 702; 2012, 74). Born of human industry after the radioactive age, the Ferromagnetics are the ultimate revenge of Gaia. They are a Newtonian reaction of a living superorganism – the Earth, or Gaia – to excessive technological activity.⁵³ Ironically, humans significantly contributed to the advent of a species that would eventually become sophisticated enough to threaten their existence. The third-person narrator describes the futility of humans trying to be the superior species, underscoring the notion of possession that comes with the transhumanist impulse of mastering biology: "They accepted to live an abject existence … simply so as not to vanish" (Rosny 2012, 110).⁵⁴ Suggesting a sense of

---

50 "un langage qui n'admettait que des termes concrets et des phrases-images" (Rosny 2011, 691).
51 "L'homme n'ayant pu regagner l'instinct, perdu pendant les ères de sa puissance, la condition actuelle du milieu le mettait aux prises avec des phénomènes que ne pouvaient guère signaler les appareils, si délicats pourtant, hérités des ancêtres, et que prévoyaient les oiseaux" (Rosny 2011, 691).
52 "nouveau règne n'a donc pu naître que grâce au milieu humain" (Rosny 2011, 702).
53 Cf. James Lovelock's *The Revenge of Gaia*. Penguin, 2007.
54 "Ils ont voulu se perpétuer dans un monde qui n'était pas le leur. Ils ont accepté une existence abjecte …, uniquement pour ne pas disparaître" (Rosny 2011, 743).

enlightenment regarding the doomed nature of the human species and the futility of attempting to adapt and survive in a dried-up world, the narrator wonders why the Last Men followed in their ancestors' footsteps: "How is it possible that we have followed their pitiful example?" (Rosny 2012, 110).[55]

The fragility of human biology when in contact with the alien Other becomes more apparent in an episode in which a member of Targ's Le Grand Planétaire community dies from exposure to the Ferromagnetics. There is a certain fear and hatred of the Ferromagnetics, described as "an obscure life form" ["une vie obscure"] and "strange magnetic creatures" ["étranges créatures magnétiques"] (Rosny 2012, 67; 2011, 694–695). As if coming full circle with the prehistoric era of *Les Xipéhuz*, alien contact in *La Mort de la Terre* initially portrays the alien Other as a Wellsian monster. Targ's community discovers that Elma la Nomade "had fallen prey to the ferromagnetics" ["était la proie des ferromagnétaux"] (Rosny 2012, 67; 2011, 694) and fainted out in the desert. Mâno, Targ's brother-in-law, exclaims: "The *Others* have *drunk* her life!" ["Les *Autres* ont *bu* sa vie!"] (Rosny 2012, 67; 2011, 695; emphasis original). Elma eventually passes away from anemia like many others who lose all of their red blood cells from the vampiric contact of the Ferromagnetics. After Elma's death, a crowd of observers "grumbled with hatred against the ferromagnetics" ["grondait de haine contre les ferromagnétaux" (Rosny 2012, 67; 2011, 695). While Targ does not hate the Ferromagnetics, he is afraid of them and their ability to not only suck dry a single human life but to eradicate the entire human species: "'This is terrifying,' the watchman [Targ] murmured. 'Were they to get into the oasis, would we not be defeated?'" (Rosny 2012, 99).[56] Targ is the singular enlightened one and does not share his people's visceral fear and animosity of the Ferromagnetics. He is a pensive character, similar to Bakhoûn or Jacques, who wishes for a different scenario that could have avoided this evolutionary clash of reigns. Targ has a desire to coexist with the alien Other, even though it is buried in a need for self-preservation:

> It [humanity] would have to destroy the enemy or make use of it. I fear that its destruction is impossible: a new kingdom necessarily carries within itself means of success that defy the predictions and

---

[55] "Comment est-il possible que nous ayons suivi leur pitoyable exemple?" (Rosny 2011, 743).

[56] "C'est effrayant, murmura le veilleur. S'ils pénétraient dans l'oasis ne serions-nous pas vaincus?" (Rosny 2011, 729).

the energy of an old kingdom. In opposite manner, why might we not find a means that would permit the two kingdoms to coexist, even to help each other? Yes, why not ... insofar as the ferromagnetic world has its origin in our industry? Is this not an indication of some deep compatibility? (Rosny 2012, 77–78)[57]

Targ's Dream: Traveling Through Deep Geological Time

La Mort de la Terre not only positions a posthumanist view of the alien Other from Targ's perspective, it also allows the reader to reimagine the human as embedded in deep geological history. Indeed, to come to terms with Anthropos's existential crisis, we must reconceptualize "collective human temporality" on several different scales: "on the scale of a human history that has generated multiple inequalities between humans, on the scale of a humanity that has become an agent as a species, and on the scale of a geological power that transforms the physical nature" (Heise 2019, 278). While Heise makes no mention of posthumanism, these reimaginings of scale align directly with its mission. Contemporary science fiction has always been able to "scale up the imagination of the human" via nonhuman agents, technological change, and discoveries of new worlds, for instance; in fact, the ability to recount narratives about the human species as a whole is a distinguishing factor of the genre (Heise 2019, 281–282).

One of the major challenges of reimagining the human in the Anthropocene is the depiction of evolutionary or deep geological time. Heise argues that science-fictional strategies such as serial protagonists – "when a work of science fiction tells stories of a leading or at least exemplary individual at a particular moment in humans' future history and then time-leaps to the next decisive period and individual" (2019, 286) – allow for narrative circumvention of the restrictions of portraying

---

[57] "Il faudrait détruire l'ennemi ou l'utiliser. Je crains que sa destruction ne soit impossible: un nouveau règne doit porter en soi des éléments de succès qui défient les prévisions et les énergies d'un règne vieilli. Au rebours, pourquoi ne trouverait-on pas une méthode qui permettrait aux deux règnes de coexister, de s'entraider même? Oui, pourquoi pas? ... puisque tout le monde ferromagnétique tire son origine de notre industrie? N'y a-t-il pas là l'indice d'une compatibilité profonde? (Puis, portant ses yeux vers les grands pics de l'Occident:) Hélas! mes rêves sont ridicules. Et pourtant ... pourtant! Ne m'aident-ils pas à vivre? ... Ne me donnent-ils pas un peu de ce jeune bonheur qui a fui pour toujours l'âme des hommes?" (Rosny 2011, 754).

hundreds of thousands of years (or more) in the space of several hundred pages. As we will see in my analysis of Chevillard's tale of species extinction in Chapter Two, the "extreme contemporary" French novel of the late twentieth and early twenty-first centuries has an abundance of experimental narrative techniques. Yet long before literature such as Chevillard's, *La Mort de la Terre* experimented with narrative perspective in a way that demonstrates deep geological time and the human species's embeddedness in Earth's history – a posthumanist maneuver. Ultimately, Rosny's narrative architecture portrays a symbiotic relationship between the human species, the planet, and the alien Other – the Ferromagnetics.

Given Targ's symbiosis with deep geological time, Rosny essentially shrinks the "scale effect," that is, "phenomena that are invisible at the normal levels of perception but only emerge as one changes the spatial or temporal scale at which the issues are framed" (Clark 2015, 22).[58] Shrinking the scale effect is not only an effective science-fictional mechanism to show deep geological time within the small space of a novella, but it also allows both readers and perhaps even Targ to separate ourselves/himself from the miniscule timeframe in which we exist as mortal human creatures. In the novella's second chapter there is a shift from Targ's third-person, limited voice to a third-person, omniscient voice in the recounting of "the story of the great catastrophes, handed down faithfully from generation to generation" (Rosny 2012, 71).[59] Chatelain and Slusser note that the section that follows "begins with a different speaking voice, that of five hundred centuries of postcatastrophe generations, with a sweep in time that goes from the 'have occupied' of postcatastrophe memory all the way back to precatastrophe memory" (2012, 140 n. 13). Indeed, the focus at this point in the text becomes that of human memory. This omniscient narrator, unbound by space-time, seems to re-emerge in the first person in the same chapter, mentioning "our species" ["notre espèce"] and even using "I" ["je"] (Rosny 2012, 74, 75; 2011, 703). Yet this narrator is familiar with Targ's innermost thoughts. Whose perspective is this, then? Chatelain and Slusser argue that "it is tempting to see this refocusing narrator as 'retracing' the

---

[58] The deep geological time of the Anthropocene could also be thought of as a "hyperobject." Jeff VanderMeer, American science fiction author of the "New Weird" strain since the early 2000s, uses philosopher Timothy Morton's concept of "hyperobjects" to refer to global warming. The term "global warming" itself is "an anchor for something difficult to picture in its entirety" (VanderMeer 2016). Hyperobjects, in my view, are part of the scaling phenomenon that both Heise and Clark examine.

[59] "l'histoire des grandes catastrophes, fidèlement transmise de génération en generation" (Rosny 2011, 698).

evolutionary path that inscribes the rise and fall of humankind, the final compression of this experience in Targ's final 'dream'" at the end of the novella (in Rosny 2012, 141 n. 13). The translators underscore that their interpretation is only one of many; what is important to note is that Rosny's narrative gives us a different perspective of evolutionary space-time. *La Mort de la Terre* allows us, in the words of Heise, to "scale up" our imagination of the human (2019, 301). Rosny does this in a way in which the individual protagonist does not become lost in the deep expanse of evolutionary time. On the contrary, Rosny's posthumanist tale allows Targ to become embedded in the evolutionary history of both the past and future. By giving Targ this narrative "superpower" of understanding collective human memory over deep geological time, Rosny positions Targ as a vehicle of posthumanist sympathy toward the alien Other, the Ferromagnetics.

This odd narrative polyphony culminates in the final pages of the novella, when Targ is the last man on the planet and finally succumbs not only to death but to the notion that humanity's golden age is long gone. As Targ fades into the darkness, "he remained buried in his sadness and his dreams" ["il demeura enseveli dans sa tristesse et dans son rêve"] (Rosny 2012, 120; 2011, 754). Targ's "dream" is in fact a clever science-fictional device that Rosny uses to allow him to travel through deep time, thus reducing the scale effect: "He made, one more time, the grand voyage back toward the beginning of time, which had so passionately enflamed his soul" (Rosny 2012, 120).[60] Targ sees the primordial soup of life from which developed "blind and deaf creatures" ["des creatures aveugles et sourdes"] (Rosny 2012, 120; 2011, 754). Massive creatures such as the giant tiger, the dinotherium, the diplodicus, were all part of an ancient reign of formidable megafauna. As each of these majestic species rose and fall, so do humans: "Now the planet favored man's ascension. His reign was the most ferocious, the most powerful of all – and the last. He became the prodigious destroyer of life. The forests died alongside their hosts without number, all beasts were exterminated or enslaved" (Rosny 2012, 120).[61] Targ's dream of evolutionary time illustrates the various reigns that have existed; in a way, Rosny anticipates the eventual discoveries of the five mass species

[60] "Il refaisait, une fois encore, le grand voyage vers l'amont des temps, qui avait si ardemment exalté son âme" (Rosny 2011, 754).

[61] "Puis, la planète laissa prospérer l'homme: son règne fut le plus féroce, le plus puissant – et le dernier. Il fut le destructeur prodigieux de la vie. Les forêts moururent et leurs hôtes sans nombre, toute bête fut exterminée ou avilie" (Rosny 2011, 754).

extinctions, which only goes to show that human extinction in *La Mort de la Terre* is no more than the "natural" course of life on Earth (Raup and Sepkoski 1982, 1502).[62]

This bird's-eye view to evolutionary history over the life of the planet serves as an effective tool for decentering Anthropos. The human becomes part of a process that operates outside of our own understanding and our own short existence; as a result, the human is no longer the apogee of a teleological view of evolution. Ultimately, what determines species superiority? For Bakhoûn and his tribe, it was the ability to observe and adapt; he found a way to destroy the Xipéhuz and survive. For Targ and the Last Men, the stakes are the same: adapt or perish. While we know that humans have evolved over hundreds of centuries in *La Mort de la Terre* – their chests and lungs growing larger to adapt to changes in the atmosphere (Rosny 2011, 699; 2012, 72) – there are certain things without which humans cannot survive, and Rosny chose the critical factor for the sustenance of carbon-based, human life: water.

Targ's dream ultimately underscores the transferal of life to another, of one reign to another, in the epic saga of the Earth. The final paragraphs of the novella reinforce this theme, where Targ reflects on how "his flesh had been transmitted, *in an unbroken line,* since the origin of things. Some thing that had once lived in the primeval sea, on emerging alluvia, in the swamps, in the forests, in the midst of savannas, and among the multitude of man's cities, had continued unbroken down to him" (2012, 121; emphasis original).[63] Like Bakhoûn and Jacques, Targ is both a careful scientific observer and a poet who sings the posthumanist praises of interspecies connectedness. Reminiscent of the final scene in *Les Xipéhuz,* where Bakhoûn gazes upward and laments the necessary destruction of the Xipéhuz to ensure human survival, Targ ruminates

---

[62] In a lecture given in 1796 on the extinction of the North American mastodon, French anatomist Georges Cuvier proposed the innovative idea that species could even go extinct. Mass extinctions signal rapid, global biodiversity loss, usually caused by major climate events. One of the concerns of the Anthropocene is that we are potentially witnessing another sixth mass extinction. The notion that there have been five mass extinctions in Earth's history was first proposed in the 1980s (Kolbert 2013). For a detailed recount of the current sixth mass extinction, see Elizabeth Kolbert's *The Sixth Extinction: An Unnatural History,* Henry Holt and Company, 2014.

[63] "sa chair s'était transmis, *sans arrêt,* depuis les origines. Quelque chose qui avait vécu dans la mer primitive, sur les limons naissants, dans les marécages, dans les forêts, au sein des savanes, et parmi les cités innombrables de l'homme, ne s'était jamais interrompu jusqu'à lui ..." (Rosny 2011, 754).

over the night sky as he slowly fades into darkness (2011, 755; 2012, 121). Knowing that death is imminent, he accepts his fate and that of the alien Other by lying down in the oasis, among the Ferromagnetics. Finally, Targ meekly offers his life to the new reign: "Then, humbly, a few small pieces of the last human life entered into the New Life" (Rosny 2012, 121).[64] Possessing knowledge of the waxing and waning of dominant species over Earth's history, Targ is better equipped to accept that humanity's reign is over. His life will now become the energy needed for the Ferromagnetics, thus subverting the vampiric, fearful image that his community evoked at the beginning of the story. Targ not only sees the nonhuman "face" of the alien Other but gives up his life to it.

Conclusion

Alien contact in *Les Xipéhuz*, *Les Navigateurs de l'infini*, and *La Mort de la Terre* forces the human protagonists to reevaluate their relationships with other species and their responsibility as citizens of planet Earth or of the solar system. In this regard, Rosny follows the French tradition of the relativity of cultures; as we saw with Cyrano and Voltaire, it is important to realize that one's moral and philosophical views are not absolute truth. The encounter of the Other questions not only our preconceived notions of how the Other thinks, acts, and looks, but also those of how the Self thinks, acts, and looks. Rosny expands upon this tradition of relativity by using the alien contact trope as a modern exploration of how the existence of and encounter with alien creatures could challenge not just human ideas but human existence as a whole. By threatening human existence, either in an urgent way in *Les Xipéhuz* and *La Mort de la Terre* or in the ecological mirror of Mars in *Les Navigateurs*, the alien Other forces a sense of respect and even admiration on the part of Bakhoûn, Targ, and the astronauts. Nevertheless, these situations represent ethical dilemmas since not all species can or should be saved, whether by the hand of humankind or not.

In this chapter, I have demonstrated that for Rosny, the technological tools of humanity are critical for species survival, yet he also engages in a posthumanist approach to the alien Other. Clashes between human and alien species illustrate transhumanist impulses to master biology, including both successes and failures. While ultimately successful, Bakhoûn's story serves as a warning that humanity's reign could end

---

[64] "Ensuite, humblement, quelques parcelles de la dernière vie humaine entrèrent dans la Vie Nouvelle" (Rosny 2011, 755).

at any given moment, thus deconstructing the image of a superior humanity or even a superior alien. In this sense, human technoscience, by means of Bakhoûn's scientific method, proves to be a way to overcome the imminent threat of extinction – a transhumanist mastery of his environment. His scientific method is also a way to view the Xipéhuz as organisms that are neither more nor less worthy of survival than humans, even though Bakhoûn ultimately and regretfully must engineer their destruction. Rosny's human astronauts of the near future are, by definition, transhumanist masters of biology. The human astronauts use their advanced technology to help the Tripeds, whose fate they see *could* presage their own in the future. Thus, their technology encourages life, potentially saving both humanity and the Tripeds from extinction. The love story between the poet-astronaut Jacques and the Triped Grace demonstrates a posthumanist understanding of the alien Other that amplifies the admittedly anthropocentric choice to help the Triped civilization. Through their relationship, we see an oscillation between fascination with and repulsion by both the human and Triped bodies. While Rosny here rejects a transhumanist aspiration toward bodily perfection, the ethereal love between Grace and Jacques complicates the posthumanist conception of the body in which the physical helps establish a human–nonhuman connection. *La Mort de la Terre*'s account of human history and Targ's personal story create a delicate tension between humanity's transhumanist impulse to master its environment and Rosny's posthumanist depiction of humanity's eventual failure to adapt and accept a new evolutionary shift.

In various ways across time and space, Rosny's human protagonists "see the face" of the alien Other and recognize the necessary evolutionary shift between species that does not always favor humans, eventually accepting the inability to adapt to a changing environment. Indeed, the idea of confrontation or cooperation between humans and alien creatures introduces problems of individual moral agency, which is within human control. But Rosny's scientific writings on *le quatrième univers* [the fourth universe] do not necessarily align with this ideology that places human agency first. In "Vers le quatrième univers" [Toward the Fourth Universe], Rosny posits that the universe is dynamic, which contradicts the commonly held theories of his time (1931, 14).[65] The

---

[65] Even Einstein, who lived approximately during the same time period as Rosny, initially believed in a static universe. In the late 1920s, Georges Lemaître (1894–1966), a Francophone Belgian Catholic priest and astronomer, hypothesized that galaxies were growing farther apart. He is credited with the formulation of the now widely accepted Big Bang theory,

celestial bodies we see are only a fraction of what exists: "Nebulae and stars with their trails are really just *a vague and infinitesimal dust* in the fraction of the total world in which they revolve" (1931, 10; emphasis original).[66] The universe possesses liminal pockets of space, consisting of alternative existences (e.g. worlds, universes, dimensions) that live independently of our own perceptible existence but with the occasional cataclysm that brings them together. The cataclysms between species within this fourth universe contribute to a greater framework of life that is completely out of human control. Thus, the desire to coexist with other species is within the realm of human agency, but the evolutionary transition of species functions beyond the will and capacity of humanity. For Rosny, these two cannot always be in harmony.

---

which explains that our continuously expanding universe exploded from an extremely hot and dense point over 13 billion years ago. The observations of American astronomer Edwin Hubble in the 1920s confirmed this expansion, and thus the dynamic nature of the universe.

[66] "Les nébuleuses et les étoiles avec leurs cortèges ne sont vraiment qu'une *vague et infinitésimale poussière* dans la fraction du monde total où elles gravitent."

Chapter Two

Becoming Orangutan: Animal Encounters in the Fiction of Éric Chevillard

In Chapter One, I showed how Rosny's work points to the zeitgeist of Western Europe in the wake of major discoveries in geology, evolution, paleontology, and other sciences that positioned the human as part of a sweeping history of the Earth and the cosmos. By shifting to an interest in prehistoric narratives (*Les Xipéhuz*; *Vamireh*, 1892; *Eyrimah*, 1893; *Nomaï*, 1897; *La Guerre du feu*, 1911) after his debut novel about the slums of London, *Nell Horn*, Rosny takes a decidedly longer view of human evolution that integrates such new scientific knowledge. While in Anglo-American SF of the 1940s and 1950s of the "hard" variety, in which many authors rely heavily on scientific extrapolation, often at the expense of not only character and plot development but also poetic language, Rosny never evacuates his literary origins from scientific extrapolation. In fact, as Clément Hummel argues, if we naively strung Rosny's narratives together with one large, thematic thread, we would be tempted to point to his evocation of science, but this would falsely link him to the "Vernian scientific novel [*roman scientifique*] from which Rosny always distanced himself, instead preferring a more poetic approach inherited from Baudelaire, which you'll encounter in Maurice Renard's definition of the scientific-marvelous [*merveilleux-scientifique*]" (2019, 12–13).[1] Charles Baudelaire, one of the most influential French poets of the modern era, is most renowned for his innovative collection *Les Fleurs du mal* (1857) [*The Flowers of Evil*], in which he explores suffering, beauty, morality, an obsession with death, and an aspiration toward an ideal world against the background of burgeoning urban life. Indeed, it is truly Rosny's "poetic writing" ["écriture poétique"] that sets him apart

---

[1] "roman scientifique à la Jules Verne, ce dont Rosny s'est toujours éloigné en préférant une démarche davantage poétique, héritée de Baudelaire, que l'on retrouvera dans la définition du merveilleux-scientifique par Maurice Renard."

from Verne and establishes a new tradition that marries the scientific with a poetic sense of wonder (Clermont 2011, 90). While this tradition seems to wane in postwar French SF, scholar Pierre Versins (1972) argues – amidst a wave of political and sociological SF on both sides of the Atlantic – for categorizing science fiction as *littérature conjécturale rationnelle*. As a result, he places science fiction next to *littérature* and thus its formal, artful pursuits, rather than below it. I trace the evolution of post-1950 French SF, including its relationship to *littérature*, in more detail in Chapter Three.

Writing a century after Rosny, Éric Chevillard similarly yokes together scientific extrapolation of human–nonhuman encounters with the poetics and literary artfulness associated with Versins's notion of *littérature*. The French author surreptitiously brings the devices of science fiction – the cognitively estranging thought experiment, in particular – to readers of literary fiction. Steeped in the new millennium's increasingly pervasive global lexicon of biodiversity loss, species extinction, and climate change, Chevillard's 2007 novel, *Sans l'orang-outan* [Without the Orangutan] speculates: what would happen if our primate cousin, the orangutan, went extinct? The author then follows the possible consequences to an extreme, estranging conclusion, resulting in a series of wildly comical and tragic scenarios of bodily, environmental, and linguistic decay. The seemingly banal death of Bagus and Mina, the last two orangutans on Earth, first triggers subtle changes that only the zookeeper, Albert Moindre, seems to notice. Everything is elongated, from the length of the meter to the distance from the Earth to the Sun: "Everything's going to move away considerably, recede behind thick mists, fall into deep nights [...] Yet I am dizzy looking at my feet. Back to the ground, and even to the slums, to the turf paths, to the cellars, to the clay tunnels between the roots. The sun is moving away, we were almost holding it" (Chevillard 2007, 17).[2] In a literary move evocative of the surreal writings of Franco-Belgian poet Henri Michaux, the landscape completely transforms into something comically eerie, a post-apocalyptic hellscape of skeleton forests and a screeching monster called "le hurlant" (Vial 2009).[3]

---

[2] "Tout va s'éloigner considérablement, reculer derrière des brumes épaisses, choir dans des nuits profondes [...] Pourtant je suis pris de vertige en regardant mes pieds. Retour au sol, et même aux bas-fonds, aux chemins de tourbe, aux caves, aux tunnels glaiseux entre les racines. Le soleil s'éloigne, on le tenait presque." Translations of *Sans l'orang-outan* are my own.

[3] The Poetry Foundation describes Henri Michaux's work as "haunting," with an emphasis on "'the strangeness of natural things and the naturalness of strange things,' as André Gide once described Michaux's philosophy. Like

Meanwhile, Albert attempts to revive the extinct species by means of behavioral modification (training his colleagues to act like orangutans) and biotechnological experiments (convincing his colleague and lover Aloïse to carry an orangutan embryo). In Albert's view, de-extinction is the best way to keep humans alive and bring the illustrious orangutan back to the balding forests.

Although other contemporary French-language writers have bridged science fiction and mainstream literature, such as in Québec (Beaulé 2019), most scholarship written in French does not recognize the connection between science fiction and the work of Chevillard (see Sermet 2019 for the one glaring exception). Anaïs Boulard calls Chevillard and Michel Houellebecq, another successful mainstream author, "writers of 'general fiction' (as opposed to fantasy or science fiction)" (2017, 218).[4] Dominique Viart explains that even though Chevillard bases his "speculative logic" on scientific extrapolations, his *œuvre* does not seem to quite fit into the "fiction" portion of SF because it is rather "an inventory of possibilities, a game of substitutions and reversals" ["un inventaire des possibles, un jeu de substitutions et de renversements"] (2014, 91). While an excellent explanation of Chevillard's modus operandi, Viart's remarks suggest a limited understanding of science fiction's capabilities. Chevillard himself has commented on others' narrow views on what literary storytelling can and should do, even though he does not equate such literary rebellions with science fiction per se (which only emphasizes the continuation of the strict SF/Literature bifurcation that Versins cited in the 1970s). In a 2008 interview in *Société Roman*, Chevillard remarked: "I think my books will forever remain impenetrable for all those who consider literature to be the art of clarifying situations and reading the real" (Riendeau 2008, 18).[5] In *Sans l'orang-outan*, Chevillard does "read the real" in the sense that he uses techniques of the speculative and absurd to *extrapolate* the ecological real – the reality of Anthropocene living – and push it to what seems to be illogical limits.

    Swift, Flaubert, and Lautreament, Michaux created imaginery [sic] lands inhabited by equally chimerical creatures" (n.d.).
[4] In a 2010 interview in *The Paris Review*, Houellebecq discussed his influences from his childhood and adolescence, like Jules Verne, American writer of horror H.P. Lovecraft, and American SF writer Clifford Simak: "If not for science fiction, my biggest influences would all belong to the nineteenth century." Houellebecq even has an entry in *The Encyclopedia of Science Fiction*: http://www.sf-encyclopedia.com/entry/houellebecq_michel.
[5] "Je pense que mes livres resteront à jamais impénétrables pour tous ceux qui considèrent que la littérature est l'art de clarifier les situations et de lire le réel."

To parody human existence with and without the orangutan, Chevillard's novel builds on a twentieth-century tradition of French literary movements that challenge narrative conventions. As I showed in Chapter One, Rosny challenged Zola's excessively materialist Naturalism, and Chevillard prolongs this challenge as a literary heir of the Absurd and *nouveau roman* movements. Publishing with Éditions de Minuit since 1987, Chevillard implicitly falls within the tradition of the *nouveau roman* of the 1950s and 1960s, which could be found at the same prestigious publishing house.[6] The *nouveau roman* sought to undermine "the continuing hegemony of classic 'Balzacian' realism, which, through its technical emphasis on plot and characterization, [authors] saw as drawing a falsely reassuring map of human experience" (Gratton 1997, 243). Instead, *nouveau roman* authors focused on "a 'higher' form of the same basic mimetic urge, such as 'psychological' realism, which prioritizes the inner world of human subjectivity, or 'phenomenological' realism, which tracks the outer world as physically experienced by a human subject" (Gratton 1997, 242). While fascinated by the stylistic qualities of psychological realism, Chevillard draws even more inspiration from the existentialist credo of the Absurd, a literary and theatrical movement that flourished among francophone playwrights such as Samuel Beckett, Henri Michaux, and Eugène Ionesco in the 1950s and 1960s. Ionesco conceptualized the Absurd as "that which is devoid of purpose [...] Cut off from his religious, metaphysical, and transcendental roots, man is lost; all his actions become senseless, absurd, useless" (qtd. in Esslin 1976, 23).[7] Indeed, without the orangutan in Chevillard's novel, life becomes meaningless, and Albert hopelessly seeks new ways to restore a sense of purpose to his world. Praising Beckett and Michaux in an interview, Chevillard described how they "were beholden to nothing. They were never bound by the demands of the system, its necessities or laws, and they never surrendered or conceded a single thing" (Waters 2017). More importantly, Beckett and Michaux break literary rules in order to reveal a sense of "shame in us

---

[6] Éditions de Minuit is historically responsible for publishing writers who would quickly become canonical novelists, playwrights, and philosophers from the 1950s to 1980s (e.g. Samuel Beckett, Marguerite Duras, Gilles Deleuze). Fleuve Noir Anticipation, a science fiction publishing house of the same time period, did not enjoy the same literary status; instead, its SF collection served as a catalyst of varying degrees of support and critique for France's mushrooming, postwar technocratic elite, as Bradford Lyau argues (1989).

[7] Cf. Eugène Ionesco. "Dans les armes de la ville." *Cahiers de la Compagnie Madeleine Renaud-Jean-Louis Barrault*, no. 20, Oct. 1957.

like a righteous punishment, like a painful realization of what we have become" (Waters 2017). What had we become? For Absurdists, we had been complicit in world wars, genocide, and the overall devaluation of human life. Displacing this view into the Anthropocene framework of animal extinction and environmental degradation in *Sans l'orang-outan*, Chevillard brings together social critique with both stylistic and thematic elements of French anti-realist tradition.

Yet Chevillard goes further than his predecessors by insisting on the anthropocentric leanings of the traditional novel; it has a tendency, in the author's view, to perpetuate lies, where humanity's existence is delicately depicted with careful language that simply maintains the status quo. Speaking about his novel *Préhistoire* (1994), Chevillard celebrates this prehistoric "time before lies" ["temps d'avant le mensonge"] before humanity writes itself into the story as the hero and perpetually recounts that same story for eons (qtd. in Daniel 2014, 68–69). As a result, humans chase every other creature out of the narrative because, as the narrator writes in *QWERTY Invectives*: "Man wants to be the only character in this world" (qtd. in Waters 2017). The French author rebels against anthropocentric thinking by densely populating his fictional universe with animals, thus prolonging the twentieth-century tradition of questioning Balzacian realism with a highly speculative fiction that is not only uninterested in the human as hero, but insists on exposing humankind's absurd, paradoxical nature. In *Palafox* (1990), a shape-shifting creature is chased after by scientists in an attempt to categorize it. *Du hérisson* (2012) [On the Hedgehog] depicts a hedgehog that distracts an author from his autobiography, and *L'Explosion de la tortue* (2019) [Explosion of the Tortoise] describes how the month-long absence of the narrator inadvertently, yet unsurprisingly, kills his pet Floridian tortoise. Animals often hijack his narratives in some form or another and displace the self-importance of humans. These animals reveal the susceptibility of our intellectual endeavors – and even of our written language – to usurpation and degradation. At times, such endeavors are stripped entirely of meaning.

In this chapter, I argue that, despite striving for a posthumanist world of permeable boundaries between human and animal, humanity reverts to transhumanist thinking in *Sans l'orang-outan*. Through the dual lenses of the Absurd and the ecocritical language of Ursula Heise, Timothy Clark, and Deleuze and Guattari, I examine two consequences of orangutan extinction in Chevillard's novel: Albert's increasingly absurd actions to de-extinct the red ape (an elaborate elegy via an "eco-shrine"; behavioral training of colleagues in order to "become" orangutans; convincing his lover Aloïse to host an orangutan embryo) and the environmental, bodily, and linguistic deteriorations in a post-orangutan world. Through the failure of Albert's posthumanist efforts – failure to preserve and enshrine the orangutans, failure to act like orangutans, failure to remember how they behave, likely failure to de-extinct the species – Chevillard highlights the inevitably transhumanist impulse to master biology, that is, the desire to overcome the ecological butterfly effect of orangutan extinction on the biosphere and rebirth the orangutan through in vitro fertilization. In order to better understand Chevillard's inventive treatment of the human–ape encounter, it is critical to first take a look at how he engages with the evolutionary and ethical contexts of human–animal relations and human animality in contemporary French thought and literature.

Human–Animal Encounters in Contemporary French Thought and Literature

In the novel, Albert underscores a human contempt for the red ape which stems from a striking similarity between humans and other primates: "There was a misunderstanding of universal forces blinded by their anger and deceived by the likeness of man and the orangutan" (Chevillard 2007, 52).[8] The extinction of the orangutan, as opposed to one of many other species that populate Chevillard's universe, carries with it both an evolutionary and cultural weight. Simians create anxiety about humans' animality, "uncannily appearing both like and unlike humans. Since Darwin, they inevitably signify evolution, reminding us – regardless of how often religion and philosophy have promoted a radical break between human and animal – of our failure to be of another order" (Vint 2009, 224). Apes are deeply embedded in Western imagery related to morality and identity. In European history, medieval imagery associated monkeys with "sin and the devil, with frivolity, folly and hideousness, with impulsivity and wantonness"; in the late nineteenth century, prostitutes and criminals were perceived as the result of an atavistic regression into primeval, ape-like behavior yet to be controlled by civilization (Corbey 1994, 129). Even though (or perhaps despite) Darwin's theory of evolution discovered a hereditary link between apes and humans, negative, monstrous imagery of apes persisted in popular culture, such as *King Kong*, a 1933 film with subsequent remakes that

---

[8] "Il y a eu méprise des forces universelles aveuglées par leur courroux et abusées par la ressemblance de l'homme et de l'orang-outan."

depicts a giant gorilla kidnapping an actress and terrorizing New York City.

Of course, a discussion about human animality in the context of a modern, civilized society cannot completely avoid Freud's thoughts on the matter. For Freud, civilization represents the control (but not complete mastery) of nature because it is one of the three main sources of suffering for humanity, the other two being one's own body, "which is doomed to decay and dissolution," and our relationships with other human beings (1989, 26). In countries that "have attained a high level of civilization," we will equally find "everything which can assist in the exploitation of the earth by man and in his protection against the forces of nature – everything, in short, which is of use to him – is attended to and effectively carried out." The community establishes a sense of control and order, which echoes the control of our instincts (Freud 1989, 45, 51–52). This anthropocentric vision situates man (notably not "the human") as symbolic of civilization and the animal as his antithesis because animal instinct is part of nature, which by Freud's definition, must be dominated by man in order to avoid suffering. *Sans l'orang-outan* challenges these notions of humanity's presumed dominance over other species. From the perspective of Chevillard's protagonist, Albert, orangutans could have easily killed us and could have chosen to "put us back in our place" ["nous remettre à notre place"], but instead "consented to our domination" ["a consenti à notre domination"] (2007, 173). Evidently, in the late twentieth and early twenty-first centuries, scientific advancements, popular culture, and social media have changed the discourse around primates, from primatologist Jane Goodall's work in the 1970s to the latest reboot of the *Planet of the Apes* film franchise (*Rise of the Planet of the Apes*, 2011).

This extremely successful franchise, whose first film starred Charlton Heston as a misanthropic, smug American astronaut, owes its existence to French author Pierre Boulle. Initially trained as an engineer at the Sorbonne, Boulle later enlisted in the French army and joined the Free French forces in Singapore during the Second World War. In 1942, Japanese forces, which had seized the French colony of Indochina during the German Occupation of metropolitan France, captured Boulle during an espionage mission. After experiencing forced labor and captivity as a prisoner of war, such themes permeated his later fiction, especially *La Planète des singes* (1963) [*Planet of the Apes*]. In the novel, human protagonist Ulysse is shipwrecked on a faraway planet in the star system of Betelgeuse and the advanced primate civilization there treats him like an animal, subjecting him to scientific experiments to test his intelligence and instincts. Boulle's novel functions as a *conte philosophique* in the tradition of Voltaire, thus emphasizing the importance of storytelling as a vehicle for exploring ideas such as evolution, intelligence, and language (Becker 1996, 71). In such a reading, Boulle subverts the dominant Freudian paradigm that equates immoral or savage behavior with apes. More broadly, in "the apocalyptic future envisioned by Boulle, humankind has been eradicated by a society with similar social structures" to 1960s France, thus demonstrating how the novel "critiques paradigms of Western capitalism" (Scott 2020, 34). Thus, like Rosny's work, *La Planète des singes* represents a cultural zeitgeist of global geopolitical tensions, technological acceleration, the collapse of old colonial empires, and the expansion of civil rights.

Equally invested in the literary, environmental, and nonhuman stakes of language, Chevillard's fiction continues the thematic interests of Boulle amidst a flurry of thinking about human–animal relationships in French philosophy and popular culture in the late twentieth century. Chevillard began writing in the late 1980s, right before a time of cultural panic surrounding the boundary between humans and animals. The cloning of Dolly the sheep in 1996 and the rise of mad cow disease "were last straws, apocalyptic events, states of exception, that led to the dismantling of the traditional concepts of the human and the animal" (Senior et al. 2015, 3). Soon after these zoonotic marvels and crises, Jacques Derrida gave a talk at the Colloque de Cérisy in 1997, "L'Animal que donc je suis" ["The Animal That Therefore I Am"].[9] Derrida's linguistic and philosophical wordplay in his talk highlights the role of language in reimagining the relationship between human and animal. The choice of "Je suis," meaning both "I am" and "I follow," is intentionally provocative; Chevillard teases out this linguistic provocation in his subversion of a teleological view of evolution from simian to human. Derrida also introduced the term *animot*, which he hoped to substitute for the generalizing term of "animaux" [animals], a French homophone. He

---

[9] Derrida was, of course, writing within an established modern tradition of French posthumanist thought, but the 1990s proved to be a time of forging new paths in philosophical thought regarding animals and, more broadly, nature. The anthropological work of Gilles Deleuze, Michel Foucault, and Élisabeth de Fontenay revealed notions of sacrifice, exchange, and an inner animality in the human (Senior et al. 2015, 4). The writings of Bruno Latour and Isabelle Stenghers, who influenced Donna Haraway and other anglophone posthumanist thinkers, investigated material practices of data collection as well as animal conditions in both scientific and agricultural settings (Senior et al. 2015, 6). Michel Serres's *Le Parasite* (1980) and *Le Contrat naturel* (1990) contributed to a shift from the universal humanism of traditional Continental philosophy toward posthumanism.

described *animot* as "Neither a species nor a gender nor an individual, it is an irreducible living multiplicity of mortals, and rather than a double clone or a portmanteau word, a sort of monstrous hybrid, a chimera waiting to be put to death by its Bellerophon" (Derrida and Wills 2002, 49).[10] Editors Matthew Senior, David L. Clark, and Carla Freccero write that "*animot* makes explicit the fact that the being of the animal always passes through the medium of words [...] *Animot* thus means granting a kind of language to animals and developing subtle, poetic expressions that capture the proximity yet separateness of humans and animals, arising in moments when animal movements, paths, and sounds intersect with human displacements and language" (2015, 2).

As both Derrida's title and Chevillard's novel suggest, language is necessary to examine the paradoxical proximity and distance of human–animal encounters. Derrida plays on the famous phrase from seventeenth-century philosopher René Descartes in his treatise *Discourse on Method*, "I think therefore I am" ["Je pense donc je suis"], which is how Descartes arrives at an understanding of consciousness (the human as a thinking, rational being aware of its own thought process). What does it mean to be simultaneously human and animal? What does it mean for the human to come after the animal? In the case of *Sans l'orang-outan*, Chevillard takes these key posthumanist questions to task. Paying tribute to Derrida's ideas and Boulle's philosophical cynicism of humans as the pinnacle of evolution, Chevillard uses the experiments of his protagonist Albert as a way to examine the uneasy coexistence and occasional "surfing" (Cary Wolfe's term) between human and ape (Wolfe 2014, 3). Ultimately, for Albert, we should become more ape-like to eradicate our (negative) human behavior. (Take that, Freud.) In fact, becoming more ape-like in the novel reaches a point at which evolution reverses itself and the orangutan comes *after* the human, thus playfully flipping Derrida's title on its head.

The Tragedy of Animal Extinction: Albert's Elegy

For Albert, the deaths of Bagus and Mina signal the end of the world. Or perhaps simply the end of the world *as we know it*. Part One of Chevillard's novel, narrated from the first-person perspective of the

---

[10] "ni une espèce, ni une genre, ni un individu, c'est une irréductible multiplicité vivante de mortels, et plutôt qu'un double clone ou un mot-valise, une sorte d'hybride monstrueux, une chimère attendant d'être mise à mort par son Bellérophon" (Derrida 1999, 292).

eccentric zookeeper, sets a catastrophic tone: "We're going to react before we get to that point, I said to myself, this disaster, this apocalypse" (2007, 9–10).[11] Why would the death of two orangutans at a zoo merit such hyperbolic language? Orangutan extinction is not a disastrous event – not immediately, at least. There is no asteroid hurtling toward the Earth; there is no alien invasion nor massive earthquake, which could set the stage for a new era in human history. In fact, people in the streets are simply going about their daily routine, which suggests a certain banality of this apocalyptic event: "Now everyone goes about their business in the city, on the edge of this yawning abyss, as if nothing had happened. Would I be the only one to have noticed their disappearance?" (Chevillard 2007, 11).[12] If anything, Albert's "insistence on the fatality of the orangutans' death seems too great to be sincere," thus potentially diminishing the gravity of the situation (Boulard 2017, 224). However, the "apocalypse" carries biblical weight, indicating both a time of moral judgment of one's thoughts and actions and the establishment of a new order. Albert indeed signals a revelation. It does not come from an otherworldly being, but rather a terrestrial being – the extinction of a nonhuman animal.

Chevillard's posthumanist move takes literary cues from his nineteenth-century French predecessors, Rosny, Flammarion, and Jean-Baptiste Cousin de Grainville. In Cousin de Grainville's *Le Dernier homme* (1805) [*The Last Man*], the first example of a secular apocalypse (albeit still with a Christian subtext), the end to humanity is the result of environmental disasters instead of an instantaneous, divine revelation typical of the genre (Alkon 1987, 160; Ransom, "The First Last Man" 2014, 314). Amy Ransom, among others, gives credit to Cousin de Grainville for launching a trend of last man narratives in both French and English literature, culminating in Mary Shelley's *The Last Man* in 1826 and Camille Flammarion's *La Fin du monde* [*Omega: The Last Days of the World*] in 1894 (Ransom, "The First Last Man" 2014, 314). Flammarion's novel, like Rosny's *La Mort de la Terre*, expands upon the notion of humanity's gradual end by underscoring our inability to survive after dramatic changes in the Earth's climate.[13] Albert is a

---

[11] "On va réagir avant d'en arriver là, je me disais, à ce désastre, à cette apocalypse."
[12] "Or chacun va à ses occupations dans la ville, au bord de ce gouffre béant, comme si rien ne s'était passé. Serais-je seul à m'être avisé de leur disparition?"
[13] In Flammarion's *La Fin du monde*, a comet that nearly collides with Earth leaves toxic gases in the atmosphere, severely altering the climate and leading to human degeneration over millions of years. The next stage in

perceptive, if not initially hyperbolic, narrator sensitive to the era of the Anthropocene; his reaction highlights both his posthumanist sympathy for the orangutan and anticipates his absurd efforts to recalibrate the ecological equilibrium affected by orangutan extinction.

Albert's lamentation and tragic discourse surrounding orangutan extinction conveys a "general sense of decline, of sweeping losses of life, diversity, knowledge, and beauty" (Heise 2016, 12). As Ursula Heise explains, the use of genre tropes aims to arouse sympathy in the reader or spectator: "Often, these stories of decline seek to mobilize readers' emotions through the lament, melancholy, and mourning that are characteristic of elegy [...] and, in a different way, of tragedy (conventionally, the story of the inevitable and partly undeserved fall of a person of high social standing; in its modern sense, the meaningless and undeserved death of innocent victims)" (2016, 34). Instead of the conventional, tragic, *human* hero, the subject of Albert's elegy is the orangutan, a species that did not deserve to die. Utilizing tragic and elegiac literary forms in the case of species extinction is a posthumanist gesture that transgresses species boundaries. Albert's prolonged elegy questions who or what is worthy of our collective mourning. For the zookeeper, we failed to recognize the orangutan's splendor and his melancholia could be, as sociologist Catriona Mortimer-Sandilands remarks of instances of melancholic grief, "a potentially politicized way of preserving that object in the midst of a culture that fails to recognize its significance" (2010, 333). Furthermore, the orangutan, a simian with an evolutionary link to *Homo sapiens*, represents a more convincing, nonhuman, tragic hero. Heise notes that for "charismatic megafauna" such as the polar bear, panda, or tiger, "the sheer size and the perceived majesty and fierceness of major predators makes it easy to cast them in narratives of tragic falls from grace" (2016, 35). While not a fierce predator, the orangutan's likeness to humans makes Albert's posthumanist prose in Part One appealing to the reader.

As part of Albert's ode to the orangutan, he eventually creates an "eco-shrine," thus highlighting the religious connotations of both the absurd and the apocalypse. In Part Three, Albert transports the corpses of Bagus and Mina from the workshop of his zoo colleague, Horvillier, to his home. The bodies draw the gaze of others in a stark reversal of

> human evolution begins when the souls of the remaining two humans on Earth are transported to Jupiter after they die. While humanity cannot be completely exonerated of the environmental changes that slowly made the planet less hospitable for human life, there are evolutionary forces out of our control, as I argued about Rosny's works in Chapter One.

the non-reaction reported by Albert at the beginning of the novel: "We innocently neglected to cover the mummies and, as soon as we were in the street and during the whole transport, they aroused a great stir among passers-by, fortunately still rare at this early hour: some fell on their knees, others pursued us, trying to touch Bagus and Mina, perhaps to convince themselves of the reality of what their eyes were seeing" (Chevillard 2007, 133).[14] This emotion exhibited by onlookers contributes to the strangely spiritual aspect of the absurd, which "deal[s] with the ultimates of the human condition not in terms of intellectual understanding but in terms of communicating a metaphysical truth through a living experience" (Esslin 1976, 424). As Albert houses Bagus and Mina in his bedroom, he begins to receive frequent visits from friends and zoo colleagues, Aloïse and Claudius, as well as his neighbor Ragonit. Others begin to crowd outside of Albert's home in the hopes of seeing the orangutans:

> Other unwanted people knocked on my door, parents and acquaintances of Claudius and Ragonit, then parents and acquaintances of these relatives and acquaintances, we are all brothers, alas, the harassment did not stop. In the morning, a line formed in front of my door. I saw happy faces, shining looks; all these people were impatient. They were going to see some orangutans again! (Chevillard 2007, 137)[15]

Because visitors want to touch Bagus and Mina, Albert worries that their mummified bodies might start to resemble "two dead fir trees, drooping shoulders and sparse hair" ["deux sapins morts, épaules tombantes et le poil rare"] (Chevillard 2007, 138). Ragonit suggests creating a museum, where visitors could look at – but not touch – Bagus and Mina, delicately placed under a glass dome. Giving Bagus and Mina a superior status as lost, tragic heroes, Albert has their bodies literally

---

[14] "Nous avons innocemment négligé de couvrir les momies et, sitôt dans la rue et durant tout le transport, elles suscitèrent un vif émoi chez les passants, heureusement rares encore en cette heure matinale, certains tombaient à genoux, d'autres nous poursuivaient, essayant de toucher Bagus et Mina pour se convaincre sans doute de la réalité de ce que leurs yeux voyaient."

[15] "D'autres indésirables frappaient à ma porte, parents et connaissances de Claudius et de Ragonit, pis parents et connaissances de ces parents et connaissances, nous sommes tous frères, hélas, le harcèlement ne cessa plus. Dès le matin, une file d'attente se formait devant ma porte. Je voyais des visage réjouis, des regards brillants; tous ces gens trépignaient d'impatience. Ils allaient revoir des orangs-outans!"

placed on a pedestal in an elegiac, posthumanist gesture: "In a large square in the center of the city, Ragonit built a stone plinth three meters high, which he overhung with a perfectly hemispherical bell" (Chevillard 2007, 139).[16] By creating an eco-shrine to the orangutan, Albert creates a new cosmic system of posthumanist values in a world devoid of meaning. As soon as the monument is erected, people ecstatically crowd around it as part of a new devotional practice: "People gathered around the monument [...] they flocked to the center of the square, noisy at first, excited, letting out cheers and shouts of joy. They were crying at the same time. Men fell to their knees. They were hugging. They were dancing" (Chevillard 2007, 139).[17] Paying homage to the eco-shrine of Bagus and Mina becomes a poetic ritual for communicating these new values: "It is the mark of all great religions that they not only possess a body of knowledge that can be taught in the form of cosmological information or ethical rules but that they also communicate the essence of this body of doctrine in the living, recurring poetic imagery of ritual" (Esslin 1976, 424). Indeed, Albert hopes to establish a new system of (posthumanist) values, beginning with the veneration of Bagus's and Mina's bodies, as if they were holy relics.

Extinction Aftershocks

Keeping with these posthumanist values, Albert goes to great lengths to explain the human influence on the biosphere that eventually led to orangutan extinction. When Albert pauses from his elegy to the orangutan in Part One to give an ode to the defunct dodo, he highlights the butterfly effect, where the smallest variations – imperceptible to humans – in interdependent systems create unpredictable outcomes. Popular culture has adopted the butterfly effect as a way to explain how a small event can set off a chain reaction of other natural events in the future. Moreover, the dodo serves as both a reminder of the ecological interconnectedness of different species on Earth and of the complicated, and occasionally harmful, relationship between humans and the environment. Like the orangutan, the dodo had a heroic

---

[16] "Sur une vaste place, au centre de la ville, Ragonit édifia un socle de pierre haut de trois mètres qu'il surplomba d'une cloche parfaitement hémisphérique."

[17] "La population se massait autour du monument [...] elle afflua vers le centre de la place, bruyante d'abord, excite, lançant des hourras et des cris de joie. On pleurait en même temps. Des hommes tombèrent à genoux. On s'étreignait. On dansait."

downfall. The dodo went extinct because of human hunting and the introduction of non-native species to its habitat; the large, flightless pigeon died out only a few decades after Dutch sailors discovered the species on the island of Mauritius in the seventeenth century. The dodo serves as a "flagship species," meaning one that is "able to occupy the hero's role, often function[ing] synecdochically by pointing to broader crises in humans' interactions with nature, especially during periods of modernization and colonization" (Heise 2016, 36). Heise remarks that the dodo's extinction was a critical indication of the effects of modernization: "The dodo looms large in many books on extinction because it was the first species whose end came to be clearly attributed to human intervention: it signals a historical turning point where the deadly ecological consequences of exploration and colonization became visible" (2016, 36).

According to Mauritian folklore, the tambalacoque tree, which was valued for its timber, could only germinate if it passed through the gut of the dodo (Witmer and Cheke 1991, 133). Albert rehearses this dodo folklore in detail (Chevillard 2007, 56). Some ecologists argue that this connection between the tambalacoque and the dodo is an "obligate mutualism," or, put simply, a coevolution. Albert shares this connection with the reader to illustrate the strong interdependence of species, including humans and nonhumans.[18] The zookeeper continues, claiming that the extinction of the dodo had an effect on orangutan extinction centuries later: "Without the turkey, no more tambalacoque in the very short term, which is the same sort of wood as the palaquium of the Indian forest, its brother in the sapotaceae family, and it is precisely the abusive exploitation of this forest, the systematic felling of the precious palaquium, which led to the disappearance of the orangutan" (Chevillard 2007, 56–57).[19] Chevillard utilizes the speculative mode to extrapolate the butterfly effect between the human-caused extinction of the dodo and that of the tambalacoque.[20] Indeed, Albert notes how "deforestation

---

[18] Witmer and Cheke note how the dodo and the tambalacoque are often pointed to in ecology courses as an example of species interdependence, but they contest the idea that a tambalacoque seed would require treatment by a dodo's gut in order to germinate (1991, 133–137).

[19] "Sans le dindon, plus de tambalacoque à très courte échéance, qui est du même bois que le palaquium de la forêt indienne, son frère dans la famille des sapotacées, et c'est précisément l'exploitation abusive de cette forêt, l'abattage systématique du précieux palaquium, qui ont entraîné la disparition de l'orang-outan."

[20] An aspect of chaos theory proposed by meteorologist Edward Lorenz to explain complex, interdependent systems in nature, the butterfly effect

accelerated its fall" ["la déforestation a précipité sa chute"] (Chevillard 2007, 57). Therefore, the deaths of Bagus and Mina "function as a synecdoche for the broader environmentalist idea of nature's decline as well as for the stories that communities and societies tell about their own modernization" (Heise 2016, 32). Even worse, Bagus and Mina ultimately die from a flu virus that they contracted from human visitors (Chevillard 2007, 12). Rather than risking exposure to zoonotic viruses, which are some of the deadliest to humans (e.g. the epidemics of swine and avian flu, and probably the COVID-19 pandemic), this posthumanist move by Chevillard instead positions humans as dangerous carriers of pathogens. Ultimately, by connecting and extrapolating upon the extinctions of the dodo and the orangutan, Albert calls attention to human responsibility for species loss.

The butterfly effect not only manifests itself in the past, though, as Albert predicts in Part One: "We will pay dearly for our indifference, I foresee great upheavals" (Chevillard 2007, 16).[21] The reader continues to see the ripple effect initiated by the deaths of Bagus and Mina, from the subtle, physical change in the length of the meter to the abrupt transition to a bleak, degraded ecosystem in Part Two: "Fallout, a chain reaction of repercussions, each creature, each thing belonging to this world was given a small shake" (Chevillard 2007, 63).[22] The reader already knows that, for Albert, orangutan extinction signals the end of *his* world, but, somehow, this becomes a collective reality as the Earth turns into a desolate wasteland. As Boulard points out, "factual details of the events that led to total chaos are missing from the narrative, and we never know why and how the death of two primates precipitated the end of the world" (2017, 220). Yet the potentially catastrophic aftermath of species extinction in the Anthropocene is an elusive referent that can be difficult to represent in fiction. Perhaps a more vertiginous shift for the reader than in Rosny's *La Mort de la Terre*, discussed in Chapter One, Chevillard's depiction of the scale effect allows the reader to understand the serious implications of what seems to have no tangible implications on an individual, human scale, at least in the short term. In other words, numerous human actions that may seem insignificant at first, such as

purports that the smallest variation in a system, which is typically imperceptible to humans, can result in unpredictable outcomes, as is the case in *Sans l'orang-outan*.
21 "Nous allons payer cher notre désinvolture, je prévois de profonds bouleversements."
22 "Contrecoups, répercussions en chaîne, chaque creature, chaque chose de ce monde reçut sa petite secousse."

clearing trees, "come together to form a new, imponderable physical event, altering the basic ecological cycles of the planet" (Clark 2015, 72).

This sudden shift to a bleak, post-apocalyptic environment in Part Two underscores a biohorror aesthetic in Chevillard's novel in which he mixes science fiction and bodily or biological changes, thus evoking our cultural anxieties regarding technology and our fears of difference. Chapter One described a precursor to biohorror in my analysis of *Les Navigateurs de l'infini*, where Jacques navigated the grotesque nature of human and Triped bodies. Biohorror is situated at the crossroads of the supernatural horror stories of H.P. Lovecraft, which produce an affect of "the terrifying and sublime conclusions to be drawn from a view of the world as an utterly unhuman world," and the Gothic aesthetic, which is grounded in the anxieties and "horrors of new technologies at the very forefront of their becoming reality, or imagining them before they have been developed" (Thacker 2010, 1; Heise-von der Lippe 2017, 5). Many Hollywood SF films contain biohorror, such as *The Fly* (David Cronenberg, 1986), in which a scientist accidentally transforms into the titular insect, or *Alien* (Ridley Scott, 1979), whose most memorable scene is when a bloody, alien creature erupts from the stomach of one of the crew members of the spaceship. These films are not only examples of anxieties about technology but also of "the incursion of the irrational into an apparently calm and ordered venue – an intrusion that in the real world we all fear with good reason; for this fear (which is for some an active desire) we may need a catharsis in harmless fictional form" (Nicholls and Clute 2019).

Biohorror is no stranger to the tradition of the Absurd. Lavery and Finburgh see the entanglement of horror and ecological awareness in Samuel Beckett, one of Chevillard's inspirations, and ultimately, in Absurd theatre as a whole: "By keeping it nebulous, Beckett conjures an unspoken sense of dread. In this way, he provokes a mood of unease, a kind of haunting that communicates a socio-historical atmosphere that the audience might otherwise prefer to repress or ignore" (2007, 11). In contemporary literary fiction, Marie Darrieussecq – another mainstream novelist using SF themes and devices like Chevillard – picks up on such themes of absurdity and biohorror in her Kafka-esque *Truismes* (1996) [*Pig Tales*] that depicts the metamorphosis of a woman into a pig. In *Sans l'orang-outan*, the absurdist sensibility surrounding ecological horror blends SF themes of apocalypse and environmental wastelands with an uneasiness regarding bodily dysmorphias. In Part One, Pelleport, a scientist at the zoo who takes on the role of taxidermist, prepares the deceased Bagus and Mina to be dissected and stuffed with "wood, plaster, moss, resin, whatever else, then it will be necessary to believe for centuries that these scarecrows were Bagus and Mina" (Chevillard 2007, 14).[23] Even the horrific possibility of orangutan consumption crosses Albert's mind when he sees Pelleport with his large blades: "Pelleport sharpens two scalpels against each other, would he eat my monkeys? I'd rather not see that" (Chevillard 2007, 19).[24] Biohorror often evokes a sense of disgust toward disfigured, monstrous, or otherwise different bodies, reaffirming a dichotomy of Self and Other. However, Albert's biohorror takes on a different form to that of the film *Alien*, for instance, instead situating the poor corpses of Bagus and Mina as the *victim* of othering and deserving of our sympathy.

In the novel's depleted, post-apocalyptic world, biohorror paradoxically elicits laughter. Piles of partially decomposed bodies serve as the only forests left to provide shade and shelter to humans, yet humans risk being crushed by them (Chevillard 2007, 73). *Le hurlant* is a cankerous, parasitic organism that lives off the wastelands of the exhausted biosphere, yet the inhabitants of Chevillard's world comically try to beat the screaming monster with a stick, which becomes a cultish ritual. At times, the earth opens up and consumes unsuspecting human victims, recalling Beckett's absurdist play *Happy Days* (1961) [*Oh les beaux jours*], where Winnie is half-buried in a mound but becomes increasingly submerged as the play progresses (73). Like *Oh les beaux jours*, *Sans l'orang-outan* combines the comic and the tragic. The reader laughs uneasily at those who are swallowed up by the sand and become partially submerged prisoners. At the same time, there is a tragic sense of humanity heroically attempting to survive in a devastating environment. It is through these notions of negativity (a post-apocalyptic world of monsters and mountains of cadavers) that Chevillard's absurd implicitly expresses the idea "that things ought to be otherwise, even when no direct green message is forthcoming" (Lavery and Finburgh 2015, 11). This element of dark humor introduces new imagery to the posthumanist nature of the novel, forcing our gaze on both the natural world and the bodies that have broken down after orangutan extinction.

The reader also begins to see the disintegration of language – in particular, the meaning-building capacities and permanence of literature, which allows us to "see to what extent the Anthropocene is a matter of reading and writing, of decoding and inscription" (Vermeulen 2020, 26). Imagine *Sans l'orang-outan* as a text that works on a temporal continuum

---

[23] "de bois, de plâtre, de mousse, de résine, que sais-je encore, puis il faudra croire pour des siècles que ces *épouvantails* furent Bagus et Mina."
[24] "Pelleport affûte deux scalpels l'un sur l'autre, voudrait-il manger mes singes? Je préfère ne pas voir ça."

between past, present, and future, where a post-apocalyptic world without literature represents a break from that historical continuum. In Rosny's *Les Xipéhuz*, Bakhoûn's story of an alien encounter, inscribed on clay tablets and translated by a fictitious modern linguist, marks a shift from prehistory to history with the invention of writing. Chatelain and Slusser describe this move as a "neat science-fictional trick" (2012, 39) that etches scientific authority into Rosny's story, thus giving literal veracity to the prehistoric timeframe of *Les Xipéhuz*. While Rosny builds a bridge of communication between eras of superstition and scientific rationality, Chevillard demolishes it. Orangutan extinction and its butterfly effects serve as a *tabula rasa*, discarding old humanist taxonomies formerly engraved in the permanent bedrock of literature. Buried in the blizzard of the novel's post-orangutan world, "our literature struggles to make its sick little voice heard. What is it saying? Pale enigma" (Chevillard 2007, 89).[25]

Nonetheless, authorial irony is always at work within Chevillard's fiction. Despite the futility and eventual deterioration of language and literature in the post-orangutan world, Albert persists. He resists the human-driven story that Chevillard loathes so much. Like the forgotten name of the dodo – "When we want to talk about it, we say turkey, we look for the right word, it slips away, we say turkey, the word escapes us better than the poultry who carried it, called *dronte*, or *dodo*, but most often we say turkey" – we will forget the words "orang" and "utan" (Chevillard 2007, 53–54).[26] But, says the overzealous Albert, if only we engraved the name of the orangutan onto the bark of young trees, then we would never forget the orangutan! Ironically, without the permanence of the word *orangutan*, "the disappearance of the orangutan would be final and irrevocable and the chances of being reborn one day absolutely zero" (Chevillard 2007, 55).[27] No longer on the precipice of Bakhoûn's relatively stable world, Albert lives in what Stephanie Wakefield calls the Anthropocene back loop (2020, 23), that is, an era of great possibility, renewal, and "unexpected synergies" between humans, the environment, and technology, all of which the zookeeper hopes to capitalize on through the rebuilding of both words and – more extremely – bodies.

---

[25] "notre littérature peine à faire entendre sa petite voix de malade. Que dit-elle? Pâle énigme."
[26] "Quand on veut parler de lui, on dit dindon, on cherche le mot juste, il se dérobe, on dit dindon, le mot nous échappe mieux que la volaille qui le portait, appelé dronte, ou dodo, mais le plus souvent on dit dindon."
[27] "la disparition de l'orang-outan serait définitive et sans recours et des chances de renaître un jour nulles absolument."

Becoming Orangutan: Albert's Behavioral Experiment

As the narrative abruptly transitions to a bleak post-apocalyptic world, the orangutan's extinction ignites a new world order where humans must continue their struggle to survive, despite the looming possibility of humanity's self-destruction. The orangutan "was not plotting its own extinction like we are slyly doing (soon, under the laws of evolution, an arm will treacherously stab us in the back)" (Chevillard 2007, 52).[28] In Part Three, Albert decides to reintroduce the orangutan by training his fellow zoo employees to act like them. By insisting on *becoming* orangutans, Albert takes Deleuze and Guattari's ecological concept of *devenir-animal* [becoming-animal] (1980, 291) quite literally, in which the philosophers propose "a theoretical way of embracing the rhizomatic – and posthumanist – texture of the environment, including the relationship between human and animal" (Lord 2020, 143). This rhizomatic relationship – like the botanical term from which the term derives, *rhizome* – insists on a non-hierarchical relationship between beings. As such, in the case of human and orangutan, *devenir-animal* attempts to undo any evolutionary stratification between the two species. In Albert's view, to fully embody orangutan existence is to achieve the goals of *devenir-animal*, that is, the creation of a different world order that does not center around humanity and its destructive habits yet is also a way to repopulate parts of the Earth in the novel (Chevillard 2007, 161). Ironically, becoming an orangutan is the only heroic way to save both human *and* simian. Training to become orangutans is thus an exercise in self-preservation; it serves the transhumanist purpose of attempting to overcome the obstacle of orangutan extinction, which has created a butterfly effect of degradation, including on humans themselves.

Without the orangutan, bodies become lethargic and cumbersome: "This sluggishness! We drag ourselves. I'm not making it up [...] Our arms no longer grip anything. Here are our lost bodies" (Chevillard 2007, 11).[29] The key objective for Albert's experiment is for humans to defy the gravitational heaviness of their bodies and live life in the trees, "suspended by a hand or a finger, celestial bodies – only our excrement and our corpses will touch the ground" (Chevillard 2007, 162).[30] Moving

---

[28] "ne complotait pas sa propre extinction comme nous le faisons sournoisement (bientôt, en vertu des lois de l'évolution, un bras nous poussera dans le dos pour nous poignarder par traîtrise)."

[29] "Cette torpeur! On se traîne. Je ne l'invente pas [...] Nos bras ne saisissent plus rien. Voilà nos corps perdus."

[30] "suspendus par une main ou un doigt, corps célestes – ne toucheront plus le sol que nos excréments et nos cadavres."

beyond the Freudian logic of humans simply walking upright to become civilized, thus elevating ourselves above the excrement of animals, Albert takes a step further, insisting on our elevation to the trees. By occupying a higher physical space, Albert calls attention to the superior status of the orangutan. As Albert coaches his team, telling them to free themselves of the clothing and shoes weighing them down or to expunge their frustration with their failure to make their bodies lighter, the reader laughs nervously at Albert's absurd reasoning that, somehow, being nude will allow his trainees to become orangutans (Chevillard 2007, 164–165).

A self-proclaimed expert on the extinct species and exempt from the training, Albert notably takes on the role of redeemer and savior of a failing humanity that must exist without the orangutan. Albert's desire to help humanity does not put him at risk, which positions him in stark contrast to other human or posthuman protagonists I examine throughout this book. His team responds somewhat begrudgingly to the authoritarian zookeeper's orders from an armchair placed between two tree trunks (Chevillard 2007, 177). He even admits to taking his ambitions too far and acting prematurely to accelerate his trainees' progress by releasing a tiger on them. The tiger first attacks an older trainee, Aldon, who plays dead. The tiger then pounces on another, Karpof, and rips off part of his face with a swipe of its paw, sinks its teeth into his throat, and drags him into the cage to finish him off. Instead of evoking a sense of horror, this pitiful scene simply invokes Albert's displeasure, and he sees it as a teachable moment for his team (Chevillard 2007, 178–179). The zookeeper's logic is nonsensical, yet calls attention to his transhumanist desire to overcome nature: how can humanity survive and reclaim existential meaning without the orangutan if, in Albert's mind, injury and possibly death represent a successful orangutan transformation? The more Albert prolongs his behavioral experiment, the more he strikes the reader as delusional, even though his increasingly absurd acts are posthumanist, challenging the hierarchical simian-ape relationship and reconceptualizing the human as the former epitome of evolution.

Albert's perspective demonstrates the protagonist's blend of posthumanist goals and transhumanist actions. Yet his attempts ultimately fail. Unlike our esteemed simian ancestors, humans cannot adapt to their new arboreal environment. Although Albert insisted that his human trainees would adapt to the forest and their bodies would morph appropriately – without surgery (!), he proclaims – this never comes to fruition. Albert wishes to, but cannot successfully shrink the scale effect of evolution (Chevillard 2007, 172). Indeed, one of his coworkers, Balmer, falls from high in the trees and dies. Albert calls him a "useful martyr for our cause" ["martyr utile à notre cause"] (Chevillard 2007, 168). Although the humans struggle to fully embody orangutans, for Albert, they can at least die like them: "Balmer was the first to perish as we will all perish, I hope, as a real orangutan and he thereby demonstrated that it was well in our power to become one" (Chevillard 2007, 169).[31] In the end, humans simply cannot transform themselves into the exceptional orangutan, despite Albert's reliance on the rhizomatic relationship between human and simian.

Through his protagonist, Albert, Chevillard muses on whether our "evolved" state as *Homo sapiens* is simply a comic irony, an evolutionary coincidence. Without the comedy, Rosny suggested a similar perspective in *Les Xipéhuz*. The confrontation with the alien forms could have easily resulted in our extinction; the Xipéhuz were worthy to replace us. In *Sans l'orang-outan*, Albert takes this a step further by saying it *should* have been humans that went extinct. Such a possible coincidence encourages a subsequent non-anthropocentric reframing of our existence. The remarks of Ragonit, one of Albert's orangutans-in-training, suggest that the universe cares about our lives: Orangutans were meant to go extinct, so imitating them puts humans at risk of extinction. Albert challenges Ragonit's anthropocentric view and says that Balmer's death can be explained by the complex laws of a balanced ecosystem: "And how can we not see, on the contrary, that it is a matter of healthy regulation within the group, natural and beneficial to the species? The males outnumber the females and this imbalance would have inevitably led us to bloody clashes" (Chevillard 2007, 170).[32] Even though both Albert and Ragonit view Balmer's death as the hidden workings of a superior order, Albert insists that this force is simply an ecological one, rather than one invested in the motives behind human actions. Albert "assumes that some truth exists in the universe which is more valuable than life itself. There must be abstract ideas and values which are worth dying and suffering for, otherwise the hero's painful quest [...] becomes absurd" (Meeker 1996, 167).

The failure of Albert and his team of orangutans-in-training comes to a head when they must ultimately choose to give up on their endeavor

---

[31] "Balmer le premier a péri comme nous périrons tous, je l'espère, en véritable orang-outan et il a par là même démontré qu'il était bien en notre pouvoir de devenir tel."

[32] "Et comment ne pas voir au contraire qu'il s'agit d'une saine régulation au sein du groupe, naturelle et profitable à l'espèce? Les mâles sont en surnombre par rapport aux femelles et ce déséquilibre nous aurait inévitablement conduits à des affrontements sanglants."

because of the limits of human memory – "Would the orangutan dilute his wine? [...] Where would he store his personal effects? Did he sometimes wear glasses?" – rather than the universal forces evoked by Ragonit, as the reason for their failure (Chevillard 2007, 183).[33] Like literature and language, human memory is also subject to degradation in *Sans l'orang-outan*:

> As time goes by, my own memories and those of my companions disintegrate. So when I ask Claudius to jump from his branch, head forward, arms outstretched, in order to acquire through exercise the qualities of an orangutan glider, he refuses to do so with the utmost energy, pretending that we never saw such a thing, that I am wrong, that I'm confused, and he protests so much and so well that he succeeds in sowing doubt in me. (Chevillard 2007, 182)[34]

The training project becomes a paradox: Albert wants a team of humans to transform into a group of orangutans but, in order to do so successfully in the dilapidated environment of the post-orangutan Anthropocene, they need a proper example, which is impossible to find. The stuffed bodies of Bagus and Mina cannot even serve as models. So preoccupied with his experiment, Albert neglects his routine care of their bodies in the eco-shrine. The ubiquitous deterioration finally spreads to Bagus and Mina: "Their shriveled skin cracks in many places, loses its hair, is now only a party dress for moths. Their neglected, verminous appearance would rather encourage one to avoid them" (Chevillard 2007, 183).[35] In a sense, this is a reminder of Albert's own mortality and that of the rest of humanity because "the prospect of looking like them one day is no longer very appealing" ["la perspective de leur ressembler un jour n'a plus autant d'attrait"] (Chevillard 2007, 183–184). Human failure to keep the orangutan alive is amplified by the failure of Albert and his team to keep the simian alive in their minds; unable to remember what

---

[33] "L'orang-outan coupait-il son vin? [...] Où rangeait-il ses effets personnels? Portait-il parfois des lunettes?"

[34] "Le temps passant, mes propres souvenirs et ceux de mes compagnons se délitent. Ainsi lorsque je demande à Claudius de sauter de sa branche, tête en avant, bras écartés, afin d'acquérir par l'exercice les qualités de planeur de l'orang-outan, s'y refuse-t-il avec la dernière énergie, prétextant que jamais on ne vit une telle chose, que je me trompe, que je confonds, et il proteste tant et si bien qu'il réussit à introduire le doute en moi."

[35] "Leur peau racornie se craquelle en maints endroits, perd son crin, n'est plus une robe de fête que pour les mites. Leur aspect négligé, vermineux, inciterait plutôt à les fuir."

the orangutans were like, the team can no longer emulate them, thus dismantling the very purpose of the behavioral experiment.

Becoming Orangutan: Albert's Biotechnological Experiment

Despite their decision to no longer attempt to become orangutans, Albert still wants to restore balance to a world without the red ape. Part Four of *Sans l'orang-outan*, one page in total, gives a brief portrait of Albert's bioengineered endeavor to reverse species extinction. Like his team for the behavioral experiment of Part Three, Albert relies on others in his quest to de-extinct the orangutan. He easily recruits Pelleport, who successfully creates an embryo in the laboratory from the frozen sperm and eggs of Bagus and Mina. Albert then convinces his lover Aloïse to be inseminated with the orangutan embryo. The in vitro experiment is ultimately what Deleuze and Guattari call "involution," a form of evolution "which occurs between heterogeneous species, on condition that we do not confuse involution with a regression. Becoming is involutive, involution is creative. To regress is to move towards the less differentiated. But to involute is to form a block that follows along its own line" (1980, 292).[36] Involution's tendency toward creation is exactly what Albert desires with his human-orangutan assemblage.

Melding simian and human together in a final effort to become orangutan, Chevillard parodies an element that supposedly distinguishes human from simian – technological progress. It is humans who embraced the progress granted by these forms of technology, but humans' overuse of technology (e.g. the deforestation that contributed to the orangutan's downfall) questions our species's superiority. Sherryl Vint describes an iconic scene in science fiction cinema in Stanley Kubrick's *2001: A Space Odyssey*, in which an ape throws a bone up into the sky and the shot transposes from bone in mid-air to a spaceship floating in orbit. This scene, argues Vint, demonstrates "man's triumphal conquest of nature through the invention of technology" (2009, 228–229). The discovery of the bone for destroying things marks the transformation into modern-day humans that Albert tries to undo throughout the novel, that is, this "emergence of man from ape" (Vint 2009, 229). Technology, then, created a rift between *Homo sapiens* and our primate

---

[36] "qui se fait entre hétérogènes, à condition que l'on ne confonde surtout pas l'involution avec une régression. Le devenir est involutif, l'involution est créatrice. Régresser, c'est aller vers le moins différencié. Mais involuer, c'est former un bloc qui file suivant sa propre ligne."

predecessor, pointing to primitivity as a lack of technological culture. Albert rectifies this misunderstanding, explaining that the orangutans were never interested in our forms of technology (Chevillard 2007, 174). Living a life in the trees, the orangutans forced humans to look upwards, aspire to the stars, and make room for our spacemen and rocket ships: "He pulled us up. He opened the sky to us, brushed aside the clouds, brought the moon closer. The orangutan cleared a path among the stars for us. Free field for our rockets, for our prayers" (Chevillard 2007, 22).[37] In fact, the orangutan's indifference to technology was mistaken as contempt, when in reality, according to Albert, the simian species encouraged and applauded our technological adventures: "Was it not, in the absence of gods and proven Martians, our only audience, with perhaps the gorilla and the chimpanzee, the only audience capable of evaluating our extraordinary adventure, of being amazed at it, of applauding us?" (Chevillard 2007, 174).[38] Wouldn't, then, the orangutans applaud Albert's technological efforts to bring them back to the trees?

In *Sans l'orang-outan*, technology ironically and quite literally brings humans back to their simian origins, revealing Chevillard's treatment of humanity and its environment as a complex blend between a posthumanist sympathy for the nonhuman Other and transhumanist impulse to overcome biology at all cost, which "assumes that all choice is likely to be an error and that survival depends upon finding accommodations that will permit all parties to endure" (Meeker 1996, 164). Could a radical human-simian assemblage repair a degraded Anthropocene, ensure human survival, and regenerate the orangutan species? The hopeful, last line of the novel – "In two hundred and forty-five days, I'm trembling with emotion, a son will be born to her who will also be the father of us all" – leaves the reader to speculate whether Aloïse will successfully carry and give birth to an orangutan (Chevillard 2007, 187).[39] By suspending the conclusion to Albert's endeavors, Chevillard draws our attention to the need for a posthumanist ethic that is more nuanced than Albert's own eco-morale. Albert's potential failure highlights the issue with a transhumanist solution to a posthumanist problem. The

---

[37] "Il nous tirait vers le haut. Il nous ouvrait le ciel, écartait les nues, rapprochait la lune. L'orang-outan nous frayait un chemin entre les astres. Champ libre pour nos fusées, pour nos prières."

[38] "N'était-il pourtant, en l'absence de dieux et de Martiens avérés, notre seul public, avec peut-être le gorille et le chimpanzé, le seul public capable de prendre la mesure de notre extraordinaire aventure, de s'en ébaudir, de nous applaudir?"

[39] "Dans deux cent quarante-cinq jours, j'en tremble d'émotion, lui naîtra un fils qui sera aussi notre père à tous."

Deleuzian assemblage is a radical reimagining of moving away from hierarchical thought between humans and nonhumans, but the novel indicates that our anthropocentric impulses can prevent us from fully achieving such a radical reconceptualization. In contrast with Albert's dreams of a new genealogy, Chevillard ultimately takes a more figurative approach to becoming-orangutan; in other words, he brings up debate about certain kinds of language that are productive to reimagining our existence in the Anthropocene.

Conclusion

In a 2004 interview, Chevillard expresses his alarm about technological acceleration, which potentially risks more species' extinction and eventually our own:

> The future we are making for ourselves is rather ominous, technology until death. We are tempted to contrast it with our rustic past for which we believe ourselves to have this strange, belated nostalgia, even though all of humanity's efforts since this prehistoric age has a tendency toward this, this technological future until death, this world fully under control. (*Scalps* 2004, 179)[40]

Once again, Chevillard connects the bucolic and the prehistoric to the contemporary, insisting on the ongoing obsession with transhumanist control over one's environment. In Rosny's corpus analyzed in Chapter One, technology and science distinguished modern humans from prehistoric ones who were stuck in animistic, irrational views of the Other. Technology transported humans to the heavens, allowing them to observe a new environment and help a species survive. But technology also brought humans back down to Earth. Water was a resource that the species could not live without, and the excesses of human technology made humanity regress to a pre-industrial society, simply trying to survive, yet eventually accepting defeat. Unlike Targ, Chevillard's Albert expresses no resignation; his zealous endeavors to undo anthropogenic species extinction, ecological wastelands, and degraded bodies only

---

[40] "L'avenir que nous nous fabriquons est plutôt inquiétant, technologie à mort. Nous sommes tentés de lui opposer notre passé rustique pour lequel nous nous prenons sur le tard d'une étrange nostalgie, alors même que tout l'effort de l'homme depuis cet âge préhistorique tend vers cela, cet avenir technologique à mort, ce monde entièrement sous contrôle."

highlight the author's parody of anthropocentric thinking, and even human existence writ large. Albert becomes desperate and takes on a pseudo-heroic role to undo this damage as everything seems to fade away and degrade into the physical and linguistic butterfly effects caused by the deaths of Bagus and Mina. Technology becomes a final resort, transforming from a weapon of domination and violence (the Ape Man from *2001: A Space Odyssey*) to one of possible creation with the Aloïse-embryo assemblage. Ironically, Albert is not the one who actually performs the physical work necessary to accomplish his absurd behavioral and biotechnological endeavors.

Both Albert's behavioral and biotechnological experiments reveal that the human body is a sometimes absurd technological tool that is used in the service of creating life and helping another species, thus problematizing the transhumanist view that technology is primarily a tool for humans to master the environment. Nevertheless, Albert tries to be the noble hero of tragic literature; his efforts simply culminate in a display of humanity's eccentricities. Chevillard satirizes the hero and reveals his foolishness, blending such satire with Albert's posthumanist sympathy. Chevillard changes the heroic narrative even further to one centered around life-giving or life-promoting sources (an eco-shrine, a womb). At the same time, the author suggests that Albert is trapped in his own world and determined to succeed despite his absurdities. By means of Albert's many failures, Chevillard highlights his protagonist's tragic, transhumanist impulses to master biology. Yet, paradoxically, Chevillard ends on a posthumanist note. The reader is encouraged to transcend Albert's story and observe that, by mocking Albert's failures, the novel calls attention to a need for a posthumanist ethic that challenges the centrality of the human and views the human as part of a symbiotic ecosystem.

Part Two

Posthuman Bodies, Posthuman Minds

Chapter Three

Cyborg Encounters in the Fiction of Jean-Claude Dunyach and Ayerdhal

The cyborg initially appears as a nightmare for posthumanist thinking, but this cybernetic creature carries the utopic potential of coexistence between humans and nonhumans. The cyborg seems to run amok with technology so that it can transcend body, mind, and the Earth. Pioneers of artificial intelligence Hans Moravec and Martin Minsky saw no difference between human and machine, even going as far as suggesting that a computer could become a repository for the human mind and eventually discard the materiality of the human body. This transhumanist quest for immortality continues into the twenty-first century with "some Silicon Valley guy" who thinks he "is transcending human being" (Morton and Boyer 2021, 69). These techno-fantasies reimagine the human as "a mere assemblage of parts and pieces, infinitely malleable by technical means [...] the fantasy of extracting the self, mind or consciousness from the flesh in order to achieve cybernetic immortality" (Pastourmatzi 2014, 275). However, this quest denies the fact that humans are embodied beings whose material existence not only connects them to the Earth but to other living entities. Such a quest ignores "the net result of thousands of years of sedimented evolutionary history" and how this history affects human thought and behavior (Hayles 1999, 284). Take Jeff Bezos, for instance. To my knowledge, he is not a cyborg, but he is, like Aloïse's orangutan embryo in Chapter Two, an assemblage of technical and human parts when he straps himself to a rocket to go to the edge of the stratosphere. By engaging in transcendent being – that is, the art of overcoming and going beyond what one is – Bezos dares to transcend "the material realm of social responsibility," as was Bernard Blanc's concern with the Vernian tradition, which I discussed in the Introduction (Vint 2006, 8). In other words, escaping Earth's gravitational pull seems synonymous with dodging social responsibility down on the ground as Amazon's practices negatively impact smaller businesses, the company's own employees, and the environment. Upon first glance, cyborgs, and their human-machine assemblages as forebears, are transcendent beings whose holistic nature makes them greater and more powerful than the sum of their parts.

Jean-Claude Dunyach and Ayerdhal's *Étoiles mourantes* (1999) [Dying Stars] offers a critical take on the transhumanist exploitation of the cyborg as a means of infinite power or even immortality for human identity. In their co-authored novel, diversified populations of cybernetic posthumans are scattered throughout the universe, each one achieving some sense of immortality at the cost of the human body, mind, or both. The first pages of the novel are reflections from the AnimalCities ["AnimauxVilles"], a massive extraterrestrial species composed of flesh and filament, now inhabited by human communities. These spacefaring creatures initially discovered the feeble human species at the beginning of the previous millennium when one of their kind suddenly appeared in the dried-up basin that used to be the Mediterranean Sea. The AnimalCities granted humans the ability to escape an Anthropocene Earth and allowed the terrestrial species to explore many new worlds. The beginnings of such explorations are documented in Dunyach's previous novel (written without Ayerdhal) that is set in the same universe, *Étoiles mortes* (1992) [Dead Stars], which won the French SF award the Prix Rosny-aîné. Humans abused this privilege, however, by only sending their elites to distant planets. An unnamed fifth faction of cyborgs was destroyed, and the AnimalCities decided to repair what they had broken, which resulted in the Dispersion of the remaining four branches so that they would never need to come in constant contact with one another. In *Étoiles mourantes*, each branch of technologically enhanced humans suggests a different facet of transhumanist exploitation of the mind-body-AI interface. The Mechanists ["Mécanistes"] are a male-dominant, warrior faction whose intelligent bodily armor is like a second skin. The Originals ["Originels"] transfer the souls of dying individuals into *personae*, which are animated holograms powered by artificial intelligence (AI).[1] The third faction consists of Organics ["Organiques"], who host parasitic nanoviruses called "embiotes." The *embiotes* force the Organics to exercise extreme physical control over their bodies. However, if the symbiotic growths are not removed, they can take over the body and turn it into a statue, to which an entire museum is dedicated in the Organic world. The final faction is the Connected ["Connectés"], who have what is called a "flagelle" at the

---

[1] The authors use the Latin nominative plural *personae* to designate a single AI hologram; this is undoubtedly a conscious choice to relay a sense of plurality of "persons" that stems from dividing the Self in the cyborg process.

base of their spine, which plugs them into a network that connects their whole society. Once permitted to quickly navigate the fabric of the "Ban," or space-time, these cyborgs have now been relegated to different corners of the universe in order to avoid contact that could quickly lead to deadly conflict. But now, the Mechanists, in their attempts to master the instant teleportation that comes so naturally to the majestic AnimalCities, threaten to unravel the threadwork of the Ban with a warship and take all living beings with it. Both xenophobic distrust of other cyborg populations and the arduous relationship between humans and artificial intelligence anchor the multi-species and multi-conscious encounters that spark this existential crisis. The transhumanist quest to master biology has come true for these factions, but such an achievement is mostly an illusion as each cyborg society struggles to find meaning in their transcendent cyborg minds and bodies.

Ultimately, Dunyach and Ayerdhal reframe the cyborg as an entity capable of posthumanist connection. While the Mechanists and the dictator of the Originals, Koriana, seek extreme transhumanist mastery of biology, four unique protagonists from each society have the potential to create posthumanist networks paradoxically *because of* and *despite* their human–machine interfaces. Take the robotic vacuum, the Roomba, for instance; its simplistic agency serves as a model for Dunyach and Ayerdhal's protagonists. It revels in what Timothy Morton and Dominic Boyer call subscendent (rather than posthuman, transcendent) life: "It knows it wants to get dirt inside of itself, everything else it has to figure out as it goes along, with a fairly limited sensory apparatus. So it sort of trundles along, bumping into walls and furniture, staying very close to the earth. Always less than itself" (2021, 41). Like the Roomba, Dunyach and Ayerdhal's protagonists are less than the sum of their parts; when the AnimalCities bring them together at the site of a supernova to save the universe from complete annihilation, the protagonists truly "see" each other through physical connection and the sharing of memories of loved ones. These moments allow them to subscend from their complex human–machine assemblages to their human qualities. Representative of the "punk" aspects of cyberpunk SF, these protagonists rebel from their factions, subverting not only the fragmented human–machine interfaces of their respective factions, but also the autonomous, anthropocentric tendencies associated with each community's transhumanist endeavors.[2] It is for this reason that they are selected by the AnimalCities to serve

---

[2] James Patrick Kelly and John Kessel explain cyberpunk's "obsessions" as "presenting a global perspective on the future, engaging with developments in infotech and biotech, especially invasive technologies that transform

as representatives of their respective societies during the climax of the novel, the explosion of a dying star. The transition from transcendence to subscendence allows the protagonists to become "more susceptible to a larger variety of things that aren't [them], most of which are nonhuman – including [their] own body to a certain extent" (Morton and Boyer 2021, 64). The cyborg does not have to be a posthumanist's nightmare. In fact, it has the utopian potential to create posthumanist relationships.

In this chapter, I demonstrate that a more embodied human–machine interface in the novel allows for a posthumanist ethic to bloom when facing the cyborg Other. My analysis expands upon the very limited academic discussion of this novel by French SF scholars in France, who have briefly noted the text's theme of posthumanist coexistence (Bréan 2012; "Histoires du futur" 2013), heavy scientific extrapolation (Vas-Deyres 2013), and emphasis on the bodily senses (Vas-Deyres 2018). With the help of the cybernetic language of Katherine Hayles, Timothy Morton, and Gilles Deleuze, I argue that the degree of cyborg embodiment – the extent to which a cyborg manifests physically – impacts how the novel's characters "see the face" of the cyborg Other, to recall Levinas's term from Chapter One: first, how the transhumanist cyborgs like the Mechanists and Koriana lack connections to the Other by neither experiencing the confines of the body nor the *connections* of the body (as biological matter to other forms of matter), and second, how the "punk" individuals from each faction and the events that transpire at the supernova show that cyborgs can make empathetic connections with other organisms due to their artificially intelligent prostheses. These prostheses, then, do not ignore their "embedded embodiment," that is, using the posthuman body to embed itself in a larger web of life (Nayar 2014, 9). In the end, in the ideal posthumanist cyborg model of Dunyach and Ayerdhal, it is a question of, in Hayles's terms, "*extending embodied awareness* in highly specific, local, and material ways that would be impossible without electronic prostheses" (Hayles 1999, 291; emphasis added). In this case, technology becomes a tool for making connections with the Other rather than simply acting as a tool for mastering (or completely discarding) the body. In order to better understand Dunyach and Ayerdhal's impressive treatment of the cyborg within a post-Second World War French SF tradition that mostly ignores supercharged scientific extrapolation, it is critical to take a look at how these authors engage with human–machine encounters in the broader cultural and literary context of twentieth-century France.

> human body/psyche, [and a] *subversive attitude that challenges traditional values*" (2007, ix; emphasis added).

Human–Machine Encounters in Contemporary French Science Fiction and Culture

In this cyberpunk space opera of sensorial delights and deprivations, the French co-authors successfully marry their separate yet overlapping interests of social critique and the ways in which scientific development – particularly cybernetic enhancement of the body – crack open questions concerning our human understanding of the relationships between mind, body, and machine. Both a scientist and a writer, Dunyach holds a doctorate in supercomputing and applied mathematics and has published nine novels and ten short story collections since the 1980s with French publishers dedicated to SF – Denoël, Fleuve Noir Anticipation, and l'Atalante. Perhaps due to the "literary" quality of Dunyach's writing, many of his short stories have been translated into English by Sheryl Curtis and Jean-Louis Trudel (Dunyach 2004; 2009). Indeed, emblematic of the "literary turn" in French SF of the 2000s, Dunyach's work showcases a "textual thickness" ["épaisseur textuelle"], that is, a greater, more explicit interest in intertextuality and metatextuality, thus "inviting readers to question the conditions of creation involving figures taken from text to text" (Bréan, "Le Rapport à l'avenir (2/2)" 2013).[3] Demonstrating a remarkable range of imagination, his fiction varies from the virtual realities and bodies of cyberpunk ("La Stratégie du requin" ["Shark"]) to Victorian steampunk where a pterodactyl creature must be conquered by a Jules Verne-like flying machine ("L'Orchidée de la nuit" ["Night Orchid"]), to the fantastic/horror subgenre when a boy accidentally swallows a fairy ("Regarde-moi quand je dors" ["Watch Me While I Sleep"]). His co-author, Ayerdhal, on the other hand, who also started writing in the late 1980s, merges thrillers, sociopolitical commentary, and SF in his body of work. The award-winning *Demain, une oasis* (1992) [Tomorrow, an Oasis] describes an alternate reality where the northern part of the world launches an expedition into space, leaving the southern hemisphere behind. *Mytale* (1991) depicts a planet of mutants, abandoned by an empire but whose contact is sought once again after a new republic emerges thousands of years later. Bréan remarks that "each novel is an episode of the broad political claim that accompanies the expansion of humankind, a road congested with oppressive systems and individual rebellions. The protagonists assert a conquering singularity, which offers a counterpoint to frozen political and social institutions" ("Histoires du futur" 2013,

---

[3] "invitant les lecteurs à s'interroger sur les conditions de la création touchant à des figures reprises de texte en texte."

para. 17).⁴ Given Ayerdhal's interest in social relations and politics and Dunyach's penchant for examining death, memory, and the human body, their co-authorship works as a natural assemblage for investigating the dystopian and utopian effects of living in a cybernetic, posthuman body.

Extrapolated from information technology and astrophysics, their novel is a rare example of hard SF in twentieth-century French fiction, whose uniqueness stems from the French's wary relationship with technology after both world wars, as I emphasized in the Introduction (Vas-Deyres 2012, 439); as a result, this deeply impacted French SF production and the themes tackled by its creators. While from an American perspective, technology bolstered national heroism on the beaches of Normandy and brought modern technological comfort to individual Americans after the Second World War, French citizens experienced its horrors up close, including totalitarian regimes and genocide (Bréan 2012, 46). As for SF production, not only did it practically come to a halt in the interwar and immediate postwar periods in France (contrary to the American SF market), but the authors who *were* successful tended to write deeply pessimistic fiction that rejected the stereotypical scientific positivism of the Vernian narrative. In some cases, technology all but disappeared from the narrative. The SF of Jacques Spitz, Régis Messac, Léon Daudet, and Théo Varlet, for instance, shifted fictional models to ones with "a more 'noble' literary heritage: that of the imaginary voyage, the *conte philosophique*, and the *roman d'hypothèse*. Accordingly, their SF works [did] not give a great deal of importance to technological inventions, which, quite often, [became] mere pretexts" (Bozzetto and Evans 1990, 7). Anti-scientific thinking during these years positioned science as leading humanity to one of only two bleak outcomes: either the apocalypse or an "ant hill" society that would obliterate individual liberties (Bozzetto and Evans 1990, 7). Take René Barjavel's successful novel *Ravage* (1943) [*Ashes, Ashes*], where strange weather causes the world's electricity to disappear, and, after a few adventures, the protagonist survives and establishes a bucolic utopia near the Mediterranean. This emblematic work of one of the most successful authors to emerge from the chaos of a war-torn France clearly reflected negative views on science and progress, and such views were shared by most French people of the time (Bozzetto and Evans 1990, 12).

---

⁴ "chaque roman est plutôt un épisode de la vaste revendication politique qui accompagne l'expansion de l'humanité, une route encombrée de systèmes oppressifs et de rébellions individuelles. Les protagonistes affirment une singularité conquérante, qui offre un contrepoint à des institutions politiques et sociales figées."

Between 1950 and 1955, American SF invaded the shores of the Hexagon with throngs of translated novels from the Anglo-American Golden Age of the 1930s and 1940s, such as Isaac Asimov, Ray Bradbury, Arthur C. Clarke, Robert Heinlein, Theodore Sturgeon, Clifford Simak, and A.E. Van Vogt; this invasion sparked not only a renewed national interest in science fiction but also a rehabilitation of the soiled image of scientific progress itself. Intellectuals like Raymond Queneau (novelist, poet, critic, founder of the experimental literary group Oulipo) and Boris Vian (musician, translator, critic, author of surrealistic SF novels) saw the literary and ideological potential of this "new" SF and spearheaded efforts of translation. In various magazine and journal articles for critics and the general public alike, Queneau and Vian, among others, welcomed American SF as a "genre likely, similar to the detective novel, to renew the way novelists look at the contemporary world" (Bréan 2012, 91).[5] The SF genre quickly became trendy along with other American imports such as Hollywood films, jazz, Coca-Cola, and chewing gum – some of which were cultural products that had previously been banned under the Nazi Occupation (Evans 1991, 235). Meanwhile, in the greater sociopolitical landscape of this time, France was losing its imperial grip in wars of independence in Indochina (1946–1954) and Algeria (1954–1962); as a result, the nation started to see itself as in steep decline on the world stage. What then emerged, despite collective national trauma from the world wars, was a concerted effort to modernize France very quickly via state-sponsored technological innovation. Such efforts became part of a national narrative of "salvation, redemption, and liberation," where "technology would save France from economic and cultural disaster" (Hecht 2009, 201). For Roger Bozzetto, American SF played a double role in this national push to redeem France and propel it into the future at warp speed. First, it reanimated a seemingly lost literary tradition in France. Second, it served as a model for Hexagonal SF – even in its many imitations of American space operas – to inject science, technology, and modernity into French society. American SF seemed to symbolize the apotheosis of a "new industrial ideology" to replace France's traditional, agrarian society (Bozzetto and Evans 1990, 13). Therefore, in the French imagination, supercharged science and technology as vectors of progress and optimism became inseparable from the United States and American SF.

[5] "genre susceptible, à l'instar du roman policier, de renouveler le regard posé par les romanciers sur le monde contemporain." For more on the connections between science fiction and Surrealism, see the collection *Surrealism, Science Fiction and Comics*, edited by Gavin Parkinson (2015).

The governmental obsession with rapid modernization inspired by an American model of techno-scientific progress and consumerism drew critiques of *machinisme* – a complete transformation of human by machine – from French intellectuals and creatives in the 1950s and 1960s who "feared that without any deliberate human agency, technological change and the lure of material goods had conspired to alter the very structure of social and political relationships" (Hecht 2009, 30; Vas-Deyres 2012, 158). No other French work expresses this zeitgeist better than Jean-Luc Godard's underappreciated film noir *Alphaville* (1965), where a technocratic society dampens human emotion and individuality. The film follows a detective named Lemmy Caution on a mission to the city of Alphaville to retrieve a fellow agent named Dickson. More importantly, Caution must either kill or bring back Professor von Braun, creator of the supercomputer Alpha 60 that reigns over Alphaville. In the city, odes to science abound from the names of streets and parks to flashing neon signs of "$E=mc^2$." The abrasive and decisively inhuman voice of Alpha 60 is ubiquitous, making itself heard throughout the entire film. Governed by the rationality of Alpha 60, the citizens seem almost as robotic as their cold oppressor. The citizens' mantra, "I'm doing well, thank you, don't mention it" ["Je vais très bien, merci, je vous en prie"], is recited often in an unexpected way during a conversation. For Godard, the only way to save these emotionless zombies is to instill in them poetic language that will eventually unlock the most profound and complex human sentiment of all – love: "Indeed, it is [Surrealist] poetry – Paul Éluard's *Capitale de la douleur* – that the fading Dickson hands to Caution as a weapon" (Utterson 2008, 57). Poetry also redeems Natasha, daughter of Professor von Braun, who does not even understand the concept of love because it is not in the dictionary – which citizens call the Bible: "Through Éluard's *Capitale de la douleur* [which Natasha reads on-screen] Caution stirs in Natasha the meaning of the words 'conscious' and 'love.' She repeats the refrain of the executed resister [who had acted 'illogically' by mourning the death of his mother ...] as she takes tentative steps toward a new lexicon of redemptive humanity, 'I ... love ... you ... I love you'" (Utterson 2008, 60). *Alphaville* not only symbolizes a national uneasiness in the face of France's mid-century blast into industrial modernity. The film also anticipates the more intense, alienating, and invasive qualities of a techno-capitalist world explored by SF authors on both sides of the Atlantic from the 1970s onwards.

The post-1968 era of French SF ushered in a different kind of storytelling that brought out the political and psychological in a way that American-style hard SF had not been doing in the immediate postwar years. This shift away from the much-imitated Anglo-American SF translated in the 1950s and 1960s was also representative of the strong anti-American, anti-capitalist sentiments present during the widespread protests of May 1968. Thus, what had been deemed American (technoscience, progress, modernity, and hard SF fueled by such concepts) was no longer in fashion (Thomas 1989, 299). Hard SF, which was popular during the American SF Golden Age, "only has very distant echoes in France" ["n'a que des échos très lointains en France"] (Bréan 2012, 84).[6] Post-1968 SF in France was full of works that focused on psychological issues, "and in particular with an individual protagonist's isolation and flight into an imaginary universe, often with Philip K. Dickian overtones [...] or sexual preoccupations" (Thomas 1989, 299). Indeed, "New French SF" authors appearing in the 1970s like Philippe Curval, Michel Jeury, Jean-Marcy Ligny, and Serge Brussolo – only loosely grouped together – often focused on the manipulation of realities and alternate worlds in a Dickian, hallucinogenic style (Dick's works appeared in French translation after 1970). These authors also drew from a variety of non-SF (or SF-adjacent) literatures, ideologies, and specific writers: Surrealism, the French Nouveau Roman, Latin American literature, Franz Kafka, Edgar Allan Poe, and Samuel Beckett (the last of whom was a major inspiration for Chevillard, as I discussed in Chapter Two) (Jouanne 1988, 227).

With this growing interest in genre-bending literatures that manipulated material and immaterial realities, the "Frenchified term *science-fiction*" was starting to take on "a meaning of its own, which would cover some of what could be termed (at least borderline) 'fantasy' in the US" (Thomas 1989, 299). Authors following this aesthetic approach in the 1980s (Jacques Barbéri, Francis Berthelot, Richard Canal, Jean-Claude Dunyach, Pierre Stolze, and Antoine Volodine) saw SF "more as a language or medium rather than an end in itself" (Jouanne 1988, 227). The same could be said for Limite, a collective of young writers of experimental fiction who wanted to broaden the SF genre by taking greater literary risks (Lanuque 2013, para. 6). The prose of these authors "is part of the continuity of experiments carried out before and especially

---

[6] Bréan uses Hal Clement and Arthur C. Clarke as examples of this lack of French interest regarding Anglo-American SF orientated toward heavily extrapolated science. He points to the limited popular success of Clement's hard-science novel, *Mission of Gravity* (1953), not translated into French until 1971 (as *Question de poids*). Clarke's more technical works are published by the "Anticipation" collection of Fleuve noir, which was dedicated to popular fiction, whereas his "softer" fiction was published by more prestigious, literary SF collections, like Denoël's "Présence du futur" and Gallimard/Hachette's "Le Rayon fantastique" (Bréan 2012, 84–85).

after 1968" (Lanuque 2013, para. 7).[7] Limite is characterized by "the at least partial expression of a postmodernism, with this desire to break down the boundaries between genres, to mix all literatures together, and a certain predilection for a very well-made, refined, even bombastic prose, where political considerations are often evanescent" (Lanuque 2013, para. 9).[8] In the 1980s, French SF turns inward ("un repli sur soi") both in terms of formal experimentation of the text itself and an exploration of psychological realities, thus representative of "a certain discouragement in the face of reality, an apparent burial of revolutionary hopes in the broad sense of 1968 and the following years" (Lanuque 2013, para. 20).[9] As such, French authors once again relegated science and technology to the background or dispensed with them altogether in the pursuit of other tropes, themes, and genres in other speculative or experimental traditions.

Authors like Dunyach, Ayerdhal, Roland C. Wagner, and Serge Lehman carry some of these trends into the last decade before the new millennium as French SF reacts to shifts in both SF writing and a reordering of the world stage. Lanuque argues that the return to the space opera narrative in the 1990s is a reflex against the avant-garde, literary experimentations among Limite that fizzled out in the 1980s (2013, para. 34). From a sociopolitical perspective, Bréan sees 1990s authors and the "new space opera" as a response to changes in global geopolitics with the fall of the Soviet Union. In particular, authors implicitly situate their worlds within the schema of Francis Fukuyama's oft-cited "end of History" proposition from 1992, in which the political scientist argues that ideological evolution has come to an end with the universalization of Western liberal democracy. For French SF authors, "History, including in the political sense, continues in their anticipations of the future, all of which includes mechanisms of oppression, domination, wars, and conflicts caused by direct descendants of the State who are taken as examples of liberal perfection, or their future equivalents" (Bréan, "Histoires du future" 2013, para 3).[10] By leaning

---

[7] "s'inscrit dans la continuité des expérimentations menées avant et surtout après 1968."
[8] "l'expression au moins partielle d'un postmodernisme, avec cette volonté d'abattre les frontières entre les genres, de mêler toutes les littératures et une certaine prédilection pour une prose très travaillée, raffinée, voire ampoulée, où les considérants politiques sont souvent évanescents."
[9] "un certain découragement face au réel, un enterrement apparent des espoirs révolutionnaires au sens large des années 68."
[10] "l'Histoire, y compris au sens politique, se poursuit dans leurs anticipations, avec tout ce que cela implique des mécanismes d'oppression, de domination,

on the resources offered by cyberpunk and the new space opera, this cohort of French writers sees possibilities of new futures that examine the friction between individual liberties, institutional powers, and social progress identified by Fukuyama (Bréan, "Histoires du future" 2013, para. 4). Dunyach and Ayerdhal's *Étoiles mourantes* portrays such tensions between the cyborg protagonists and the traditions and institutional power of their societies as they struggle to find a posthumanist coexistence among all inhabitants of their universe.

Cyberpunk-inspired works like Dunyach and Ayerdhal's novel investigate the toll that biotechnologies and information technologies take on human psyche and body in a way that highlights the idiosyncrasies of Gallic cyberpunk in the 1990s. For American SF authors toward the end of the century, like Greg Bear or Vernor Vinge, "technology once again becomes an operator of miracles, in particular nanotechnologies which give complete control over human organisms, and even brains" (Bréan, "Le Rapport à l'avenir (1/2)" 2013).[11] Gallic cyberpunk, however, takes a more measured approach to new technologies, balancing a careful optimism with residual technological cynicism. Because these authors take advantage of cybernetic imagery "to make humans the solution to an infotechnological problem" ["pour faire de l'humain la solution d'un problème de nature informatique"], a common thread among French cyberpunks reveals itself to be the attention given to emotions and desires (Bréan 2017, para. 27). Indeed, this is the crowning moment for Dunyach and Ayerdhal's protagonists in *Étoiles mourantes* when they meet each other at the supernova and can only "see" each other in the Levinasian sense when they emotionally, and even physically, connect. Writing about American cyberpunks in a 1996 essay, Dunyach praises their creation of "a sensual mapping of cyberspace" ["une cartographie sensuelle du Cyberespace"] (98). What is interesting here is Dunyach's use of the word *sensuelle* to describe the new sensorial experiences granted by cyberspace, and biotechnology writ large. In *Étoiles mourantes*, the extraterrestrial AnimalCities describe humankind's inability to understand the Ban and its limitations as a sensory failing, rather than an intellectual one: "Humans were deaf to the universe, and their poor senses were too easily fooled by the mirages of space-time. Little did they know that space smelled musty, like a prison. They did

de guerres et conflits, causé par les descendants directs des États pris pour exemples de perfection libérale, ou leurs équivalents futurs."

[11] "la technologie redevient un opérateur de miracles, en particulier les nanotechnologies qui donnent un contrôle complet sur les organismes, voire les cerveaux, humains."

not see its insurmountable limits" (Ayerdhal and Dunyach 1999, 11).[12] Contemporary French SF is, in Dunyach's own words, "often stuffed with smells, noises, tastes." The French, he goes on, "are people of the food, the touch, the smell. We're a country of perfumers, of cooks, and it can be seen in our literature; therefore, in our science fiction, people work on that sensoriality" (qtd. in Vas-Deyres 2018, 49). Humankind's sensory failing in the novel, due to cyborg disembodiment, leads to a lack of sensory awareness and emotional connection with not only the Ban but the cyborg Other.

The Mechanists: Tecamac

Despite achieving the transhumanist dream of mastering the body via artificial intelligence, the Mechanists must cope with the intrusive nature of their carbex armor. The armor covers the men completely from head to toe and is an intelligent second skin in constant symbiosis with the flesh, thus completely enhancing and weaponizing the body (Goffette 2007, 45–46). But this comes at a cost. Wearers share their mental space with the artificial intelligence that powers the carbex, which either amplifies or limits the human occupant's physical power. When a government official named Xuyinco grabs the wrists of the engineer Hualpa, the latter can feel the intrusion of the carbex: "the Engineer felt his carbex stiffen and his neck buckle under the weight of what poured into his brain. The feelings of dullness and flooding were fictitious, caused by the lack of references of his nervous system coupled to the armorial processor" (Ayerdhal and Dunyach 1999, 41).[13] The Mechanists' desire for bodily control is merely an illusion because they are unable to truly exercise autonomous will.

This lack of autonomous will is a consequence of the severity of the Mechanists' "distributed cognition," a term used by Hayles. All warriors inherit a carbex armor "teeming with the ghosts of ten, twenty or a hundred Mechanists" ["grouillante des fantômes de dix, vingt ou cent Mécanistes"] (Ayerdhal and Dunyach 1999, 19). As such, we cannot

---

[12] "Les hommes étaient sourds à l'univers et leurs pauvres sens se laissaient trop facilement abuser par les mirages de l'espace-temps. Ils ignoraient que l'espace avait une odeur de renfermé, pareille à celle d'une prison. Ils n'en distinguaient pas les limites infranchissables."

[13] "l'Ingénieur sentit son carbex se raider et sa nuque ployer sous le poids de ce qui se déversa dans son encéphale. Les sensations d'alourdissement et d'inondation étaient factices, engendrées par le manque de références de son système nerveux couplé au processeur armorial."

assume "that there is an agency, desire, or will belonging to the self and clearly distinguished from the 'wills of others'"; in other words, the Mechanists' "collective heterogenous quality implies a distributed cognition located in disparate parts that may be in only tenuous communication with one another" (Hayles 1999, 3–4). For instance, master Chetelpec, a Mechanist who trains younger generations, wears old armor whose original human occupant severely affected the succession of occupants over decades: "For six centuries, the armor had walled in the narcissistic personality of its first wearer and hated, humiliated, mistreated those who wore it. All had died young, paranoid to the last degree, drained of strength and energy, parched" (Ayerdhal and Dunyach 1999, 27).[14] The Mechanists' distributed cognition can even lead to complete dysfunction and eventual self-destruction. Iztoatl[44] and Hualpa[33] (whose superscripts in the text designate the number of generations of humans serving within the carbex armor) are Mechanist engineers who become entangled in an aggressive confrontation with Organics 20 years prior to the events of the novel. After making a deal with the Connected to use their nanotechnology to create a new generation of armor, Organics intercept the Mechanists' ship with the precious cargo. For unknown reasons, IZTOATL and HUALPA, distinguished as separate, artificially intelligent entities in the text in all capitals, destroy each other; while the Mechanists save IZTOATL's human occupant, he survives for only a year after his transplant into a "virgin" suit of armor with no previous occupants (Ayerdhal and Dunyach 1999, 31). Despite surviving this extraction and quasi-self-destruction, this generation of Iztoatl eventually "succumbed to his schizophrenia in a new armor" ["a succombé à sa schizophrénie dans une nouvelle armure"] (Ayerdhal and Dunyach 1999, 39). Between the ghosts of previous human occupants of a carbex armor, and the intrusive, hostile nature of the artificial intelligence itself, these disparate parts of the Mechanist cyborg can lead to dysfunction, and possibly self-destruction.

The hostility that comes from sharing both mind and body with an artificial intelligence transforms into a hostility toward other cyborg factions when the Mechanists attempt to control other networks of life, including the very fabric of space-time itself, the Ban.[15] To

---

[14] "Depuis six siècles, l'armure s'était murée dans la personnalité narcissique de son premier porteur et exécrait, humiliait, malmenait ceux qui l'endossaient. Tous étaient morts jeunes, paranoïaques au dernier degré, vidés de force et d'énergie, desséchées."

[15] The term "Ban" comes from the ancient Japanese game of Go that uses a grid of 19-by-19 lines, called a *goban* (Goffette 2007, 50).

describe the Ban, Dunyach and Ayerdhal use the idea of a "trame," or threadwork, which provides a modern, scientific visualization of what is often called the fabric of space-time. AnimalCities navigate the various knots, called Alephs, in the Ban threadwork, thus permitting them instantaneous travel throughout space. Recalling the mysterious, invisible recesses of space-time of Rosny's *quatrième univers,* discussed in Chapter One, the Ban evades complete human comprehension. However, the Mechanists have crafted the warship *Zéro Plus* as a way to master what they see as the AnimalCities' monopoly of instantaneous travel throughout space. This ship, though, threatens to rip apart the "fabric" of the Ban, thus endangering all the other life systems that are connected to it, including the AnimalCities. The *Zéro Plus* "was able to plow the web of underlying mathematical reality until it screamed. It was designed to tear apart, to destroy even the very foundations of Ban harmony. By mutilating the universe forever" (Ayerdhal and Dunyach 1999, 11).[16] Koriana, an Original who will make a deal with the Mechanists for his own personal gains, observes: "The Mechanists always wanted to destroy what they couldn't control" (Ayerdhal and Dunyach 1999, 135).[17]

Tecamac's cognitive assemblage of human flesh and carbex is more symbiotic, and thus, more life-enhancing, than his fellow Mechanists. He wears a virgin suit of armor without the conscious remnants of previous human occupants. While Tecamac occasionally struggles with his carbex's interference, he does not experience the painful plurality of master Chetelpec, or worse, the schizophrenia of Iztoatl. Like any other "primanyme," Tecamac's strong personality serves as a shell to host generations of new warriors, which keeps these warriors from developing their own unique personalities (Ayerdhal and Dunyach 1999, 63–64).[18] Tecamac's human–machine interface is so seamless that the AI is able to disguise itself in such a way that it appears to Tecamac as if he is speaking to himself: "Finally, it had disguised itself as an exogenous consciousness and it had *spoken*, as dreams speak, without really spoken words, stimulating the senses, and it had been as if Tecamac was talking

---

[16] "était capable de labourer la trame de la réalité mathématique sous-jacente jusqu'à ce qu'elle hurle. Il était conçu pour déchirer, pour détruire jusqu'aux fondements mêmes de l'harmonie du Ban. En mutilant à jamais l'univers."
[17] "Les Mécanistes ont toujours voulu détruire ce qu'ils ne parvenaient pas à contrôler."
[18] "Sa première fonction est de s'assurer que les successeurs de son primanyme ne développeront pas leur propre personnalité, ou à défaut, que l'armure pourra la canaliser."

to himself" (Ayerdhal and Dunyach 1999, 20; emphasis original).[19] Therefore, Tecamac's well-integrated interface raises less problematic questions about how agency is distributed, including "how and in what ways actors contribute to systemic dynamics, and consequently how responsibilities – technical, social, legal, ethical – should be apportioned" (Hayles 2017, 119).

This posthumanist network of inorganic and organic parts distinguishes Tecamac from his fellow warriors in that he is more capable of loving and "seeing" the face of the Other. His subversive nature truly shows in the very act of loving a woman named Zezlu. In the male-dominated Mechanist society, women cannot be warriors, nor can they hold positions in administration or government. Zezlu is a Geisha, one of three castes of women, and she fulfills the need for sexual reproduction. For Tecamac and Zezlu, sexual relations further intensify the intersubjectivity of Tecamac and his carbex armor. Tecamac's flesh is left exposed "[a]s the armor opened, warped, sucked the Geisha towards the Warrior and closed behind her, until it completely encompassed him" (Ayerdhal and Dunyach 1999, 50).[20] The carbex armor is the one in control as it takes over as the human Self: "The movements, the ripples, the massages were the work of the armor and the energy that Zezlu's desire consumed was supplied by the armor."[21] Nevertheless, Tecamac realizes that he can love Zezlu, which in itself is an act of revolt against Mechanist society given Zezlu's status: "It seemed to him then that love was both simpler and more important than what the Mechanism claimed, that it was in any case different from the Mechanistic vocation" (Ayerdhal and Dunyach 1999, 51, 52).[22] When Zezlu is assassinated by government officials in an attempt to put an end to the feminist movement in which she heavily participated, Tecamac rebels once again by slaughtering her assassins. When the police come to arrest him, although he plans to go willingly with them, "he did not wish to become more criminal than he was already considered, but he had to make them understand [...] that there was no longer any authority

---

[19] "Enfin, elle s'était déguisée en conscience exogène et elle avait *parlé*, ainsi que les rêves parlent, sans mots vraiment prononcés, en stimulant les sens, et cela avait été comme si Tecamac se parlait à lui-même."

[20] "plus l'armure s'ouvrait, se déformait, aspirait la Geisha vers le Guerrier et se refermait derrière elle, jusqu'à l'englober tout à fait."

[21] "Les mouvements, les ondulations, les massages étaient l'œuvre de l'armure et l'énergie que le désir de Zezlu consommait était fournie par l'armure."

[22] "Il lui sembla alors que l'amour était à la fois plus simple et plus important que ce que le Mécanisme prétendait, qu'il était en tout cas différent de la vocation Mécaniste."

anywhere capable of restraining him" (Ayerdhal and Dunyach 1999, 56).[23] This stubborn self-determination, which allows his cyborg identity to have a more symbiotic human–machine interface, will allow him to evolve past the Mechanists' transhumanist xenophobia of other cyborg factions. Indeed, as master Chetelpec says to Tecamac in anticipation of his encounter with other cyborgs at the site of the supernova: "You will probably be the first Mechanist to approach the Organics without hate. Do what I couldn't: don't judge them, above all, don't judge us" (Ayerdhal and Dunyach 1999, 312).[24]

The Originals: Gadjio and Koriana

For Koriana, dictator of the 28 worlds of Original society, the quest for human physical transcendence is no less blatant than in the Mechanist faction; the tyrant simply refuses the cyborg limitations of his own faction. Within Original society, the souls of dying individuals are transferred into cyborg *personae*, animated holograms powered by artificial intelligence. While this process allows Originals to transcend physical death, the personae can only be a copy of the human Self with rudimentary personality traits and limited memory: "Many humans found it easier to leave knowing that they were leaving behind a simplified copy of themselves, immutable, immortal, and talkative [...] Even though their autonomy diminished as they got farther from their graves, even if the oldest tended to ramble, personae represented the ultimate snub to Death" (Ayerdhal and Dunyach 1999, 72).[25] The Originals recognize that, although far from ideal, these personae allow them to escape death. However, the personae process is too imperfect for Koriana. In his view, the body is weak and vulnerable, yet it also maintains the power of the mind: memory. Consequently, he holds onto

---

[23] "il ne souhaitait pas devenir plus criminel qu'on ne le considérait déjà, mais il devait leur faire comprendre [...] qu'il n'existait plus d'autorité nulle part capable de le contraindre."
[24] "Tu seras probablement le premier Mécaniste à approcher des Organiques sans haine. Fais ce que je ne pourrais pas me permettre: ne les juge pas, surtout, ne nous juge pas."
[25] "Beaucoup d'hommes trouvaient plus facile de partir en sachant qu'ils laissaient derrière eux une copie simplifiée d'eux-mêmes, immuable, immortelle, et bavarde [...] Même si leur autonomie diminuait au fur et à mesure qu'elles s'éloignaient de leur tombe, même si les plus anciennes avaient tendance à radoter, les personae représentaient l'ultime pied de nez à la face de la Mort."

his decrepit body, refusing to die as his cells rebel and devour his insides (Ayerdhal and Dunyach 1999, 72). In his refusal to accept the limitations of his faction, Koriana insists on losing nothing in the delicate process of transferring his soul to a personae, including his full memory.

Ironically, Gadjio, who assists other Originals in the pursuit of immortality from human to cyborg personae, is truly the immortal one; it is his privilege and right as a "Passeur" to remember everything about his clients. The difficult process of transferring a dying person's essence into a machine requires the artistic touch of a Passeur, that "was as much psychology as it was dissection – which called for a subtle blend of cruelty and compassion" (Ayerdhal and Dunyach 1999, 73).[26] Koriana has hired Gadjio to work with him over the course of several years, demanding that he create one of his usual "babbling, animated dolls as close to life as technology [...] will allow," to which Koriana will officially offer his human essence.[27] The world will forget him and his body of flesh will finally vanish. But the important difference in Koriana's demand is that Gadjio must forget *him* because Gadjio's memory would reveal Koriana as artifice (Ayerdhal and Dunyach 1999, 79). Such erasure of his recent memory would include the knowledge that his terminally ill daughter, Marine, has passed away, yet still lives on the fleshy walls of Our Mother of Bones ["Notre Mère des Os"], an AnimalCity with whom Gadjio has a special connection. Knowing that Marine was far too young to be transferred into a personae, Our Mother of Bones decided to collect her essence from her body and host it in her own flesh. Memory is then truly the distinguishing factor between human and machine: "To have memory is to have history; it is also to develop empathy. The distinction between human and android produces an ontology grounded in *mortality* and not *biology* [...] The continuity of memory thus implies a kind of immortality, in which the vicissitudes of the flesh become irrelevant" (Bukatman 1993, 248–249; emphasis original). Memory thus complicates the transhumanist quest for immortality through disembodiment because if a cyborg can retain its full human memory, it has the capability to make posthumanist connections with the Other.

In contrast to Gadjio's preserved body and memory, which engenders his posthumanist character, Koriana will stop at nothing to achieve true transhumanist immortality beyond the disembodiment of the personae

---

[26] "relevait autant de la psychologie que de la dissection – qui réclamait un mélange subtil de cruauté et de compassion."
[27] "poupées animées et babillantes, aussi proche de la vie que la technologie [...] permettra."

process by acquiring a carbex armor for himself from the Mechanists. In a scene where Gadjio must unexpectedly confront this armor, the carbex is torn in half, attaching part of itself to Gadjio; Our Mother of Bones takes Gadjio away to the "Retrouvailles" [Rediscoveries], where the supernova will soon occur. When Koriana discovers what has happened, he seeks out Noone, an AnimalCity with whom he has a special relationship. Their conversation reveals Koriana's deal to acquire the carbex armor, exposing his vulnerability. As the epitome of transhumanist ideology, Koriana clings to human exceptionalism – or rather, his *own* human exceptionalism – and biological enhancement. His respect for Noone forces him to find a way to explain himself and his desire to live forever, which ultimately has consequences on the AnimalCities and the other cyborg factions: "I betrayed your species and mine for the only chance of immortality I could find" (Ayerdhal and Dunyach 1999, 132).[28] Koriana seeks to truly transcend the body, without sacrificing any part of his Self in the process; yet "the body is what makes us mortal and weak, but it is this very vulnerability that should make us take care of ourselves, one another, and the planet we live on" (Vint 2006, 10).

Koriana's refusal to accept his vulnerability makes him willing to sacrifice *others*. He goes on to explain that his researchers have discovered how the Ban works. The Alephs – holograms that are multidimensional portals in space allowing access to the Ban – all "hum" the same "melody," and when one knows how to "sing" in unison with them, they transport one to another part of the universe. The cyborgs cannot hear this song but AnimalCities can. The AnimalCity Noone does not understand why this matters since her kind are happy to take the cyborgs anywhere. However, the problem is that the Mechanists, and their Original ally Koriana, do not like depending on another life system to go where they please. The universe belongs to the AnimalCities, says Koriana, "while we [humans] are prisoners of the gravitational pull of a handful of planets" (Ayerdhal and Dunyach 1999, 133).[29] Both Koriana and the Mechanists see themselves as prisoners of the natural order of the universe that keeps them from prolonging their lives beyond the means of their societies. Therefore, in his desperation to transcend both physical and memorial death, Koriana made a deal with the Mechanists to give them all his information on the Ban in return for

---

[28] "J'ai trahi ton espèce et la mienne pour la seule chance d'immortalité que j'ai pu découvrir."
[29] "alors que nous sommes prisonniers du puits gravifique d'une poignée de planètes."

a virgin carbex armor, which highlights the dictator's disdain for the interconnectedness of posthumanism (Ayerdhal and Dunyach 1999, 134). His transhumanist pursuit of perfect immortality emphasizes a blatant disregard for the Other, whether this be other cyborg factions or the AnimalCities as a whole.

The Connected: Nadiane

The societal structure of the Connected allows its members a greater understanding of a posthumanist interconnectedness, yet it comes at the cost of the body. In imagery that invokes *The Matrix* (Wackowskis, 1999), the Connected plug into a virtual network, the "Symbiase," via a biomechanical extension of their spines called a "flagelle." To reach this "utopia of communication" ["utopie de communication"], the cyborgs must frequently plug in (Vas-Deyres 2012, 442). This seamless stream of data between all members of the faction contrasts with the Mechanists and Originals, who live in greater isolation, despite the plurality of consciousnesses within their respective human–machine interfaces. The Mechanists have no sense of connection between one another, except for the inherited phantoms of their armor. Most of the Original population are also like phantoms. But a transhumanist desire to transform the body into a tool still fuels the Connected's communicative utopia. Anticipating and extrapolating the effects of twenty-first-century social media, disconnection from the Symbiase network for longer than four hours generates "a feeling of tightness, soon followed by intolerable itching accompanied by olfactory hallucinations. Then the body signals went wild. The person [...] would drown in their own sweat or choke on their saliva after unsuccessfully trying to swallow their tongue" (Ayerdhal and Dunyach 1999, 212).[30] The Connected body has been manipulated and deformed in such a way that it is completely dependent on the machine, thus privileging informational patterns – the informational space of the network – over bodily material.

Defining the posthuman as informational patterns affirms the dreams of transhumanist technologists like Marvin Minsky or Ray Kurzweil, but such a definition does not necessarily reject the body entirely. In fact, the symbiosis of Connected society, thanks to their virtual network,

---

[30] "une sensation d'oppression, bientôt suivie de démangeaisons intolérables accompagnées de mirages olfactifs. Puis les signaux corporels s'affolaient. La personne [...] se noyait dans sa propre sueur ou s'étouffait avec sa salive après avoir vainement tenté d'avaler sa langue."

"then takes on its full meaning within the narrative thread of the novel, which must unite the different branches and annihilate their isolation" (Vas-Deyres 2012, 442).[31] The protagonist Nadiane's increased bodily awareness – and, by extension, vulnerability – emphasizes a greater utopian potential for the posthuman that she can extend to the rest of the cyborg societies. Nadiane's exceptional resistance to disconnection exhibits her power to adapt beyond her faction, so she is chosen to go to the Retrouvailles, the meeting of representatives from all four factions to witness a supernova. Nevertheless, her disconnection can only last a few hours, and this physical vulnerability simultaneously symbolizes the weakness of the entire Connected faction. Nadiane's brother, Joanelis, explains this vulnerability to her in relation to the threat that the Mechanists pose to their society: "Our vulnerability … your vulnerability, little sister, is your best protection. Nevertheless, the Mechanism is quite capable of destroying our ecosystem, inadvertently, out of spite or simply carried away by its momentum" (Ayerdhal and Dunyach 1999, 359–360).[32]

While Nadiane can withstand being apart from the Symbiase network for longer, her translucent skin exhibits her body's fragility if she remains disconnected for too long. She pushes her disconnection to its limit in an effort to be forthright about her physical brittleness while at the Retrouvailles: "she realized she was half naked, the pixels of her skin dormant like electronic snow inside a hologram. She wasn't emitting anything, she was almost transparent" (Ayerdhal and Dunyach 1999, 363, 434).[33] Ultimately, her posthumanist gesture of saving both her own and the other cyborg factions by sacrificing herself in the blast of the supernova at the Retrouvailles stems from this ability to disconnect and display her bodily weakness. This image starkly contrasts with the desire of Koriana and the Mechanists to control bodily mortality by deconstructing the human Self. Nadiane, instead, has a more symbiotic interface that allows her to feel empathy for them. By offering a new vision of the posthuman interface through the Connected's communicative network of docile, and ultimately

---

[31] "prend alors tout son sens au sein du programme narrative du roman qui se doit d'unir les différents Rameaux et annihiler leur isolement."

[32] "Notre vulnérabilité … *ta* vulnérabilité, petite sœur, est ta meilleure protection. Il n'empêche que le Mécanisme est tout à fait capable de détruire notre écosystème, par inadvertance, par dépit ou simplement emporté par son élan."

[33] "elle réalisa qu'elle était à moitié nue, les pixels de sa peau inactifs comme de la neige électronique au cœur d'un hologramme. Elle n'émettait rien, elle était presque transparente."

redemptive, technology, the authors "integrate upheavals due to technological progress while remaining universal and humanist. The interest of such a novel is to see how the singularity of cyberspace can appear to be positive and a generator of social hope" (Vas-Deyres 2012, 444).[34]

The Organics: Érythrée

As is the case for the other societies, the anarchist Organics also value extending the life of the body in their human–machine interface. They host parasitic nanoviruses called *embiotes* that infiltrate their nervous systems, allowing them to heal quickly and live longer lives: "During the first six years of their symbiosis, the ectoparasite grew faster than its host [...] then it became an endoparasite, permeating the epidermis until it disappears, digesting the nervous network, replacing/combining all the organic functions with its embiotic system. Around the age of ten, the symbiosis was complete" (Ayerdhal and Dunyach 1999, 144).[35] Yet this form of symbiosis in the human–machine interface "problematizes notions of monadic identity through genetics and biochemistry" (Ransom, "The New French SF" 2014). Once reaching puberty, the symbiotic growth must be removed and given away as a gift, or the Organics risk their personalities being completely consumed by artificial intelligence: "[one had to] dispossess oneself, to prevent the *embiote* from taking possession of their body and dissolving their personality into hers. It was the price of symbiosis. The *embiote* optimizes vital functions, the *embiote* prolongs life and youth" (Ayerdhal and Dunyach 1999, 146).[36] There is a sense of bodily control that must be mastered by the Organics; however, the Mechanists' carbex is much more hostile, and thus more dominant within the human/machine interface.

---

[34] "intègre les bouleversements dus au progrès technologique tout en restant universelle et humaniste. L'intérêt d'un tel roman est de voir comment la singularité du cyberspace peut apparaître comme positive et génératrice d'espérance sociale."

[35] "Pendant les six premières années de leur symbiose, l'ectoparasite grandissait plus vite que son hôte [...] puis il se faisait endoparasite, imprégnant l'épiderme jusqu'à disparaître en lui, digérant le réseau nerveux, suppléant/associant toutes les fonctions organiques avec son système embiotique. Vers dix ans, la symbiose était achevée."

[36] "[il fallait] se déposseder, pour empêcher l'embiote de s'approprier leur corps et dissoudre leur personnalité dans la sienne. C'était le prix de la symbiose. L'embiote optimisait les fonctions vitales, l'embiote prolongeait la vie et la jeunesse."

The petrified bodies of those who give in to the *embiote* growth are placed in an art museum, which, like the Originals, exalts the artistic process within cybernetic immortality and is ultimately a microcosm of humanity's rise and fall within the Anthropocene. The positions of these petrified human figures "were horrible, the forms were shapeless, bristling with odious growths, tortures of impossible arabesques, inhuman even in suffering" (Ayerdhal and Dunyach 1999, 148).[37] Claire Colebrook writes that art is the relationship between humanity and extinction: "Far from extinction or human annihilation being solely a twenty-first-century event (although it is that too), art is tied essentially to the nonexistence of man" (2014, 142). Similar to Albert's eco-shrine, which I discussed in Chapter Two, bodies of these "artefacteurs" are put on display forever. However, unlike the degradation of Bagus's and Mina's mummified bodies, the statues of *artefacteurs* are preserved under a carbonite film for hundreds of years. As Tachine, the mother of protagonist and rebellious Érythrée, notes when she is at the museum, the bodies are all in tormented positions: "There was the one whose skull melted on his shoulders. There was the one who dug through his guts with both hands" (Ayerdhal and Dunyach 1999, 189).[38] Biohorror thus persists in these fossilized bodies that resist the weathering effects of time – a physical manifestation of the everlasting memory that Koriana seeks. The museum and its bodily artifacts represent the paradox of the Anthropocene – one that raises the human to a geological, powerful force yet participates in a discourse of doom. In other words, we have achieved our fullest sense of greatness by having an epoch bear our name, yet this simultaneously entails our undoing. While these *artefacteur* statues have mastered body and environment, they have met their demise via artistic and technological means in order to do so. Thus, one of the painful Organic definitions of the posthuman focuses on technology as art to be displayed and thus extending the Organics' immortality. Such a reimagining of the human complicates the notion of technology as tool for mastering the body. It reveals how the body and AI paradoxically work together to create an external material object that is placed in a museum and serves as a cultural container to bring energy home (rather than push it outwards

---

[37] "étaient horribles, les formes étaient informes, hérissées d'excroissances odieuses, tortures d'arabesques impossibles, inhumaines jusque dans la souffrance."
[38] "Il y avait celui dont le crâne fondait sur les épaules. Il y avait celui qui se foullaient les tripes de ses deux mains."

like the Mechanist carbex). Art is tied, paradoxically, to both human mortality and immortality.

Érythrée, however, sees this societal custom as suffocating and dreams of different ways of being and of seeing others, not unlike the countercultural youth of 1960s France and subsequent French SF. The anti-establishment, anti-capitalist, and anti-war sentiments of young people in 1960s France came to an explosive head in mass protests in May 1968. The movement sparked a generation of hopeful authors influenced by both the utopic ideas of May '68 and their American counterparts. This utopian vision declined in the 1980s, perhaps, as Vas-Deyres speculates, "due to the fact that many people of the counter-culture believed that the dream of a utopia had come true with the election of François Mitterrand in 1981" (2018, 48). Yet a second French SF golden age emerged in the 1990s, in which Dunyach and Ayerdhal took part, and new visions of humanity appeared in the vast reaches of outer space; these authors "suggest a destiny for humanity, which manages to overcome the technical and cultural impasses attaching it to a potentially exhausted Earth" (Bréan, "Le Rapport à l'avenir (1/2)" 2013).[39] In this regard, Érythrée sees the potential in harmonious expansion, thus subverting transhumanist ideals of expansion at all costs, as did Rosny's gravity-defying astronauts in Chapter One.

Érythrée's rebellious desire for growth beyond her faction even takes political shape in her activism in Contre-Ut, a movement that seeks to abolish the disparate cyborg factions and reunite all cyborgs. Her mother Tachine, however, who symbolizes an older generation against which 1960s youth clashed, warns Érythrée of such utopian desires that echo new economic and geopolitical changes in a France on the precipice of the millennium: the creation of the euro, further unifying continental Europe, and the imminent enlargement of the Schengen Area to encompass more European nations in its visa-free zone of now 27 countries, thus allowing more freedom of movement across national borders. In Tachine's view, the idea of mixing the branches is as shocking as the wars that took place before the Dispersion. While the Dispersion was meant to protect humans from themselves, the resulting segregation only reinforced their vast cyborg differences. Tachine has seen this for herself on occasional visits to other factions, arguing that

> The Originals, for example, are not gentle mystics who cultivate the memory of the dead, take advice from centuries-old holograms,

---

[39] "postulent un destin pour l'humanité, qui parvient à dépasser les blocages techniques et culturels l'attachant à une Terre potentiellement épuisée."

and are ruled by a family oligarchy [...] You will never see children in their streets, children are disembodied very early and raised to the state of Astrals so that their bodies are not soiled with carnal contact. (Ayerdhal and Dunyach 1999, 153–154).[40]

In her sarcastic response to her mother's xenophobic comments, Érythrée calls the Mechanists a mere mix of thugs and samurais whose armor is meant to eliminate everything else, while the Connected are a groupthink society of "digital collectivism" ["collectivisme informatique"]. The most posthumanist of the four punk protagonists due to her yearning to see the face of the cyborg Other, Érythrée insists that she will make her own judgments: "I'll go see to what extent they're inhuman and degenerate" ["j'irai voir chez eux à quel point ils sont inhumains et dégéneres"] (Ayerdhal and Dunyach 1999, 154).

Facing the Cyborg Other: *Les Retrouvailles*

In the second half of the novel, "Les Retrouvailles" [Rediscoveries], the reader gets a greater sense of how certain forms of artificial intelligence in the novel are more aggressive, and thus more prone to dissolving the human Self. When Koriana's procured carbex armor splits itself in two, and half attaches itself to Gadjio, his symbiotic cyborg interface is endangered. As was the case for most Mechanists, the carbex threatens to take over Gadjio's personality, even though he cannot feel it, thus demonstrating the anti-posthumanist nature of the carbex; its innate hostility divides the human Self in such a way that it renders Gadjio hostile as well. Indeed, Gadjio finds the Organics dangerous and manipulative, but the AnimalCity Our Mother of Bones intervenes, reminding Gadjio that the carbex armor is capitalizing on such fears: "It prompts you to challenge them to weaken your fear of it. Look at them better [...] with your Passeur eyes" (Ayerdhal and Dunyach 1999, 341).[41] To stop the carbex from manipulating Gadjio's mind, an *embiote*, the form of nano- and biotechnology upon which the Organics' society is based,

---

[40] "Les Originels, par exemple, ne sont pas de gentils mystiques qui cultivent la mémoire des morts, prennent conseil auprès des hologrammes pluriséculaires et sont dirigés par une oligarchie familiale [...] Jamais tu ne verras d'enfants dans leurs rues, les enfants sont désincarnés très tôt et élevés à l'état d'Astraux pour que leurs corps ne se souillent pas de contacts charnels."

[41] "Il te pousse à te défier d'elles pour affaiblir ta crainte de lui. Regarde-les mieux [...] avec tes yeux de Passeur."

must be grafted onto Gadjio's neck, after which, "he felt no pain and there was no link between his terrorized conscience and the haven of peace that his subconscious had become" (Ayerdhal and Dunyach 1999, 399).[42] Thus, Gadjio's quasi-schizophrenic suffering, similar to that of most Mechanists, is temporarily alleviated by the addition of another layer to his human–machine interface. Increasing the heterogeneity of consciousnesses within Gadjio, thanks to the restorative nature of the *embiote*, does not create further division of the Self. As Hayles points out, if we look carefully at how such a cognitive assemblage comes together, it is easier to parse out how decision-making and power are distributed in the system (2017, 119). While the *embiote* manipulates the body and has the potential to take over it completely, it does not create such a schism within the mind-body dynamic of the cyborg that it would result in hostility toward the Other. In other words, the posthumanist *embiote* restores Gadjio's symbiotic interface, thus remedying his lack of agency over his own cognitive processes.

Nevertheless, the *embiote* still sparks a fear of the cyborg Other. When a Mechanist, Sletloc, hits Koriana in the head, Érythrée assesses the damage by inserting her hand into his skull; her human–ectoparasite interface allows her certain metamorphic capabilities. This stirs Tecamac's repulsion: "She turned to him and moved away slightly so that he saw her hand on the Charon's face, her hand whose fingers were disappearing into the old man's skull. Tecamac recoiled. He had been told a lot about the repulsive faculties of the Organics! But that was something else!" (Ayerdhal and Dunyach 1999, 436).[43] The sight of the *embiote* and its capability to deform the body in a way that is unique to the Organics evokes a less provocative biohorror than that examined in Chapter Two. With Tecamac, biohorror is truly fear of the bodily difference of the Other. Yet it becomes muddied when such difference attaches itself to one's own body. Both the torn carbex armor and the newly grafted *embiote* have deformed Gadjio's body, rendering it "both fascinating and grotesque" ["à la fois fascinant et horrible"]: "His back looked like a tableau of molten gel, epidermis, and metal, and the epidemic spread to his arms, pelvis, and flanks. The carbex softened on the parts it dominated to spread in the flesh that he had not reached himself"

---

[42] "il n'éprouvait aucune douleur et il n'existait pas de lien entre sa conscience, terrorisée, et le havre de paix qu'était devenu son subconscient."

[43] "Elle se tourna vers lui et s'écarta légèrement pour qu'il vît sa main sur le visage du Charon, sa main dont les doigts disparaissaient dans le crane du vieillard. Tecamac eut un geste de recul. On lui en avait pourtant beaucoup dit sur les facultés répugnantes des Organiques! Mais ça!"

(Ayerdhal and Dunyach 1999, 400).[44] The *embiote* is like a "magic wand" ["baguette magique"] that can change Gadjio into anything he desires, but he must learn to control it, to which he exclaims: "Now I am a monster!" ["Maintenant, je suis un monstre!"] (Ayerdhal and Dunyach 1999, 400). Gadjio sees his newly disfigured body not only as a deviance from his previous, more "humanlike" one but also as a deviance from his own cultural norm, as an Original, of what the physical characteristics of the body should look like. Ultimately, by calling himself a monster, Gadjio affirms the alterity of not only the AI but the Organics' society that the *embiote* represents.

Despite Tecamac's and Gadjio's repulsion at such crossings of the boundary of the body – experienced as a type of biohorror – the collaboration between the different cyborg protagonists allows them to form a connection. While Tecamac, Gadjio, Nadiane, and Érythrée share the trait of a more symbiotic human–machine interface that distinguishes each one from their respective factions, what truly unites them are their memories of loved ones, thus highlighting the human half of their interfaces. They each have someone they admire. Just as Bakhoûn, Rosny's prehistoric scientist, was able to project his Self onto the face of the alien Other (see Chapter One), these cyborg protagonists are able to do the same through their anecdotes of caring: "Through the memories they exchanged, the relationship that formed between them resembled what Érythrée imagined the Retrouvailles would be, and beyond that, what she hoped for a real fusion between the factions."[45] Tecamac loves Zezlu, thus "verifying [his] human fragility" ["vérifiant l'humaine fragilité"]. Nadiane talks about her admiration for her brother, Joanelis, which "verged on a love that transcended fraternity" ["confinait à un amour transcendant la fraternité"] (Ayerdhal and Dunyach 1999, 444). Even though Gadjio is not present during this exchange, his love for his daughter, Marine, is also a demonstration of his humanity. Érythrée, however, does not feel the need to prove her love and compassion from memories of her life in the Organic faction, given that she is the most posthumanist of the representatives at the Retrouvailles. Indeed, she proves herself by helping others. She even awakens Tecamac's ethical responsibility for the Other when he decides that he will help Nadiane

---

[44] "Son dos ressemblait à un camaïeu de gel, d'épiderme et de métal fondus, et l'épidémie se propageait à ses bras, à son bassin et à ses flancs, le carbex s'atténuait sur les parties qu'il dominait pour se répandre dans les chairs qu'il n'avait pas atteintes de lui-même."

[45] "À travers les souvenirs qu'ils échangeaient, la relation qui s'établissait entre eux ressemblait à l'idée qu'Érythrée s'était faite des Retrouvailles, et au-delà, à ce qu'elle espérait d'une réelle fusion entre les Rameaux."

as she fades from her disconnection (Ayerdhal and Dunyach 1999, 458). Yet Nadiane cannot be saved; her ship of "nanones" is the only thing that can reduce the impact of the Mechanists' warship on the Ban and, as a result, she must sacrifice herself to save the others. Indeed, after the explosion of the dying star, Tecamac recognizes her immense selflessness (Ayerdhal and Dunyach 1999, 530).

Like the miniature network that develops between the four protagonists, the reconfiguration of the Ban after the star's death emphasizes both the fragility and interconnectedness of all systems of life. Pushing beyond the limits of an Anthropocene Earth, the universe, as an AnimalCity puts it "is an ecosystem, as unstable and fragile as a planetary biotope. It is perpetually evolving [...] Some alterations are 'visibly' local, such as those caused by a supernova. Others [are] regional [...] But none at all are independent" (Ayerdhal and Dunyach 1999, 423).[46] A symbol of rebirth, the supernova equally promises a new era of increased connections between cyborg factions. Indeed, an indication of the possible changes to come is Tecamac's affection for Érythrée, which anticipates a new kind of diversity and exchange between the various cyborg factions. Their inter-factional love subverts a maternal authority in the case of Érythrée, and for Tecamac, a hierarchical and misogynist one. In the final scene of the novel, Érythrée takes Tecamac's hand and the carbex armor retracts to expose Tecamac's flesh, reminding the reader that the body – not only the shared memory of loved ones – can serve as an empathetic tool of posthumanist connection. Érythrée and Tecamac form an unexpected cognitive assemblage that brings together their disparate organic and cybernetic parts with the effect of spreading Érythrée's code of embedded embodiment: "In its impetus, with the help of the Cities, Érythrée would carry humanity toward this mode of configuration that it practiced with so much ease and that it called sharing" (Ayerdhal and Dunyach 1999, 538).[47] As was the case for Rosny in Chapter One, Ayerdhal and Dunyach are cautiously optimistic about the future of the cyborg factions and their protagonists, which offers the same hopeful outlook as much of French SF produced right before the new millennium, as Bréan argues ("Le Rapport à l'avenir (1/2)" 2013). Nonetheless, the dénouement of the novel suggests that the conflict

---

[46] "est un écosystème, aussi instable et fragile qu'un biotope planétaire. Il évolue perpétuellement [...] Certaines altérations sont 'visiblement' locales, comme celles provoquées par une supernova. D'autres [sont] régionales [...] Mais aucune n'est indépendante du tout."

[47] "Dans son élan, avec le concours des Villes, Érythrée allait emporter l'humanité vers ce mode de configuration qu'elle pratiquait avec tant d'aisance et que lui appelait partage."

between factions has only been temporarily resolved, as Tecamac's final reflections exhibit: "When would old antagonisms reappear or brand-new jealousies arise?" (Ayerdhal and Dunyach 1999, 538).[48] Even though it is possible that these cyborg factions could return to their transhumanist ways of isolation and distrust of the Other, the events around the dying star promise that a new type of posthumanity can be born, both in its reconfiguration of the human–machine interface and in its new moral code.

Conclusion

In Part One of the present study, the body served as a technological apparatus to potentially save or destroy a species or make empathetic connections with the nonhuman Other. As I have mapped out in this first chapter of Part Two, we can see how the posthuman complicates human–nonhuman encounters within a posthumanist and transhumanist framework. As technologically enhanced humans with different types of human–machine interfaces, the cyborgs in *Étoiles mourantes* all experience bodily connections to their surroundings, to others in their own communities, and to those outside their own societies in very diverse ways. This novel thus engages with two types of archetypal encounters in science fiction: first, the intimate, cyberpunk encounter between human and artificial intelligence. Such an encounter challenges and questions human identity in a way that was not possible for human–animal or human–alien encounters given their less mentally and physically intrusive nature. Second, following the tradition of the space opera, the authors place populations of cyborgs with various human–AI interfaces in conflict with one another. How the cyborg Self relates to and confronts the cyborg Other is based on their human–AI interface.

Ultimately, for Ayerdhal and Dunyach, a more symbiotic human–AI interface allows for a posthumanist ethic to bloom when facing the cyborg Other. Most importantly, the subscendent status of the cybernetic posthuman in *Étoiles mourantes* nuances the transhumanist quest to master both the Self and its environment. Dunyach touches upon such subscendence in his 1992 prequel, *Étoiles mortes*, as his characters instantly travel from one AnimalCity to another; the artist, Closter, tries to recover his memories after each teleportation, while Marika, in an astral form similar to the Originals, looks for her body

---

[48] "Quand resurgiraient de vieux antagonismes ou que naîtraient des jalousies toutes neuves?"

as she wanders from one fleshy AnimalCity to the next. Although they are not the cybernetic posthumans developed in *Étoiles mourantes*, both characters seek subscendent existence, that is, a holistic identity of mind and flesh. Equally, if we return to the image of Jeff Bezos-as-astronaut at the beginning of this chapter, we notice a stark difference between his transhumanist transcendence and that of Ayerdhal and Dunyach's cyborg protagonists. The Bezos-rocket assemblage is much more powerful than the sum of its parts. You could perhaps say the same for the Tecamac-Érythrée assemblage, but it exerts a different kind of power. Its transhumanist power derives from Morton and Boyer's art of subscendence, that is, a Roomba-like attitude of being close to the Earth. In the novel, subscendent maneuvers focus on 1) bodily vulnerability and 2) "seeing" the face of the cyborg Other, both of which reduce the cyborg to less than the sum of its parts.

Each cyborg faction exhibits the degree to which the body's tentacular connections to the human mind and AI affects contact with the cyborg Other. While the Mechanists enjoy the physical power and endurance of carbex armor, they suffer from the fragmentation of their minds, and they are the most hostile of the factions. The Originals download their simplified consciousness into AI holograms, yet lose part of their human identity since their full memory cannot remain intact. The Mechanist and Original societies demonstrate human vulnerability and weakness and seek to overcome it either through discarding or deformation of the body within the human–machine interface, which gives them a greater chance at transhumanist immortality and perfectibility. However, the Organics and Connected are already much less obsessed with the transhumanist dream, either depending on technology to maintain their physical youth and heal or being physically unable to survive outside their virtual world. Both seek self-preservation. The Mechanists treat the Organics like prey, for instance, using them as a training exercise for young Mechanists. The Connected seek immortality by making a copy of their entire Symbiase network. They too partially act in defensive self-preservation since the Mechanists' quest for complete domination could destroy them as well. In due course, this contrast between the cyborg factions and their protagonists in revolt demonstrates Ayerdhal and Dunyach's vision of accepting human vulnerability, of which the body is emblematic.

Indeed, for Érythrée, it is the "face" of the cyborg Other that brings out the human within posthumanism, which highlights the Gallic cyberpunk attributes of Dunyach and Ayerdhal's work. Echoing Godard's technological anxieties about the machine's suppression of human emotion and poetic expression, the French authors focus on the "humanity" of different cyborgs – that is, their memories of loved ones. Once together, Tecamac, Nadiane, Gadjio, and Érythrée see this shared quality in each other, allowing them to have a greater understanding of the Other. Érythrée understands the "difficulties of intersubjective communication, the ways in which we are all trapped in our own skulls and unable to know if the Other has an inner life similar to our own, a problem that persists even if this Other is 'us'" (Vint 2006, 10). Despite the carbex's threat to Gadjio's symbiotic identity, he decides in the end to unite Koriana's *personae* with Noone, the AnimalCity with whom he has a strong relationship (Ayerdhal and Dunyach 1999, 534). This gesture shows the same posthumanist code of ethics to which Érythrée subscribes; it is a code that is "based not on ability, activity, agency, and empowerment but on a compassion that is rooted in our vulnerability and passivity [...] the ethical act might instead be construed as one that is freely extended without hope of reciprocation by the other" (Wolfe 2009, 141). Yes, cyborgs can certainly be posthumanists (and Donna Haraway already made this abundantly clear in her frequently cited feminist work). As the present study's final chapter on Luc Besson's female protagonists outlines, the female posthuman, as Érythrée and Nadiane have demonstrated, reinforces the posthumanist project of reshaping the ontological boundaries of Anthropos in crisis. For Besson's superheroines, transcending mind and body takes on a new meaning in a world of masculine techno-fantasies.

Chapter Four

Encounters with Posthuman Women in the Films of Luc Besson

In a scene from Luc Besson's colorful space opera *The Fifth Element* (1997), the spectator's gaze aligns with that of male hero Korben Dallas as he gently touches the face of an unconscious Leeloo, a revered engineered cyborg with extraterrestrial origins. Symbol of light, life, and goodness, Leeloo is the greatest weapon against evil as the titular "fifth element," combining her powers with four sacred stones that represent the natural elements of earth, air, water, and fire. Leeloo has just escaped her captors, and Korben believes he has saved a damsel in distress, kissing her to wake her up. In an extreme close-up, Leeloo's eyes quickly open, focusing on Korben's face pressed against hers. She puts Korben's massive revolver to his head, saying in her divine language, "Never without my permission," which echoes a biblical scene between Mary Magdalene and Jesus after his resurrection, where he says to her, "Noli mi tangere," or "Do not touch me." As Laura Mulvey wrote in her landmark 1975 article on the cinematic male gaze, "women are simultaneously looked at and displayed, with their appearance coded for strong visual and erotic impact so that they can be said to connote *to-be-looked-at-ness*" (2006, 346; emphasis original). While subscendence valorized the notion of becoming less than the sum of one's parts in order to locate humanness in the cyborgs of Chapter Three, the introduction of the cinematic gaze complicates the value of subscendence for the posthuman woman. She occupies a liminal space between human and nonhuman because of her enhanced mental and/or physical abilities, yet she still has the bodily appearance of a human woman to both the viewer and the characters around her. In other words, woman, like the alien, animal, and machine, is Other. Nevertheless, this moment between Leeloo and Korben not only underscores her status as humanity's otherworldly savior but also highlights the posthuman woman's *countergaze*, a characteristic of Besson's films *The Fifth Element* and *Lucy* (2014) rejecting the objectifying male gaze.

By bringing an SF archetypal figure like the posthuman woman to center stage and positioning her in a powerful cinematographic stance, Luc Besson pays tribute both to French auteurism and Hollywood film. Strongly associated with 1960s New Wave filmmakers like François Truffaut and Jean-Luc Godard, auteurism sees filmmaking "as an artistic and intellectual practice, whose methods and goals are juxtaposed to those of mainstream cinema, Hollywood in particular" (Maule 2008, 13–14). Despite scoffing at the restrictive nature of French auteurism that typically disregards popular genres, such as the action film, or their SF tropes, like the cyborg, Besson is himself an auteur – or, I would argue, a neo-auteur – in both his style and characterization, as other scholars and film critics have noted (Rabin 2017; Magerstädt 2018). Besson's visual aesthetics are excessively stylized pastiches of various genres (film noir, action, SF) and media (advertisements, video games, comics) with bold costume design and characters (Hayward 2006; Cousins 2008; Buckland 2000; Sojcher 2002). His characters are "larger than life, often inordinately powerful physically – be they men or women – much like the comic strip characters to whom their genesis owes a great deal" (Hayward 2002, 56–57). Indeed, Besson has drawn much inspiration from the *bande dessinée* [comics], considered an important and culturally precious art form in France, along with cinema. In fact, rather than going to the Parisian cinematheque like his predecessors to learn about the masters of French cinema, Besson's childhood was spent reading *bandes dessinées* and watching *Star Wars* and *Indiana Jones* (Brooks 2006; Rogers 2017; Hayward 1998). As a result, his films are a Frankenstein patchwork of international elements, packaged in an easily digestible format for Anglo-American audiences (Hayward 1999, 257). In *The Fifth Element*, for instance, the décor conceived by French cartoonists Jean-Claude Mézières and Moebius merge with French designer Jean-Paul Gaultier's elaborate costume designs that are worn by English-speaking stars like Bruce Willis. As such, Besson's SF films can "scale up" their visual imagination to include humans, nonhumans, posthumans, and even whole civilizations on the brink of extinction.

Such existential crises telescope between Anthropos as a collective entity and the individual woman who is reconfigured by masculine-coded technology, and as a result risks being completely "bleached out" by it (Hayward 2002, 57). In Besson's neo-noir thriller shot in French, *La Femme Nikita* (1990), Nikita is reconstituted from a childish junkie into a heavily surveilled government assassin.[1] When Nikita's final mission

---

[1] This film has inspired two television adaptations in English: the Canadian series *Nikita* (1997–2001) and the American series *La Femme Nikita* (2010–2013).

implodes, she disappears, refusing to be wiped out by state-sponsored technology of weapons and surveillance, and ultimately, her identity. In *The Fifth Element*, Leeloo is rebuilt with technology; she uses her powers to save the world from a catastrophic Evil, even though her cyborg capability of downloading information temporarily traumatizes her when she learns about twentieth-century human war. *Lucy* takes place in a postmodern world, where the protagonist can simulate her image on a TV screen to communicate with others. Before she transforms into a flash drive, she transforms her body and mind into a supercomputer to give her knowledge to humanity. Thus, Besson's films – especially, but not exclusively his SF work – have been infiltrated with an "SF-consciousness, the constant awareness that origins are subject to recall, that almost anything may be technically constructible, and that there may be no inherent limits to what technological civilizations, and technologically transformed bodies, are capable of" (Csicsery-Ronay 1991, 391). This SF awareness is critical for formulating a more complex understanding of Besson's neo-auterism, projecting it into Simone de Beauvoir's theoretical territory (women must construct themselves), Donna Haraway's science-fictional theory of the cyborg (women must construct themselves into cyborgs), and posthumanism (women cyborgs contest various ontological borders, opening pathways to human/nonhuman interconnectedness, which insists on an interrelation and co-evolution between human and nonhuman).

While Besson brings into focus the female posthuman woman as a powerful figure who has the potential to save others from complete annihilation, these women can only rebuild their worlds by "rebuilding" themselves through projects of self-identity construction. This chapter examines two of Luc Besson's films within the framework of gendered archetypes in cinema, such as the *man*-made female robot (e.g. created by men, not women), the femme fatale, or the hypermasculine cyborg. I argue that Besson's films evoke and subvert these gendered posthuman archetypes because his female characters ultimately reject the male-projected techno-identities projected onto them. Moreover, I show that his female posthuman/ist protagonists evolve in their projects of self-identity construction, which I examine via the theories of Simone de Beauvoir and Donna Haraway. In *The Fifth Element*, Leeloo rejects the definitions of identity imposed or projected onto her by countering the male gaze and appropriating "masculine" violence. At the same time, she symbolizes what Olive Richard calls the "female love power" of William Marston's superheroine Wonder Woman because Leeloo represents the need for love in a masculine world (Richard 1942; Cocca 2016, 26). Love is a crucial part of Besson's fictional worlds, functioning as "a virtue that guides the actions of the leading characters" (Magerstädt 2018, 2); he envisions his female characters to be both a rejection of male-projected identities and a demonstration of feminine-coded heroism rooted in love. In other words, they do not just adopt masculine-coded violence but subvert it by adding elements traditionally coded as feminine. In *Lucy* (2014), the titular character starts as an average human but gradually becomes posthuman in both her physical strength and intellect due to the effects of an illicit drug surgically inserted into her abdomen. Initially seeking vengeance on those who tried to use her as a drug mule, Lucy refuses to be "remade" by men and showcases Besson's signature countergaze rejecting the male gaze. As the film progresses, she can increasingly manipulate the laws of physics with her mind, but she realizes that she cannot stop her mind from reaching 100 percent capacity. She makes it her mission to share her posthuman knowledge of undiscovered laws of physics with humanity before her mind consumes her. Whereas Leeloo uses her posthuman identity to rebuild the world of men through love, Lucy uses her posthumanness to offer to rebuild the world through knowledge, suggesting that learning is a tool for survival.

Scholars have analyzed these various elements disparately yet have not brought them together under the auspices of posthumanist, science-fictional storytelling (e.g. human–nonhuman contact narratives) nor under what I am arguing is Besson's "neo-auteurism," that is, a hybrid cinema that transgresses both genre and national boundaries. Susan Hayward is the most prolific scholar of Luc Besson's work, addressing his themes of alienation, youth in crisis, and the recycling or adaptation of his characters ("Luc Besson's *Cinquième Élément*" 2000, "Recycled Woman" 2000). Hayward has produced extensive studies on *La Femme Nikita*, including a book-length analysis (2010), which is partly why I do not dedicate a significant amount of space to the neo-noir thriller in this chapter. (It is also worth noting that Nikita is fully human throughout the film; she is, in a way, a metaphorical cyborg as she is forced to manipulate weapons as an assassin serving the French state.) Scholarship in French and English has offered perceptive remarks on Besson's themes of "loving our extraterrestrial neighbours" (Magerstädt 2018, 2), anthropogenic damage to the Earth (André 2014; Hayward 2006), and his transgressive characters with fluid identities (the camp, gender queer Ruby Rhod or the cyborgness of the evil corporatist Zorg in *The Fifth Element*) (Hayward 1999, "Luc Besson's *Cinquième Élément*" 2000, "Recycled Woman" 2000, 2006; Ott 2004; Brown 2007). Studies on *Lucy* in particular often focus on Scarlett Johansson's casting in the titular role, situating the star within her other nonhuman/posthuman characters (Loreck et al. 2019; Shetley 2018) in their analyses of her face as technology (Dinnen and McBean 2018), her disembodied voice (Tunbridge 2016), or her representation of knowledge (Kent 2020; Stevens 2018). I build on this work by taking a broader view of Besson's *œuvre* within the context of female posthuman protagonists and SF genre conventions, including current conversations on technology and the Anthropocene. Furthermore, my posthumanist and transhumanist theoretical framework focuses on the composite parts of Leeloo and Lucy that allow them to rebuild themselves à la Haraway and Beauvoir and rebuild the worlds around them. Here, I would argue that such an approach resonates with Besson's cinematic style, which in itself is made of heterogenous parts.

Dangerous Women: From Femme Fatales to Cyborgs in French Storytelling

Leeloo and Lucy occupy a space of intertextuality and postmodern recycling of female archetypal characterizations that date back to antiquity, particularly the man-made female. Whether woman or science-fictional posthuman woman, female archetypes have often been portrayed as bodies to be exploited, sexualized, and dependent. As Simone de Beauvoir writes in *Le deuxième sexe* (1949) [*The Second Sex*], the Christian creation story remains anchored in the collective imagination of Western culture: "Eve wasn't created at the same time as man [...] she was taken from the side of the first male. Her very birth was not autonomous" (II: 233).[2] Eve is not an independent human being. She was created from Adam's rib so that he did not have to be alone. These two aspects of Eve's existence establish a sense of dependency of women's identity on men. This aspect of dependence can also be traced to non-biblical mythology, as the man-made artificial female appears in Ovid's epic the *Metamorphoses*. Pygmalion falls in love with the statue of a woman he has carved and gives offerings to the goddess Venus, asking her for a wife who resembles the statue. Venus brings the statue to life, and Pygmalion marries her (10.243–297). In the French literary tradition, Villiers de l'Isle-Adam's novel *L'Ève future* (1878) [*Tomorrow's Eve*] exemplifies this Pygmalion/Eve impulse in SF. In *L'Ève future*, Lord Ewald, a character reminiscent of the melancholic archetype of Romanticism, despairs that he is in love with a beautiful singer named Alicia Clary who unfortunately lacks wit and intelligence. His friend,

---

[2] "Ève n'a pas été façonnée en même temps que l'homme [...] elle a été tirée du flanc du premier mâle. Sa naissance même n'est pas autonome."

famous inventor Thomas Edison, makes him an artificial woman, Hadaly, with the same physical characteristics as Alicia but a completely different mind that is powered by supernatural forces. Hadaly is just as beautiful but engages in thoughtful discussion with Ewald. Bringing an artificial woman to life to satisfy the desire of a man establishes a gender-coded paradigm where technology grants men the power to create a human-like machine that is also the ideal woman.

As gender roles morph and technological anxieties increase in the twentieth century, recycled archetypes of women permeate film in the form of the femme fatale in film noir (and borrowed in SF film) and female robot or cyborg in late twentieth-century film, encompassing Beauvoir's argument that women are either feared or desired. Cultural shifts during and after the Second World War inspire the femme fatale archetype on both sides of the Atlantic, symbolizing an imperiled masculinity as women permeate the workplace and gain more socio-economic freedom. Duplicitous female characters like Elsa Bannister in *The Lady from Shanghai* (Orson Welles, 1947) manipulate men with their sexuality and break up conventional households, representing an assault on family values. While the self-seeking American femme fatale consciously plots the demise of the male protagonist, the French femme fatale seems to set herself apart from her American counterpart with "her overriding and unshakeable emotional attachment to a male protagonist" (Rolls 2009, 135). In other words, she will stop at nothing to get or keep her male paramour, such as Alice's quest to frame an innocent victim in order to save her guilty lover in *Panique* (Julien Duvivier, 1947). Besson's emphasis on female love power, then, suggests a stronger connection to the French cinematic portrayal of femme fatales. Yet his female protagonists are not the French spider-women who serve as "unwitting and tragic instrument[s] of doom" (Rolls 2009, 134). In fact, their attachment to humanity positions them as powerful instruments of life and survival.

Female robot archetypes in SF prolong this notion of the dangerous, yet sexually desired woman meant to serve men: the ideal, subservient housewife in *The Stepford Wives* (2004), the female replicants in *Blade Runner* (1982) who are "basic pleasure models," or the female robots in the HBO series *Westworld* (2016–2022) who cater to wealthy male patrons' sexual desires in an Old West-themed amusement park populated by robots. As Morton and Boyer put it in twenty-first-century, transhumanist terms, "This whole techno-fantasy is really about transcending the physical in the final analysis. What's scary about artificial intelligence being smarter than you is what's scary about women being more powerful than you. I suspect the whole singularity fantasy [of uploading ourselves into machines] is a displaced reaction to feminism" (2021,

69). Indeed, both the femme fatale and man-constructed woman are patriarchal reactions to the combined "dangers" of both rapid technological and feminist social change.

While the French tradition pioneered science fiction film, there are unfortunately no examples of female posthumans in the form of robots, superheroes, or cyborgs. Georges Méliès's *Un voyage dans la lune* (1902) [*A Trip to the Moon*], the first science fiction film, is an homage to Jules Verne's *From the Earth to the Moon* and thus showcases the scientism prevalent in France before the world wars. At the same time, the film takes fantastical directions and speculates beyond Verne's text with the introduction of playful, mischievous Selenite aliens who resemble demons. The dreamy films of Jean Cocteau, such as his reimagining of the classic French fairy tale *La Belle et la bête* (1946) [*Beauty and the Beast*] as well as the underworld travels of a poet in his film *Orphée* (1950) [*Orpheus*], evoke the influence of Surrealism in French cinema. SF themes with a touch of Surrealist aesthetics return to the silver screen in the mid-twentieth century with Godard's *Alphaville*, which I discussed in Chapter Three. René Laloux's psychedelic animated film *La Planète sauvage* (1973) [*Fantastic Planet*] portrays an advanced society of gigantic blue beings, Traags, who treat human beings as animals, keeping them as pets or slaughtering them. Based on French author Stefan Wul's novel *Oms en série* (1957), the film is an explicit allegory of human rights and racial tensions in post-Second World War and soon-to-be-postcolonial France. Despite the French heritage of SF film, most French filmmakers have shown little interest in its expansive possibilities to explore not only social and technological change but also the question of what constitutes art.

French distancing from SF filmmaking can be pinned on its perceived association with Hollywood, including the action-packed films that, from a French perspective, represent the very opposite of auteur cinema. Hollywood saturated the SF film market post-Second World War with both B-movies (*Invasion of the Body Snatchers*, 1956; *The Day the Earth Stood Still*, 1951) and critically acclaimed, big-budget hits such as *Alien* (Ridley Scott, 1979), *Blade Runner*, (1982), *Jurassic Park* (Steven Spielberg, 1993), or *The Matrix* (Wachowskis, 1999). These later blockbusters in the 1980s and 1990s began to coincide with French concerns about American "cultural penetration" within the Hexagon. American films were tightening their grip on the French box office, with receipts increasing from 35 to 54 percent between 1980 and 1993 (Kuisel 2012, 313–314). Moreover, companies identified with American identity like Coca-Cola, McDonald's, and Disney began expanding throughout France (Mazgaj 2012, 316). Efforts to preserve a once-hegemonic French culture (whereby "French" is loaded with Gallic, falsely homogenous notions of Frenchness) in order to establish a sense of global cultural diversity began as early as 1982, when French Minister of Culture Jack Lang gave a speech at a UNESCO conference in Mexico City. He attacked what he viewed as an American imposition of homogenized culture but received little sympathy from journalists and the intellectual elite at the time (Kuisel 2012, 45–64). However, protectionist efforts accelerated in the 1990s, including quotas placed on American television programs and English-language music on the radio. Whether acting defensively or not, the French viewed American cultural imperialism as synonymous with the commodification of culture, which subsequently threatened French specificity in cultural products, like film (Mazgaj 2012, 316, 317). Indeed, cinema is part of what Jack Lang called the French "cultural exception." Rather than perceiving American cinema as a threat, including SF themes and archetypes, Luc Besson saw an opportunity to compete with Hollywood. In fact, he was part of a young cohort of emerging filmmakers in the 1980s and 1990s responsible for the *cinéma du look*, which emphasized visual style over sophisticated narratives that often featured young, alienated individuals. Moreover, Besson wanted French film to be entertaining to watch, technically sophisticated, and not necessarily fixate on French themes, which pushed back against the French cultural exception that Jack Lang and many others championed (Tremblay 1985).

Certainly, given Besson's transnational, transmedial, transgeneric films, it is easy for critics to dismiss his work as paradoxically either too French or too American. Among francophones, some focus on Besson's on-screen choices of stylized action that seem, upon face-value, to fit formulaic, Hollywood blockbusters that appeal to general audiences (Boillat 2019; Regnier 2017; Brooks 2006) but, in the words of prominent film critic Michel Ciment of *Positif*, Besson's œuvre "lacks anything substantial to say" (qtd. in Hayward 1998, 8). Yet Besson's work closely resembles the filmmaking practices of the French Poetic Realists of the 1930s, like Marcel Carné and Jean Renoir, because of the movement's tradition of "film production as a collective undertaking" (Hayward 1998, 10). As such, Besson subtly wedges himself into French cinematic tradition. Even the cineaste's own proclaimed connection to the rebellious New Wave filmmakers of the 1960s establishes a link with French cinema, if only for channeling their spirit of, in Besson's words, "rebelling against existing cultural values" and leading the new revolution "to change the look of movies by making them better, more convincing and pleasurable to watch" (Tremblay 1985).[3] This connection, while tenuous,

---

[3] In a 2017 interview, Besson mentions his ritual of reading the script every morning before going on set because he must often shoot his films out of

underscores that his fast-paced, highly stylized films were no more a radical change than New Wave cinema from its predecessor of *cinéma de qualité*, which consisted mainly of literary adaptations and costume dramas that had a seemingly fixed idea "of what constituted literature, history, or vaudeville" (Lanzoni 2002, 159).[4] Moreover, Besson's films are quite different from mainstream Hollywood SF blockbusters (Magerstädt 2018, 2), to an extent that can sometimes alienate American viewers, as was the case with Besson's 2017 space opera, *Valerian and the City of a Thousand Planets*, which was less of a financial success than *The Fifth Element* (Rabin 2017). Anglophone reviewers do not overlook the clunky dialogue or confusing plot in *Valerian*, where a sinister force threatens Alpha, a vast metropolis and home to species from a thousand planets. But some still appreciate the director's vision, flaws and all: "You've got to admire him for risking it all to make an exuberantly bonkers comic-book movie" (Rose 2017). As an anglophone myself, in this chapter I take a similar view to Rose and other critics like Rogers, who calls *The Fifth Element* "delightfully un-American," a category to which I would add Besson's other SF films, *Valerian* and *Lucy*.

What is "delightfully un-American" about Besson's neo-auteurist films is his *bande dessinée* (BD) aesthetic of inordinately powerful characters – especially, but not exclusively, women – inspired by the Franco-Belgian tradition with which an average anglophone reader or spectator might be less familiar. Of course, mid-century American comics are known for their powerful and ubiquitous male superheroes, but Besson would spend many of his teenaged hours staring at French-language comics published in the first major magazine targeted at adults, *Pilote* (1959–1989), from which he would later take inspiration in his

---

chronological order, with the exception of *La Femme Nikita* (Hayward 1998, 14–15). However, New Wave directors like Godard would have their actors improvise on the set: "he often showed up in the morning with sketchy notes for the actors, who were expected to improvise as the camera shot them from various angles, experimenting in order better to capture their loose performances" (Neupert 2010, 211). Besson and the *cinéma du look* represent a move away from their New Wave predecessors not only in the emphasis on script but also in the collective effort of all of those involved in the film process, including technicians and actors: "Although Besson scripts and produces his films as well as directs them, he does not see himself as an auteur [...] Besson works with a fairly constant crew of technicians and group of actors and readily acknowledges their role in the production of meaning in his films" (Hayward 1998, 10).

4   Indeed, in *Les Cahiers du cinéma* in 1954, a young François Truffaut criticized the tradition of this *qualité française* prevalent in 1950s cinema for lacking artistic creativity and cinematographic originality (Lanzoni 2002, 161).

creation of heroines (Quillien, "Interview (Part 2)" 2016, 6). In the history of twentieth-century BD, female characters "have notoriously, tended to be absent [...] or to depend for their existence on adolescent male fantasies in which it is difficult for women to recognize themselves" (Miller 2007, 150).[5] *Bande dessinée* readership skewed mostly male and women creators were extremely underrepresented for decades; the situation started to only change slightly in the 1990s (Bousquet et al. 2018, 50; Miller 2007, 150). As a result, portrayals of women were prone to objectification and fragmentation by the male gaze.

While in the late 1960s and 1970s, when Besson was growing up, women were becoming more active and more equal agents in the private sphere (e.g. abortion and contraception rights) and in public, BD mostly lagged behind with a few exceptions of heroines in SF. First came the mildly erotic and subsequently banned *Barbarella* in 1964; author Jean-Claude Forest modeled the titular character on the actress and international sex symbol, Brigitte Bardot.[6] As an interplanetary adventurer willing to seduce and be seduced, Barbarella represented the modern, independent, and emancipated woman – that is, a sexual agent on her own terms rather than the femmes fatales of yesteryear whose seduction was deemed dangerous yet still desirable by men. The subversive and graphically innovative SF comics series *Métal hurlant* (1975–1987) showcased the talents of cartoonists Moebius and Philippe Druillet, for instance, but objectifying portrayals of women also dominated its pages.[7] Chantal Montellier, the only female contributor to *Métal hurlant*, took a different stylistic and thematic approach to her comics, instead examining the disposability of human bodies (of any gender) in dystopian futures whose inky, colorless panels contributed to the gloomy, yet salient themes in some of her *Métal hurlant* work (Montellier 2003).[8]

---

[5] It is for this reason that many francophone women cartoonists turned to the autobiography genre in the 1990s as a way to investigate and uphold both individual and group identities on their own terms (Miller 2007, 231).

[6] During the 1960s, *bandes dessinées* began to shed their reputation as a medium for children as part of the revolutionary spirit of May 1968. However, a publication law that sought to protect French youth – in place since 1949 – was quick to censor or ban BD. *Barbarella* was promptly reissued with the heroine drawn partially clothed in scenes that had previously depicted her as completely nude (Miller 2007, 22).

[7] Literally translated as "Screaming Metal," this comics magazine anthology was exported and translated into English under the name "Heavy Metal" in the United States beginning in 1977.

[8] Montellier was later a major voice among other female cartoonists in the denunciation of trends of pornographic sex and brutal violence in BD; to be clear, she did not propose a restriction on freedom of expression, nor

The female protagonist Laureline, who made her debut in Pierre Christin and Jean-Claude Mézières's groundbreaking French SF comics *Valérian et Laureline* in 1967, stands out as intelligent, wise, and guided by a female love power rooted in compassion and justice. Besson voraciously read these comics while he was growing up, and he asserts that they "participated a lot in my emotional education, because of the relationship [Valerian and Laureline] have and the fact that [Laureline's] the boss" (Riesman 2017). Besson clearly drew much inspiration from Laureline when imagining Leeloo's character not only in looks – as Leeloo's bright orange hair takes cues from Laureline's auburn locks – but also in terms of personality and circumstances: "she is misaligned with the time in which she arrives, she learns the language very quickly, the history, the mores and customs, she shows how quickly she can adapt to her environment" (André 2014, para. 12).[9] Laureline also served as a model for Besson's female characters in his non-SF work. Take his action film *The Professional* (1994), whose female protagonist is a pre-teen child, Mathilda, played by a young Natalie Portman. Mathilda's power is multifaceted – intellectual, emotional, and even physical. She learns how to wield a gun from the hitman Léon, played by Jean Reno (a French actor of Spanish roots with a career as transnational as Besson's cinema), as a way to protect herself – and eventually Léon – from dangerous adults in her surroundings.

Besson's portrayal of women does not just bring Laureline into the late twentieth and early twenty-first century via Leeloo, and later, an actual Laureline played by supermodel Cara Delevigne in his 2017 film; such depictions reinscribe female protagonists into an otherwise misogynistic tradition of science fiction BD. Yet the filmmaker's BD aesthetic of scaling up female protagonists into colossal figures on screen continues to be paradoxical. It is worth noting how the casting of women like Milla Jovovich, Scarlett Johansson, or Cara Delevigne – whose physical attractiveness or even Hollywood bombshell status becomes inextricably linked to their successful careers in acting and modeling – in his SF films can be problematic under such claims given their "to-be-looked-at-ness," to use Laura Mulvey's term. But, as this chapter reveals, a closer analysis of the protagonists they play undermines this one-dimensionality of

---

was she promoting prudishness. Rather, she took issue with the expectation that authors (especially new ones) must conform to such trends in order to be published (Br. F. 1985; "Navrant" 1985; Miller 2007, 33–34).

9 "elle est en décalage avec l'époque dans laquelle elle arrive, elle apprend très rapidement la langue, l'histoire, les mœurs et coutumes, elle fait preuve d'une grande rapidité d'adaptation à son environnement."

female attractiveness and sexuality expected by the viewer. Besson's posthuman characters Leeloo and Lucy subvert the male gaze with powerful cinematographic positions while simultaneously persisting in their signature empathy for the oppressed or for humanity writ large, sometimes portrayed as at odds with traditional, virile male heroes. And very often, such deconstruction on the part of Johansson-as-Lucy or Jovovich-as-Leeloo aligns with Besson's eccentric cinematic style that maintains a "sense of playfulness" while successfully "attacking weighty themes" (Lambert and Morris 2014). As such, these characters are taking a Beauvoirian stance where they refuse to have their feminine selfhood defined only by their bodies.[10]

The transmedial process of putting such formidable characters on the big screen is what amplifies Besson's well-noted stylistic choices as part of what I call his BD aesthetic. In *The Fifth Element* in particular, bright colors mimic the visually stimulating and almost visual overload of a single page of a BD volume. What is different, of course, is the ways in which the reader or viewer experiences the two mediums. *Bande dessinée* images can be digested at the reader's own pace whereas the cinematic experience delivers such images quickly, as Besson describes in an interview alongside *Valérian*'s co-creators: "You can read a graphic novel in half an hour, whereas a film is usually between one-and-a-half and two hours long. So there comes a point where I have to 'blow up' the story in order to develop the book's themes in another way" (qtd. in Quillien, "Interview (Part 1)" 2016, 6). He clarifies that for every film spectator in the room, time passes at the same speed:

> You can't take your time, as you would with a book. A comic, now, that's different. When you finish reading the right-hand page, you take a last look at the left-hand one before turning it. The reader can bask in the pictures and the text; they can fully savour them one last time before moving on to the next page. In film the spectator has a clock that goes tick-tock for two hours and

---

[10] Besson's male-directed approach converges with the female-directed one in *Wonder Woman* (2017), the first Hollywood female-led superhero film directed by a woman, Patty Jenkins. For Jenkins, nonconformity to gender expectations of superwomen (in terms of physique or personality) should not automatically be a rejection of attractiveness either (@pattyjenks, 2017). Most importantly, Wonder Woman, or any heroine for that matter, "can be drawn [in comics, or in cinema] to be attractive without looking like she's posed for immediate sexual activity with the reader [or viewer]. She can convey strength, heroism, leadership, and humanity in a female body. She can be a hero to a variety of readers" (Cocca 2016, 53).

they can't stop it! It's the whole difference between free style and imposed style. A reader is free to read at their own pace. (qtd. in Quillien, "Interview (Part 1)" 2016, 6)

By explicitly applying the fantastic, otherworldly, vivid colors and oversized characters and settings of BD to his SF films like *The Fifth Element* (quite literally, since Moebius and Mézières worked on the storyboard), *Lucy*, or *Valerian*, Besson magnifies his neo-auteurism that transcends boundaries of nation, genre, and gender. Moreover, he furtively exposes anglophone audiences to a rich and subversive francophone tradition of *bande dessinée*, which as Rogers bluntly puts it, "eschewed primary-colored spandex-clad do-gooders [of US comics] in favor of science fiction, weirdness, and sex" (2017).[11]

Besson has made his career out of mixing nationalities and genres in big-budget films, but a select number of other high-profile French filmmakers have dabbled in the SF genre over the past 25 years. As for traditionally auteur filmmakers who have done some work in SF, very often, the script is written in English, such as Jean-Pierre Jeunet's fourth installment of the *Alien* series (*Alien Resurrection*, 1997) or Claire Denis's *High Life* (2019). For Denis, English was the logical choice because "In space, you speak either Russian or American, that is it" (qtd. in Fagerholm 2019). Delighted by Denis's revival of existential SF themes like the depths of the unknown and nothingness, French critics saw *High Life* as a cinematic masterpiece, placing it alongside the likes of space-sweeping epics like *2001: A Space Odyssey* (Stanley Kubrick, 1968), *Interstellar* (Christopher Nolan, 2014), and *Solaris* (Andrei Tarkovsky, 1972). A space odyssey with no prospect of return, *High Life* depicts a spaceship of criminals on death row, en route to a black hole to extract its energy. They are accompanied by Dr. Dibs, a criminal in her own right, "a sort of illuminated priestess of reproduction, figure of immemorial fertility, collector of sperm, witch of resurrection" (Mandelbaum 2018).[12] Through a disturbing process of rape and artificial insemination, the celibate male protagonist Monte becomes the father of a little girl, and the two become the only remaining passengers after a series of murders and suicides on board. In a similar vein to Albert's in vitro experiment with an orangutan embryo discussed in Chapter Two, *High Life* is a reflection of both the intimate world of familial

---

[11] "Weird" has often been a descriptor for Besson's films by anglophones (Lambert and Morris 2014) and even by Besson himself (Schaefer 2017), which points to both their otherworldliness and bombastic nature.
[12] "une sorte de prêtresse illuminée de la reproduction, figure de la fécondité immémoriale, collectrice de sperme, sorcière de la résurrection."

relations and the philosophical contemplation of human origins and its future. The film seems to linger on the question, "Why do we reproduce when there is no more hope, no more myths, no one?" (Franck-Dumas and Piette 2018).[13] While Dr. Dibs is not a femme fatale or a Pygmalion construction per se, she is a transhumanist vehicle of the quest for bodily control, desperately clutching to the potential to create life, no matter who may suffer in the process.

Feminists have historically been skeptical of the transhumanist project. The cyborg in particular can be a problematic figure for feminists, "for whom the overcoming of the body has largely been a piece [of] the most violent projects of modernity (including patriarchal domination, colonization, resource extraction, and exploitation)" (Lynes and Symes 2016, 122). Some feminists view these "violent projects" as ones of male domination because women, non-white Europeans, and nature are all branded as Other in an andro- and Eurocentric paradigm of power dynamics. These figures of Otherness are "the human and nonhuman referents of negative difference [...] who are reduced, both socially and symbolically – to the less than human status of disposable bodies" (Braidotti 2016, 677). Feminism and posthumanism intersect as a critique of both "the humanist ideal of 'Man' as the representative ideal of the human" and of humanism's anthropocentrism, instead seeking an interconnectedness and destruction of hierarchies between humans and nonhumans (Braidotti 2016, 673). These critiques have extended to discussions of the Anthropocene, which scales up the imagination to examine interconnected structural inequalities and socio-economic systems like capitalism: who is Anthropos? Who is responsible for climate change, biodiversity loss, and the impending sixth mass extinction? An oversimplified answer to "who is Anthropos?" is not far removed from a similar problem plaguing humanism: men and their machines. Even in Besson's work, technology is at times masculine-coded and acts as an ominous shadow, intercepting the identity-building, world-saving mission of strong-willed female protagonists: in *La Femme Nikita*, Nikita is constantly subjected to surveillance cameras that act as avatars of a masculine-led state; the antagonist Zorg in *The Fifth Element* represents a nefarious corporatist who conducts arms deals in order to steal the sacred stones (a rather subtle critique of 1990s American geopolitics in the Middle East that is buried amidst the colorful visuals and special effects of the film).

Yet Besson's protagonists Lucy and Leeloo utilize the transhumanist project to (re)construct their identities in order to reconstruct and even

---

[13] "Pourquoi se reproduit-on quand il n'y a plus d'espoir, plus de mythes, et plus personne?"

transcend the Anthropocene world. Constructing a female identity independent of men was Simone de Beauvoir's emphasis in *Le deuxième sexe*, where she made her famous proclamation that that we *become* our gender: "One is not born a woman; one becomes one" ["On ne naît pas femme: on le devient"] (1949, II: 13). Beauvoir emphasizes the notion of taking action to construct one's own identity beyond the cultural confines of what constitutes a woman (or a man, for that matter). Beauvoir's identity project is one of "reconstitution and interpretation," which intersects with Besson's tropes of posthuman women who are recycled and regenerated (Butler 1998, 34). Donna Haraway's landmark work, "A Cyborg Manifesto: Science, Technology, and Socialist-Feminism in the Late Twentieth Century" (1984), takes Beauvoir's solution one step further by proposing that women must construct themselves into metaphorical cyborgs not only to have control over their identity but to transgress multiple, socially constructed boundaries such as man/woman and human/nonhuman. Her cyborg myth projects Beauvoir's notion of self-construction into high-tech culture and the gender-coded archetypes of science fiction, like the man-made woman, the femme fatale, the hypermasculine cyborg, and the superhero. Leeloo and Lucy thus symbolize a relegitimization of the transhumanist project of overcoming the body.

The Fifth Element
Leeloo's Origin Story

In a liminal space between human and nonhuman, Leeloo's mysterious origins allow her to "surf" between categories of the divine, the extraterrestrial, and, as we later discover, the cybernetic. She seems to not be of this world as both a holy and alien being, a conflation examined in Rosny's *Les Xipéhuz* (see Chapter One). The film opens with an exploitation of the desert landscape as an astral site of contemplation, that is, one that evokes the contemporary, spiritual mecca of Sedona, Arizona; the mythology of UFO conspiracies and sightings (e.g. Roswell, New Mexico, and Area 51 in Nevada) as well as fictional astral projections to Mars (Edgar Rice Burrough's *A Princess of Mars*, 1917); astronomical research (the desert landscapes of Arizona and New Mexico host the overwhelming majority of American optical telescopes); a delicate ecosystem that both harbors life and destroys it (notable desert portrayals in fiction include Frank Herbert's *Dune* [1965] and its audiovisually rich adaptation by Québécois filmmaker Denis Villeneuve [2021]; French Nobel laureate writer J.M.G. Le Clézio's *Désert* [1980]).

The Fifth Element effectively brings these ethereal and posthumanist elements together given that its desert harbors a secret about Leeloo, a life-affirming creature not of this world, hidden in the depths of an ancient place of worship, an Egyptian temple. A professor of archeology believes he has deciphered Leeloo's existence as a dormant, yet powerful religious artifact in the Egyptian desert of 1914; yet, as viewers, we never truly discover who or what originally created Leeloo. The white-haired professor analyzes a series of hieroglyphics in the dim light of a temple, deducing that there is a person who, when surrounded by the four elements of earth, water, fire, and air, is the ultimate weapon against a Great Evil. As he admits, Besson's inspiration for this film was a childhood spent watching *Star Wars, Indiana Jones*, and reading *bandes dessinées* (Brooks 2006).[14] Unlike the famous professor of archeology played by Harrison Ford – who is able to outwit a different manifestation of Evil, the Nazis when they try to unleash the divine power of the Ark of the Covenant (*Raiders of the Lost Ark*, 1981) – Besson's professor is an insignificant human in the greater cosmic dynamics of Good and Evil. A devout human priest whose sect protects the secrets of the fifth element tries to poison Besson's professor. Representatives of the guardian species of the fifth element, the Mondoshawans, land moments after the professor's discovery in order to take the body from the temple to a safer location. Through all of these failed and successful interventions from scholars, priests, and aliens, Leeloo's enigmatic origins, powers, and purpose prepare us for her swift navigation between human and posthuman categories throughout the film.

Leeloo's mysterious origins are further complicated when she is reconstructed by male scientists upon her rediscovery in the twenty-third century, when the main action of the film takes place. As a prophesied black hole reopens and threatens to swallow the Earth, Leeloo's power

---

[14] It is worth noting that Besson likely uses an Egyptian desert in particular for the country's cultural value – utilized in film especially – as a land of superior civilizations that can harbor potentially dangerous, nonhuman creatures. Hollywood films like *The Mummy* (Freund, 1932) and its two reboots in 1999 and 2017, where ancient mummies come back to life to terrorize modern society, are examples of the mysterious, immortal power attributed to ancient Egyptian civilizations in Western popular fictions. Egypt thus serves as an ideal location in which to discover an ancient deity, Leeloo, who must reawaken every 5,000 years. However, Besson subverts this cinematic cliché of the discovery of the destructive mummy with that of a nonhuman creature meant to protect, not destroy. Francophone BD creator Enki Bilal also uses the cultural power of ancient Egypt in his *Nikopol* trilogy (1980–1992).

as a postmodern divinity is sought after by competing entities of Good and Evil. The aggressive Mangalores are on a mission to locate the sacred stones that represent the four elements; in exchange for the stones, Zorg will supply the Mangalores with the latest weapons technology. The Mangalores destroy the guardian Mondoshawans' ship, which not only has the sacred stones on board but also the fifth element. Only Leeloo's hand remains, but there are enough cells alive to completely regenerate her. The lead scientist observes the fifth element's posthuman features and discovers her biological superiority to humans, that is, "almost like this being was engineered," he says. Thus, Leeloo is not truly "man-made," unlike the android of Villiers de l'Isle-Adam's *L'Ève future*. Indeed, part of the issue with the female posthuman archetype is that she has no control over her origins and such origins are often at the hands of men who create her to be an object of sexual desire. Leeloo's ambiguous origin story ultimately allows her to bypass this archetypal expectation and gives her more freedom to reject male-projected identity and serve her mission as a weapon against Evil.

Nevertheless, it is important to consider that Leeloo's regeneration occurs at the hands of human men, which briefly repositions her as the object of a "scientific" gaze that still treats her as an object instead of a person, that is, a biotechnological marvel. Leeloo's rebirth goes through various phases, including reconstruction of bones, muscles and tissues, and skin. As a shield is removed to reveal Leeloo's final form, the camera first focuses on her hand, which is still incased in metal from her original armor-like shell. This close-up shot initially fragments Leeloo's body to emphasize her cyborg nature – a bioengineered, posthuman being. To both the engineer's and general's surprise, this reconstructed superior being is a woman; the revelation of her nude female form is a single medium shot causes them to pause and admire Leeloo. The camera then refocuses on the two men, the engineer reiterating her perfection numerous times, underscoring his male scientific gaze as well as the masculine-coded gaze of the spectator. Leeloo's presence is "an indispensable element of spectacle in normal narrative film, yet her visual presence tends to work against the development of a story-line, to freeze the flow of action in moments of erotic contemplation" (Mulvey 2006, 346). The scientific male gaze briefly renders Leeloo's body an "object of investigation," attempting to contain her (Hayward 1998, 91).

This scopic containment translates into a physical, spatial containment, which Leeloo rejects by becoming an active subject with a countergaze. Because she has been dormant for thousands of years, Leeloo's surroundings completely startle her. Speaking a foreign language, she crawls around and slams her hands against the glass. The general approaches her and says she will need to develop her communication skills if she wants to get out, which further establishes his attempt to contain her by telling her which language she must speak. In a medium close-up shot, Leeloo reacts with a look that counters the male scopic regime, lowering her head, palms against the glass. In a tilt shot, her downward gaze places her in a position of dominance as the camera begins to zoom in on her face. The countershot quickly shifts to show the smiling, unsuspecting general, then returns to Leeloo in a close-up as she breaks through the supposedly unbreakable barrier with a single punch. She grabs the general, hits his head on the glass containing her, and flips the switch to free herself from containment. The camera then becomes an extension of Leeloo's countergaze. In a rapid sequence of shots mimicking Leeloo's quickly blinking gaze, she assesses her obstacles (men) in video game-like fashion. Taking control of the typically male gaze places Leeloo in a dominant, masculine position because "the gaze is not necessarily male (literally), but to own and activate the gaze, given our language and the structure of the unconscious, is to be in the masculine position" (Kaplan 2005, 130). As chaos breaks out, sirens sounding, Leeloo dives through the wall into the ventilation shafts. This moment evokes an SF cinematic trope from *Star Wars: A New Hope* (1977) – that Besson also utilizes in his crime thriller *La Femme Nikita* – when Princess Leia, Luke Skywalker, and Han Solo jump down a chute into a garbage compacting room in order to escape Storm Troopers. While Hayward notes generally that Leeloo "is the (male) scientist's dream cyborg: truly contained and not threatening to man," this initial scene proves otherwise (Hayward 1999, 254). It is true that she is the dream cyborg and object of the "scientific" gaze, whose DNA structure is a biological marvel to the lead scientist. Yet her escape underscores that she is a force that cannot be confined.

Leeloo's Techno-Body

As object of both the traditional and scientific male gaze, Leeloo's techno-body is put on display, emphasizing how she surpasses physiological expectations for a female human body and for the posthuman archetype, such as the superhero. Initially showcased with Jean-Paul Gaultier's bondage-inspired costume design, Leeloo's sexualized body appears to only transgress as an idea. The viewer is "led to believe that she is amazingly strong (her hand-to-gun combat on the paradise planet/ space-hotel Fhloston), but she has none of the muscularity and vigorous health we associate with techno-bodies. Cyborg bodies are supposedly hyper-built, not just DNA structures in excess" (Hayward 1999, 254). However, Leeloo's techno-body is transgressive *because* it does not fit the Hollywood mold of hypermasculine cyborgness, such as the Terminator, which is "pure body, and yet artificially enhanced"; it is played by Arnold Schwarzenegger, known for his bodybuilding, a sport that strives for its own sense of cyborgness through bodily modification (Graham 2002, 208). But the fact that male cyborg bodies like the Terminator are visibly muscular is ironic and unnecessary, "overcompensating for the fact that such physical strength and muscularity is redundant in a world of microcircuitry in which small is likely to mean quicker and more powerful" (Graham 2002, 210).

Indeed, Leeloo – played by actress and supermodel Milla Jovovich – lacks the muscular physique of a male cyborg (or male superhero), yet she is physically strong, which betrays any gendered stereotypes of how strength should manifest itself. When she witnesses the Mangalores barge into the Diva's hotel room in search of the sacred stones, she has a brief flashback to the destruction of the Mondoshawans' ship, which had reduced her to a single arm and left the Mondoshawans dead. Instilled with a desire for cyborg revenge, Leeloo bursts into the hotel room. She uses her cyborg skills in martial arts to defeat the Mangalores. Rather than charging into the room with a pistol, Leeloo demonstrates her ability to perform hand-to-hand combat, quickly blocking attacks and maneuvering out of the way with ease. The camera moves swiftly to follow the pace of Leeloo's kicks, punches, and jumps, positioning her as an active Subject. Leeloo's human form thus symbolizes one of invisible strength, a rejection of the masculine-coded techno-body.

Taking a broader view to Jovovich's role as the Bessonian female posthuman, the actress later went on to be cast as the lead protagonist, Alice, in the successful *Resident Evil* franchise (2002–2016), based on the Japanese video game of the same name. The series begins with a virus outbreak in a secret genetic research facility owned by the Umbrella Corporation, which turns its unsuspecting victims into flesh-eating zombies. Alice, initially a security operative working for the facility, is the sole survivor by the end of the first film; in fact, in a penultimate scene that alludes to Leeloo's reconstruction by male scientists in *The Fifth Element*, Alice wakes up alone in a lab with wires attached to her body. Mirroring the same ingenuity and fortitude used by Leeloo to escape the regeneration lab, Alice frantically pulls the wires out and uses her once-dormant cybersecurity skills to hack the locked door and escape her white-walled prison. As the film franchise continues, Alice transforms into a posthuman as she acquires telekinetic powers, thus shifting away from the Leeloo techno-body model of invisible, physical strength towards the later Bessonian female hypermind represented by Lucy.

The Bessonian female techno-body blends the image of a bioengineered being that is physically or mentally strong in some ways but weak in others – in other words, possessing human vulnerability. Leeloo has much information to download after lying dormant for 5,000 years, so while still on the ship back to Earth, she uses a computer to learn more about humanity. She is now on "W" in her digital encyclopedia and decides to type in "war." Images flash on the screen, ranging from nuclear missiles, lynched African-Americans and hooded Ku Klux Klan members with burning crosses, men of various nationalities with guns, injured men on crutches. The images accelerate as Leeloo absorbs them, her eyes wide open, head shaking, a tear streaming down her cheek. The computer finally stops on an image of a mushroom cloud from an atomic bomb. The camera zooms in on the image, evoking Leeloo's previous observations about humanity: "Everything you create is used to destroy." Like Targ's condensed experience of evolutionary space-time discussed in Chapter One, Leeloo engages with larger expanses of time during which she was not alive. Her cybernetic construction allows her to intensely absorb images of war and violence from the twentieth century. This scene is a shift from Beauvoir's self-construction project of rejecting projected identities to Haraway's cyborg myth of a Self of heterogeneous parts that can traverse human/nonhuman boundaries: "Far from signaling a walling off of people from other living beings, cyborgs signal a disturbingly and pleasurably tight coupling [...] A cyborg world might be about lived social and bodily realities in which people are not afraid of their joint kinship with animals and machines, not afraid of permanently partial identities and contradictory standpoints" (2000, 293, 295). The scale effect via Leeloo's cyborg downloading allows her to experience a condensed space-time of collective human suffering and destruction, thus establishing connections between human and posthuman. Nevertheless, in a superhero moment, Leeloo has encountered her kryptonite in the form of systemic human violence which complicates her programming of fighting evil and demonstrating her vulnerability. Why, then, are men worth saving?

For Besson (as for Ayerdhal and Dunyach), the answer is love, which underscores the empathetic, emotional connections that Besson seeks to inject into his fictional worlds. The penultimate scene of posthuman salvation in *The Fifth Element* resuscitates the superhero trope, which Besson destabilizes by underscoring the interdependence of the male and female protagonists. Once the male hero Korben, the eccentric radio DJ Ruby Rhod, and Father Cornelius decipher how to activate the sacred stones that represent the four elements, there is only a minute left before the Great Evil, a massive ball of fire hurtling through space, makes contact with Earth and destroys everything. Leeloo, traumatized by human war and violence, has "short-circuited." She says: "What's the use in saving life when you see what you do with it?" When Korben insists that there are beautiful things worth saving, he is the first one to declare his love, allowing Leeloo to activate her celestial powers and save humankind from extinction. While this sentimental reveal may be an expected and even clichéd one, it stems from a transformational moment for Korben at an opera house on the planet of Fhloston Paradise. Korben is moved by the alien singer Diva's musical performance and as soon as she finishes, he is the first to give her a standing ovation.[15] The voice of the Diva "prompts a genuine emotional change in the film's maverick male protagonist, nudging him from being a hard-edged renegade into something much more openhearted" (Sims 2017). In the end, Korben cannot save the world without Leeloo, nor can Leeloo save the world without Korben (André 2014, para. 30); *The Fifth Element* thus provides both protagonists a more gender-balanced heroism and establishes a posthumanist connection between them, wherein, "As opposed to survival of the fittest, Luc Besson proposes mutual aid and sociability as a factor of evolution and survival" (André 2014, para. 27).[16]

As the embodiment of female love power, Besson's fifth element itself demonstrates a feminine-coded heroism rooted in love, a vision also shared by Patty Jenkins, the first female director of a Hollywood superhero film, *Wonder Woman* (2017). Both *The Fifth Element* and *Wonder Woman* interpret the superhero trope through a powerful female posthuman who is alien to the war-ravaged world of men and who serves as a redeemer. Leeloo and Diana share the same dilemma in the context of love, war, and violence. Leeloo explicitly asks: why are humans worth saving if everything they create is used for destruction? Diana, who witnesses the horrors of the First World War, equally questions whether the world of men is worth saving. Conceived as a way to balance out "masculine violence," William Marston created *Wonder Woman* in 1941 to emphasize her ability to teach humans the values of peace, love, and equality – a posthumanist gesture between human and nonhuman (Cocca 2016, 26). This perspective may underscore the Otherness of Woman and

---

[15] The Diva is an allusion to Jean-Jacques Beineix's thriller, *Diva* (1981), whose titular character is a celebrated American opera singer. Beineix, like Besson, belongs to the *cinéma du look*.

[16] "À l'opposé de la loi du plus fort, Luc Besson propose l'entraide et la sociabilité comme facteur d'évolution et de survie."

thus continue to subjugate her to less-than-human status in relation to the human man. Yet the posthuman woman, like Wonder Woman or Leeloo, appropriates this feminine "otherworldliness" and positions herself outside of (or perhaps above) ontological dualisms of man/woman and human/nonhuman. Transcending such reductive categories altogether, the posthuman woman, who acts as savior of a humanity on the brink of extinction, leads the way toward a utopian world, not unlike the mission of Érythrée seen in Chapter Three, or Aloïse's life-giving potential in Chapter Two. Despite the impulse to destroy each other and the planet, "somewhere in us there is a grain of humanity and love can, if we persist, bring about an evolution in the social order of things, however small" (Hayward 2006, 93). Ironically, that grain of humanity may just be found within the alienness of the posthuman woman.

Lucy

In *Lucy*, the Bessonian driving force of female love power remains, yet it evolves into stoic acts performed by posthuman Scarlett-Johansson-as-Lucy as a reminder of her former humanity; here, Johansson's signature "underperformance is mobilised as the performance of technological 'other'" (Dinnen and McBean 2018, 128). Members of a drug cartel forcibly insert a powerful nootropic drug called CPH4 into the abdomen of Lucy, a young American expatriate in Taiwan. When the drug accidentally leaks into her bloodstream, it unlocks her brain's potential, thus extrapolating the pseudoscientific myth that we only use 10 percent of our brains. As she begins to develop superhuman powers like superior strength, telepathy, and telekinesis, her display of emotions seems to wane and produces a robotic exterior similar to Godard's Natasha von Braun in *Alphaville*, analyzed in Chapter Three. Nevertheless, love – as a virtue rather than just an emotion, as Magerstädt underscores (2018, 3) – is still a present force. For instance, in a scene where Lucy forces a surgeon to remove the CPH4 packet from her body, she calls her mother to tell her that she loves her. In a gesture that sets him apart from Hollywood, Besson distinguishes Lucy from American superheroes, as Bilge Ebiri (2018) underscores in his film review: "When was the last time an American superhero called her mom to tearfully tell her she could suddenly remember what her breast milk tasted like?" Moreover, this moment marks the break between the human Lucy and the posthuman Lucy.

Yet, unlike Leeloo, posthuman Lucy does not rely on the love of a male character to give her strength to save the world. She treats a

Parisian police detective, Del Rio, as her sidekick. Played by Amr Waked, Besson acknowledges here the increasing integration of Maghrebi and Middle Eastern cultures into mainstream French culture; as such, Del Rio represents the contemporary multicultural Parisian. After she initially warns him about the drug traffickers who attempted to transform her into their drug mule, Del Rio joins forces with her. Realizing the extent of her superhuman powers, he later tells Lucy that he does not even think that she needs him. In response to the detective's observation, the indifferent expression on her face softens ever so slightly, and she kisses him apathetically, telling him that he is a "reminder," that is, of her former human self. Indeed, evocative of Besson's own professed emotional education from the comics *Valérian et Laureline*, it is clear that she is the one in control. This scene demonstrates "the characteristic insouciance of the superhero or action star, a type that stretches from Sean Connery as Bond to Robert Downey Jr. as Iron Man and beyond" (Shetley 2018, 14). Indeed, Lucy's accelerated stoicism as her powers increase showcases Besson's neo-auteurism of gendered power reversals and inserts an element of extreme self-awareness into Lucy's character. Such tender scenes ironically devoid of human emotion keep Lucy grounded and connected to humanity as she eventually transitions into an all-powerful hypermind and the effects of the drug completely consume her.

Before Lucy can fulfill her mission of finding a way to share her knowledge, she must first "construct" herself by rejecting male-driven control of biology. When male drug lords insert the dangerous narcotics into her body, Lucy "is, in effect, impregnated by the gangsters" and her body is "used as a temporary shelter and transportation device for an important payload" (Shetley 2018, 14). Yet their plan to force Lucy to board a plane to Europe with the smuggled drugs in her body ultimately backfires. In a scene where Lucy's captors take a bag off her head and touch her face, she angrily shakes them off, adding: "I'm not in the mood." In response, one of the men violently slaps her in the face and kicks her in the stomach before momentarily leaving the room. As she gasps for air while curled up on the ground, the spectator sees the blood from her reopened surgical wound. The CPH4 has leaked into her system. The viewer then observes a sequence of crosscuts between Lucy briefly losing control of her body and computer-generated simulations of the blue drug exploding and traveling through her bloodstream. In a literalization of her mind starting to take over her body, Lucy's body convulses and travels up the wall and onto the ceiling in a manner reminiscent of Hollywood representations of a paranormal possession. This transhumanist manipulation of the body, unintendedly induced by male drug lords, ironically unravels their efforts to contain Lucy's body and use it for their own means.

With her newfound posthuman powers, Lucy begins to glide through the physical world with a Bessonian countergaze as she seeks revenge for the gangsters' transhumanist bodily manipulation. She goes to a hospital and forces a surgeon to take what remains of the package out of her body at gunpoint, thus demanding a metaphorical abortion of the "fetus" she carries for the drug lords (Shetley 2018, 14). After the surgeon has finished, she returns to the hotel where she was "impregnated" with CPH4. In a sequence of shots in slow-motion, the viewer follows Lucy walking down the hallway in a shot that shows her from the waist down, her hospital gown flowing behind her like a superhero's cape, her arms slightly extended from her sides with guns clutched. This scene crosscuts to the unsuspecting boss who has headphones on, cucumber slices on his eyes, in the middle of receiving a new tattoo. When Lucy arrives, after shooting a few gangsters in her path, she pulls two knives from her back and thrusts them into both hands of the crime boss, pinning him to his seat. Damaging and containing *his* body, as he did to her, is her final act of retribution, thus reclaiming agency to "reconstruct" her fragmented body.

Despite this violent act of bodily reclamation, Lucy is characteristic of the Bessonian female posthuman for whom the notion of both love and sacrifice play a crucial role. On her path to sharing her knowledge with humanity, Lucy contacts a prominent scientist, Professor Norman, played by Morgan Freeman, whose casting exemplifies a significant decentering of white male scientific privilege. Still being pursued by drug dealers, she meets with Professor Norman – who has spent his life working on cerebral capacity – and a team of exclusively male scientists at the end of the film. She tells them that she will build a computer and download all of her knowledge to it so humans can have access, which is the final stage in her evolution from hypermind to complete disembodiment. Aware of the gravity of such a posthumanist act, the professor responds: "I just hope we are worthy of your sacrifice." Such a comment aims to undo the extreme lengths to which Lucy has pushed the femme fatale trope since, as Sophia Nguyen (2014) notes, she is willing to shoot anyone who gets in her way throughout the film. Lucy nonetheless achieves the "redemptive role as mother of knowledge," which may suggest a relinquishment of female power into male hands (Stevens 2018, 26). As part of this service to humanity, "Lucy must also surrender her body – and thereby her ability to wield the power she has attained" (Stevens 2018, 26). While embodiment is critical for both posthumanist and feminist thinking, Lucy's surrender of her power offers only a partial view of Besson's posthuman women in relation to his neo-auteurism; in Besson's own words, the message here "is that when you have power, the best thing to do is to share it," no matter the gender (or, in this case, posthuman status) of those who wield such power (qtd. in Godfrey 2014). Besson pushes this even further, emphasizing the process of his characters' genre/gender transgressions throughout his films, insisting that their power should ultimately be shared with the world in order to reconstruct and improve it.

Lucy relegitimizes the masculine-coded transhumanist project of overcoming one's body to simultaneously achieve Beauvoirian freedom and reassert the posthumanist project. Taking a broader view of recent female posthuman characters played by Scarlett Johansson, Gittell argues that in *Lucy*, *Under the Skin* (Glazer, 2013; an alien in a woman's skin who sexually lures men to their death), and *Her* (Jonze, 2013; a disembodied AI that serves as a companion and eventual lover to the male protagonist, but ultimately leaves him), these are women "who society has assigned a singular goal of serving men. Their journey is to transcend that purpose, and the process is often painful" (2014).[17] Indeed, Lucy's process is quite literally painful, from the surgical insertion of CPH4 to her newfound ability to remember the painful sound of her bones growing as a child, for instance. As Lucy reconstructs her identity, she transcends her own body – a body that "exists as a utilitarian instrument of revenge" – but also transcends gendered archetypes of women in SF cinema and rejects the Pygmalion impulse of male-projected identity (Gittell 2014). At the same time, her escape comes at what seems at first glance to be a transhumanist cost of having to leave the body behind. Although transcendence appears to be a masculine project, Judith Butler suggests viewing Beauvoir's self-construction project as one that "urge[s] women to assume the model of freedom currently embodied by the masculine gender. In other words, because women have been identified with their anatomy [...] they ought now to identify with 'consciousness,' that transcending activity unrestrained to the body" (1998, 36–37). Indeed, referring to Tunbridge, Stevens writes that Lucy's transition from hypermind to disembodiment is "a feminist tale of empowerment for its protagonist. In escaping from her body, Lucy gains incredible physical and intellectual powers" (Stevens 2018, 144).

[17] See Stevens, Loreck, and Monaghan's edited collection on Scarlett Johansson's stardom for a more in-depth discussion of the actress's career "through a multitude of roles that play to and subvert cultural norms around her recognisable femininity," including playing "characters that are themselves in transition" (Stevens et al. 2019, 3).

As such, Scarlett-Johansson-as-Lucy unravels the SF trope that connects feminine beauty to perfection, particularly the star's own "much-celebrated appearance" that is "linked to posthuman marvelousness" (Stevens et al. 2019, 16).

Lucy overcomes the masculine hegemony of existing knowledge systems represented by the group of male scientists, including Professor Norman (Francis 2016; Kent 2020, 297). This "xenofeminist" maneuver not only moves away from the body, but "names reason as an engine of feminist emancipation, and declares the right of everyone to speak as no one in particular" (Cuboniks 2018). A representation of Haraway's cyborg myth of crossing human/nonhuman boundaries, Lucy's transition into a supercomputer ultimately breaks away from the highly empathetic, posthumanist model of Leeloo and even those of the other works analyzed in this book; her final sacrifice "engages with a historical project of passing on and developing learning and knowledge" (Kent 2020, 289). Transhumanism in *Lucy*, then, functions to reassert the posthumanist project of interconnectedness between humans, nonhumans, and posthumans via a much more rationalist approach, rather than the empathetic one à la Levinas.

Moreover, similarly to the works of the other French creators analyzed in this study, *Lucy* anchors this posthumanist and transhumanist dialectic on an Anthropocene spatio-temporal scale. *Lucy* "scales up the imagination" not only with BD-esque characters and audacious visuals, as I explained earlier in the chapter; the film also "scales down," shrinking the scale effect in a similar way to Leeloo, where her alien techno-body allows her to experience everything, everywhere, all at once. Yet, unlike Leeloo or the orangutans Bagus and Mina in Chapter Two, Lucy is not a figure of alterity, at least from the beginning of the film. Instead, her body and mind are clearly anchored in cosmic time and space, as the final scenes of the film visually show her almost reaching 100 percent brain capacity and connecting with the first female humanoid, an evolutionary reference to the 3-million-year-old fossil nicknamed Lucy that was discovered in Ethiopia in 1974. As Johansson-as-Lucy dissolves into a flash drive, she "unbinds rationality from the constraints of her prior animality" (Kent 2020, 291). For Rosny's prehistoric protagonist, Bakhoûn, discussed in Chapter One, reason is the ultimate tool for posthumanist understanding yet paradoxical demise of the alien Other; in Lucy's case, however, her own human form must be the collateral damage in the pursuit of reason and knowledge as an evolutionary bridge from humanoid to human to posthuman.

Conclusion

Leeloo and Lucy's posthuman bodies carry Beauvoir's self-construction project into Donna Haraway's theoretical universe of science fiction iconography. In other words, Haraway's cyborg moves from a humanist territory, bound by interrelations between humans alone, to a posthumanist one, thus extending relations to nonhuman entities. Leeloo and Lucy are "connection-making" entities who reject identities imposed on them by men (Braidotti 2016, 680). They reject the Pygmalion myth, where a woman's creation is not autonomous. The denunciation of the Pygmalion impulse manifests itself via both Leeloo's divine status (human men did not create her, although they do regenerate her) and her countergaze which fragments the male scopic regime. Leeloo's final project is to reconstruct the world through love, redeeming male humanity of its sins of technological warfare and destruction. Lucy refuses the Pygmalion impulse by turning the tables against the male drug lords who "impregnated" her with the powerful drug CPH4. Like Leeloo, Lucy's inner self project transforms into a greater project of helping the human Other based on a connection with a greater good. Here, Besson positions knowledge and learning as essential to human survival.

Thus, there is a sense of humanism that persists in Besson's posthumanist science fiction film. He uses the posthuman experience of the enhanced human as a way to relocate the core Cartesian values of reason and consciousness shared by all human beings. This commonality represents a human universal that could, theoretically, transcend differences of race, ethnicity, gender, and language. However, humanism seems to have failed us, as I outlined in the Introduction. Historically marginalized groups like Jews, LGBTQ+, women, and Blacks, for instance, were positioned outside of the human category that, in practice, was not so universal after all – at least, in the eyes of those in power. For posthumanists, the root of this problem lies in an anthropocentric conception of the world, which contributed to stricter ontological categorizations that humanism at its core sought to avoid. Humanism treats the single human individual as one whose features are rationality, autonomy, agency, and authority. He – and now she – has the freedom to make a choice to pursue his or her own wishes (Nayar 2014, 5). In this regard, Besson's celebration of the purported freedom that humanism allows the individual to construct him or herself converges with Beauvoir's feminist existentialist argument for women to reject identities projected onto them by men.

Moreover, posthumanism takes this one step further and insists on the "embedded embodiment" of the human in other systems, which

Besson demonstrates with his female posthumans (Nayar 2014, 9). Leeloo is an "embedded" posthuman because she uses her powers to save other organisms (humanity, in particular), thus inserting herself in the web of humanity, outside of which she exists. Lucy goes even further as a representation of Besson's hybridization: transhumanism's espousal of disembodiment in contrast to posthumanism's insistence on embodiment ("the world is what we perceive through our senses") (Nayar 2014, 9). Lucy's posthuman development is a sensory hyper-awareness and instills posthumanist values in her. Her final transhumanist disembodiment is paradoxically the result of her posthumanist choice to share her knowledge, which Besson underscores in a 2014 interview in the *Guardian*: "What's interesting is the definition of humanity [...] Watch the news tonight. When you see the state of humanity today ... I mean, come on, it's a mess." Over the course of his career, Besson has evolved into an optimist, seeing utopian possibilities in the world, which contrasts with his first feature-length film, a post-apocalyptic dystopia shot in black and white, *Le dernier combat* (1983) [*The Last Battle*]. While he does not reference this dystopic film in a separate 2017 interview, he does explain his evolved worldview, readily admitting

> that there are problems, especially with the environment. But let's work on it. Let's make it better. Alpha, the city of a thousand planets [in the 2017 film *Valerian*], is basically the United Nations. They're trying to live together in peace and share the science they have. We think it's hard between a couple of different races on Earth? Try it with 8,000 aliens, just try. We see Asian and black people, Muslims, and so on, and we're like, "Whoa." But okay, let's imagine tomorrow there's 8,000 different species coming from space. You come back to Earth and you say, "Oh my God, it's easy. I love everyone." (Riesman 2017)

Conclusion

My last chapter, especially in the case of *Lucy*, points to how technoscience is subject to mistrust among posthumanists given its historical exploitation of both bodies and the environment. Speculative thinker and writer Ursula Le Guin is equally skeptical of transhumanism's "metanarrative" of technology – to use Jean-François Lyotard's term – within the "Hero's" adventure.[1] In "The Carrier Bag Theory of Fiction," she writes that "'Technology' or 'modern science' [...] is a heroic undertaking, Herculean, Promethean, conceived as a triumph, hence ultimately a tragedy" (Le Guin 1996, 154). In science-fictional terms, this translates into narratives of human conquest of Earth, other planets, and outer space (Rosny's novellas discussed in Chapter One presented carefully nuanced scenarios of human conquest regarding aliens and alien worlds), or human conquest of death (Ayerdhal and Dunyach's novel analyzed in Chapter Three demonstrated the conflict between the quest for immortality via artificial intelligence versus a capacity for interspecies coexistence). Within the popular imagination, the image of prehistoric times is associated with hunting wild bison or wooly mammoths, thus molding the narrative of human civilization around a spear. As a modern, visual example, Le Guin evokes Stanley Kubrick's iconic scene in *2001: A Space Odyssey* of a hominid discovering that a bone (a long, hard object) can serve as a tool; more specifically, the bone is a tool for bashing, whacking, and killing. Society has belonged to those

---

[1] "By legitimizing knowledge by means of a metanarrative, which implies a philosophy of history, we're driven to questioning the validity of institutions that preside over social bonds [...] To oversimplify, we can take the notion of 'postmodern' as skepticism of metanarratives" ["En légitimant le savoir par un métarécit, qui implique une philosophie de l'histoire, on est conduit à se questionner sur la validité des institutions qui régissent le lien social (...) En simplifiant à l'extrême, on tient pour 'postmoderne' l'incrédulité à l'égard des métarécits"] (Lyotard 1979, 7–8; translation mine).

with the killing tools and it encapsulates what it means to be human (Le Guin 1996, 151). Indeed, as the first author to develop the prehistoric novel, Rosny used this image of the ancient human's tool; nonetheless, as discussed in Chapter One, Rosny's commitment to evolution in *Les Xipéhuz* and even *La Mort de la Terre* (whose far-future setting evokes an atavistic, decadent civilization) ultimately allows him to embrace the progressive, nonanthropocentric goals of posthumanism by looking backward and forward in time. The problem with the killer story, in Le Guin's view, is that "we've all let ourselves become part of [it], and so we may get finished along with it" (1996, 152), thus culminating in the existential crisis evoked by the Anthropocene.

The French SF stories I have analyzed all recount human entanglement in the killer story and the posthumanist impulse to break free from it. Le Guin counters the killer story with the "life story" as represented by the container, the first "cultural device," rather than the spear, stick, or bone described in the Hero's stories. Contemporary images of prehistoric life dominated by hunting do not represent how humans spent the majority of their time. In fact, human survival mostly comprised gathering vegetables and grains, snaring fish, and catching rabbits in temperate and tropical regions.[2] However, gathering nuts and berries, and placing them in a carrier bag of some sort, Le Guin quips, does not make for an enticing story (1996, 149–150). The narratives of Rosny, Chevillard, Dunyach and Ayerdhal, and Besson are cultural containers, where the life story eventually prevails, "holding things in a particular, powerful relation to one another and us" (Le Guin 1996, 153). In Chapter One, the technological tools of a prehistoric or spacefaring humanity are critical for the species's survival. Yet sophisticated technology in *La Mort de la Terre* eventually leads to climate change, bodily vulnerability to microbes, and the development of a more adaptive species. Rosny's stories reveal a strange paradox between the killer story and the life story because one species's triumphant survival was another's annihilation. Chapter Two demonstrates how *Sans l'orang-outan* underscores the ironic nature of humanity coping with species extinction in the Anthropocene. Chevillard shifts the SF metanarrative surrounding technology from a killer story to a life story when Albert convinces his colleague and lover Aloïse to be artificially inseminated with an orangutan embryo, thus making her human womb a "container" to rebirth the orangutan species. A "tool that brings energy home" (Le Guin 1996, 151), Aloïse's

---

[2] Le Guin borrows the terms "cultural carrier bag" and "Carrier Bag Theory of human evolution" from Elizabeth Fisher's 1975 text *Women's Creation* (see Le Guin 1996, 150–151).

uterus has the life-giving capacities that Albert seeks. Chapter Three outlines how, for the Mechanists, technology becomes a weapon of domination for manipulating other factions and the women of their own society, as well as for controlling the fabric of space-time called the Ban, thus participating in Le Guin's killer story. However, Érythrée's efforts to work with other faction representatives and see their innate humanity encourages the life story. As Chapter Four illustrates, Leeloo's devastation upon downloading information about human-caused war and destruction in the twentieth century conveys the metanarrative of technology as a weapon of domination, yet Leeloo counters this notion by means of her very existence. She is a "container" of life-giving matter because she is, after all, the fifth element, which aligns her with the four natural elements of earth, water, air, and fire. Like Leeloo, Lucy is a version of Le Guin's technological container as a knowledge-sharing entity. Rather than continuing on a path of destruction and power by means of her posthuman capabilities of mental and physical strength, the conclusion of *Lucy* promotes the life story.

By gradually relegitimizing the technological metanarrative espoused by transhumanism, these stories demonstrate how technology can, in fact, be a life-giving force and a tool for change. It can be an instrument for radiating energy outwards and a transhumanist tool for overcoming Nature's obstacles, whether the human body (like the cyborgs in *Étoiles mourantes*) or orangutan extinction. It can also be an instrument for containing things and channeling energy inwards, such as Besson's posthuman female protagonists or Jenkins's Wonder Woman. Technology can also serve as a posthumanist tool for establishing connections between humans, nonhumans, and even posthumans, such as Bakhoûn's scientific method in *Les Xipéhuz*, Leeloo's cyborg capabilities in *The Fifth Element*, and Lucy's posthuman knowledge. Technology can serve as a tool for regrounding us in the complex and interconnected ecosystem of "Nature," which we saw especially with Dunyach and Ayerdhal's cyborg universe.

Reactions to existential threats to the life story in the works I have analyzed range from the nihilistic or even absurd to the sanguine, thus showcasing a mix of French and American approaches to techno-scientific change. For Bréan, techno-scientific anomalies in Anglo-American SF preceding his period of study, 1950–1980, often lead to "thrilling adventures and new perspectives" ["aventures exaltantes et des perspectives nouvelles"] (2012, 72). Indeed, postwar American SF can be characterized by its optimistic outlook toward the future, and it was in this moment that this brand of SF invaded French bookstores. In contrast to their American counterparts, French authors tended to portray such scientific wonders as provoking a certain level of anguish, revealing "the troubling limits of science" ["les limites inquiétantes de la science"] (Bréan 2012, 72). As is the case with many generalizations and stereotypes about a given nation, there is a nugget of truth that can be sifted out regarding trends of American techno-optimism and French techno-pessimism. As a young nation without the weight of history, Americans are always moving forward ("toujours en avant") and "fearlessly throwing themselves toward the new and modern" ["se lancent sans crainte vers le nouveau, le moderne"], from a French perspective (Brière et al. 2021, 5).

Of course, as I discussed in my Introduction, French thinkers are nonetheless fascinated by this techno-optimism and how it translates into a transhumanist reimagining of Anthropos, as Luc Ferry and others have dedicated studies to analyzing roots of transhumanism in Silicon Valley. Part of this fascination stems from a universalist, humanist tradition that is anchored not only in French philosophical thought but in French values at large, including the foundation of French democracy itself: all French citizens are equal in the eyes of the state. This value of universalism – and thus an undifferentiated humanist ethos contrary to posthumanism – finds its way into the narratives I have analyzed. In Part Two, Besson and Dunyach and Ayerdhal's works show how the posthuman is actually a way to rebound to the universalizing notion of the human. Even in Part One, part of the posthumanist strategy of seeing the nonhuman Other is recognizing human-like traits while accepting others that could never be fully grasped by the limits of the human mind and senses. Although this book is not a study of "Frenchness," a posthumanist and transhumanist approach to my corpus reveals a blend of worldviews and values espoused by Americans and the French, especially national attitudes towards techno-scientific change.

As writers and other intellectuals increasingly associate the state of society with that of the planet, they further push public discourse into species-level thinking, and it is here that the perceived tension between "French" and "American" worldviews slightly dissipates. As my last chapter suggested, there is a sense of hope when considering how to reimagine Anthropos during an age of physical and philosophical existential threat. The utopian outlook espoused by Besson and Dunyach/Ayerdhal, in particular, offers a glimpse of how trends in contemporary science fiction in France have been interested in moving away from a dystopian, apocalyptic tone that dominates contemporary discourse surrounding the Anthropocene and its discontents. SF "has always been a literature of hope" ["a toujours été une littérature de l'espoir"], remarks Mireille Rivalland, editor of publishing house L'Atalante. But until recently, she notes, "it mostly proposed survival. However, the turning point that's coming is the transition to life" (Thévenet 2020).[3] Indeed, the life story, rather than the story of simple survival, fuels the short manifesto of Le collectif Zanzabar, a group of contemporary French SF writers. It proclaims:

> Despite the potential tools and futurology offices of large companies, despite the ubiquitous rhetoric that tomorrow will be the same as today, yesterday, or just not,
> we remain convinced that our futures – common and individual – belong to us,
> and that we have the power to imagine them, to play with them, to experiment with them and to build them as we please.
> We are a collective of science fiction writers.
> We dream of our texts as places where to meet, think, and start extricating the future. ("Minifeste" n.d.)[4]

The striking choice of the verb in the original French "désincarcérer" (which I have translated as "extricating") suggests an enduring imprisonment; the writers instead propose the liberational act of imagining a future on one's own terms. This collective of SF authors, then, working in a similar vein to American Afrofuturists or even American solarpunk authors, envisions the future of the human species and of the planet as one that belongs to all of us – a posthumanist impulse.[5] In the Anglo-American sphere, such thinking points to a significant breakdown

---

[3] "elle nous a principalement proposé de la survie. Or, le tournant qui arrive, c'est le passage à la vie."

[4] "Malgré les outils de prospectives et les cabinets de futurologie des grands [sic] entreprises, malgré l'omniprésence du discours voulant que demain soit pareil à aujourd'hui, à hier, ou ne soit tout simplement pas, nous restons convaincus que nos avenirs – communs et individuels – nous appartiennent, et que nous avons le pouvoir de les imaginer, de jouer avec, de les expérimenter et les construire à notre guise. Nous sommes un collectif d'auteurs de science-fiction. Nous rêvons nos textes comme des endroits où se rencontrer, où penser et commencer à désincarcérer le futur."

[5] Steinkopf-Frank (2021) describes solarpunk as having a "more optimistic, regenerative vision of the future" with a "pleasant aesthetic," yet still containing a radical message of dismantling a global capitalist system that led to environmental destruction. Afrofuturism, a term coined in 1993 by Mark Dery, is "an unending fight by black people for human inclusion across time and space [which] produces precisely such a networked consciousness connecting the past, present, and future via creative production" (Lavender 2018, 567). Afrofuturism has become an increasingly

in the once-monolithic dominant SF of the Golden Age through as late as the 1980s. Moreover, these anglophone and francophone authors envision SF as a tool to reimagine and reconstruct our world.

This hopeful vision stands in stark contrast to the trendy, fatalist one of the *collapsologues*. Popularized in France by Pablo Servigne, collapsology explores the vulnerability of our societies to various systemic risks, including financial crises, resource depletion, and climate change, which threaten society with collapse in the near future.[6] Like Targ's acceptance of the inevitable in *La Mort de la Terre* seen in Chapter One, collapsologists are neither apologists of the apocalypse nor transhumanist *progressistes* such as philosophers Luc Ferry or Pascal Bruckner. Horrified by a sense of catastrophism that fuels ecological thinking, Bruckner (2013) underscores a new sense of fear of both the future and science and technology, thus "reflect[ing] a time when humanity, and especially Western humanity, has taken a sudden dislike to itself." Bruckner laments that "saving the world requires us to denigrate everything that has to do with the spirit of enterprise and the taste for discovery" and therefore takes a transhumanist stance toward technological progress and innovation.[7]

Perhaps fueled by a blend of these various trends in SF thinking, the French military – spearheaded by the Agence de l'innovation de la défense (AID) – hired a dozen French SF authors in 2019 to anticipate and strategize future existential threats. In the United States, the Pentagon has shown interest in using the ideas of SF to anticipate security threats. The geopolitical strategy of the Reagan administration in the 1980s was named Star Wars, after George Lucas's film franchise, and even had SF authors as consultants. However, France is the first nation to systematically put "fictional intelligence" into practice. Christened "La Red Team," the band of speculative thinkers began their work in 2020, creating various scenarios that could threaten national security and global stability, ranging from pirate nations more advanced than the Islamic State to the hacking of a naval officer's neural implant. Such scenarios push traditional defense strategies further into the future yet remain anchored in empirical reality. Speaking on behalf of the authors on the team, Laurent Genefort emphasizes that "what interests us are the mechanics of the real, that is, societal ruptures that disrupt

---

transmedia phenomenon, ranging from the successful Marvel film *Black Panther* (2018) to the work of musician Janelle Monaé.
[6] Cf. Servigne and Stevens 2015.
[7] For more on Bruckner and other contemporary ecologically minded French thinkers, see the final chapter "Ecological Ends" in Posthumus (2017).

everything" rather than the creation of weapons (Rérolle 2021).[8] Given the progressive and often anti-militaristic stance in much SF, known Red Team members such as Genefort were criticized by other members of the French community, which Genefort describes as coming from "a radical political fringe of SF that has adopted the language and methods of cancel culture, or rather, shaming" (Rérolle 2021).[9] Despite these criticisms, Red Team authors see themselves as civil servants. Virginie Tournay, a trained biologist, SF author, and director of the largest public research organization in France, the Centre national du recherche scientifique (CNRS) notes that her participation in the French army's efforts support "the pact of the Republic, which is a certain idea of equity, social justice, and universalism" (Rérolle 2021).[10] Authors thus see SF as a tool that can serve the values and institutions of the French state, which contributes to global cooperation and peace. Moreover, what is remarkable about this project is that the head of the AID, Emmanuel Chiva, conceived of this idea when his wife took him to the largest SF convention in France, Les Utopiales, in Nantes. From fandom to defense strategy, the Red Team initiative underscores how SF storytelling, to borrow Glotfelty's words, "does not float above the material world in some aesthetic ether, but, rather, plays a part in an immensely complex global system, in which energy, matter, *and ideas* interact" (1996, xix; emphasis original).

Rather than anticipating future threats from a strategic and militaristic point of view, many high-profile and award-winning authors in France have exploited speculation as a tool for both literary experimentation and a radical reimagining of near-future states, humans, and potential posthumans. Hervé Le Tellier, the 2020 laureate of the prestigious Prix Goncourt, experiments with doubles and bizarre realities in his genre-bending *L'Anomalie* [*The Anomaly*], which became a literary sensation during France's initial lockdown at the beginning of the COVID-19 pandemic. Bringing together disparate characters from a contract killer to an architect, the novel eventually reveals that the protagonists were on the same turbulent March 2021 flight from Paris to New York. The reader experiences an avian déjà vu; the same protagonists and the same flight, which encounters the exact

---

[8] "Ce qui nous intéresse, ce sont les mécanismes du réel, des ruptures sociétales qui bouleversent tout" rather than the creation of weapons."
[9] "une petite frange militante politique de la SF, qui adopte le langage et les méthodes de la cancel culture, ou plutôt du shaming [opprobre]."
[10] "le pacte républicain, soit une certaine idée de l'équité, de la justice sociale et de l'universalisme."

same damage inflicted by a storm en route to the American east coast, occurs the following year in 2022. A member of the experimental and speculatively minded literary group Oulipo since 1992, Le Tellier brings together the *oulipien* tools of literary playfulness and his training as a science journalist (Leyris 2020). His work serves as an indication of how SF allows artists to experiment with narrative form – especially the experience of time, as Ursula Heise has argued. Other contemporary authors, such as Antoine Volodine (a former Oulipien) and Marie Darrieussecq, engage in speculative thinking as a tool for exploring the internal world of consciousness and its entanglement with the surveillance state, thus echoing the technocratic fears of French intellectuals in the mid-twentieth century. In Darrieussecq's novel *Notre vie dans les forêts* [*Our Life in the Forest*] (2017), artificial intelligences are the tools and perhaps even the architects of a deeply sinister dystopia of data mining and clones whose organs are harvested for the deteriorating bodies of their "real" human doubles. Darrieussecq, Volodine, and Le Tellier are only a few examples of a larger trend in contemporary French literature that uses science-fictional methods to deal with the global – that is, French anxieties over the past 20 years regarding the nation's relationship to the European Union, climate change, American cultural imperialism, large tech and data corporations, and the state of Islam in a French secular state (a pertinent example of the latter being Michel Houellebecq's controversial 2015 novel, *La Soumission* [*Submission*], where the then future 2022 presidential election brings political victory to Islamic demagogues in France). As a result of putting literature "in global terms – the species, the world, history – and the local – the individual, country, life," the intellectual nature of what constitutes Anthropos inevitably and imperceptibly is transformed (Blanckeman 2014, 13).[11] What is worth noting here in these examples of the Red Team, the Zanzibar collective, and the works of the French literary elite is that SF – as a visual and literary art form, as a way of thinking and postulating about hypothetical scenarios now and in the future – is increasingly being viewed in France as a tool in and of itself, symbolizing an apparatus of human ingenuity and of adaptation.

What emerges from the pertinent questions investigated in the literary thought experiments of today's French creatives is the need to engage with more feminist and decolonialist frameworks within French science fiction. Although my theoretical approach of posthumanism was grounded in an intellectual framework that recognizes that the term

---

[11] "en termes globaux – l'espèce, le monde, l'histoire – et locaux – l'individu, le pays, la vie."

CONCLUSION

"human" historically neglected many marginalized communities who did not fit the "ideal" model of the white, European, cisgendered man, the authors and filmmaker studied in this book are all white men; as in American SF, the speculative literary and cinematic landscape in France has often been dominated by male voices. Of course, powerful female voices shine through, such as contemporary writer Elisabeth Vonarburg, cineaste Claire Denis, or Chantal Montellier, whom I discussed in Chapter Four. As a way to balance my corpus of male creatives, I have sought to engage with female thinkers such as Simone de Beauvoir, Donna Haraway, Katherine Hayles, and Laura Mulvey. Moreover, I did not want to neglect the role of female characters throughout my analyses of human–nonhuman contact events. It became increasingly clear to me that these human and posthuman women were both "containers" and "tools," yet always life-giving. Such reflections lead to more questions about the potential directions in speculative storytelling in French. The recent work of Franco-Cameroonian writer Léonara Miano, whose 2019 novel *Rouge impératrice* [Red Empress] was nominated for the Prix Goncourt, hints at the possibilities to come. In a similar move to American authors of Afrofuturism, Miano's novel envisions an African federation one hundred years in the future that is free of neocolonial divisions and interventions. My hope is that my book contributes to the conversation among both anglophone and francophone scholars regarding the role of speculative thinking in different national literatures and cinema as a tool for reimagining liberational pasts, presents, and futures for all kinds of humans and nonhumans. Our Anthropocene existence depends on it.

Bibliography

@pattyjenks. "James Cameron's Inability …" *Twitter*, 24 Aug. 2017, 8:08 p.m., https://twitter.com/PattyJenks/status/900917648015405062.

Abad-Santos, Alex. "Wonder Woman's 'No Man's Land' Scene Was the Best Superhero Moment of 2017." *Vox*, 15 Dec. 2017, https://www.vox.com/2017-in-review/2017/12/15/16767902/wonder-womans-no-mans-land-scene. Accessed 23 Feb. 2018.

Adorno, Theodor, and Michael Jones. "Trying to Understand Endgame." *New German Critique*, no. 26, 1982, pp. 119–150.

Aldiss, Brian. "Introduction" (1973). *Space Opera: An Anthology of Way-Back-When Futures*. Doubleday & Company, 1975, pp. ix–xiii.

Alkon, Paul J. "The Secularization of Apocalypse." *Origins of Futuristic Fiction*. University of Georgia Press, 1987, pp. 158–191.

Allamand, Carole. "Du sommaire au moindre: l'humanité en fuite." *Contemporary French and Francophone Studies*, vol. 16, no. 4, 2012, pp. 517–524.

André, Danièle. "*Le Dernier Combat* et *Le Cinquième Elément* – terre balbutiante et *space opéra*: de l'humain au plus qu'humain ou la science-fiction de Luc Besson." *Les Dieux cachés de la science-fiction française et francophone (1950–2010)*, edited by Natacha Vas-Deyres et al., Presses universitaires de Bordeaux, 2014, pp. 135–147.

Anthony, Andrew. "Yuval Noah Harari: 'Homo Sapiens as We Know Them Will Disappear in a Century or So'." Interview. *Guardian*, 19 Mar. 2017, https://www.theguardian.com/culture/2017/mar/19/yuval-harari-sapiens-readers-questions-lucy-prebble-arianna-huffington-future-of-humanity. Accessed 26 Apr. 2018.

Ashley, Mike, and Peter Nicholls. "Golden Age of SF." *The Encyclopedia of Science Fiction*, 9 Apr. 2015, https://sf-encyclopedia.com/entry/golden_age_of_sf. Accessed 17 Jul. 2017.

Ayerdhal. "Ayerdhal: 'La science-fiction, c'est un petit peu le successeur de la philosophie'." Interview by Deborah Gay. *Daily Mars*, 26 Oct. 2015, https://dailymars.net/interview-ayerdhal-science-fiction/. Accessed 5 Jul. 2017.

——. *Demain, une oasis*. Fleuve Noir, 1993.

———. *Mytale*. J'ai lu, 1998.
Ayerdhal and Jean-Claude Dunyach. *Étoiles mourantes*. J'ai lu, 1999.
Badiou, Alain. "Français." *Vocabulaire européen des philosophies: dictionnaire des intraduisables*, edited by Barbara Cassin, Éditions du Seuil, 2004, pp. 465–473.
Badmington, Neil. *Alien Chic: Posthumanism and the Other Within*. Routledge, 2004.
Bakhtin, Mikhail. *Rabelais and His World*. Translated by Hélène Iswolsky, Indiana University Press, 1984.
Barnosky, Anthony D., et al. "Has the Earth's Sixth Mass Extinction Already Arrived?" *Nature*, no. 471, 3 Mar. 2011, pp. 51–57.
Baron, Anne-Marie. *Balzac occulte: alchimie, magnétisme, sociétés secrètes*. Éditions L'Âge d'Homme, 2012.
Barthes, Roland. *Mythologies*. Éditions du Seuil, 1957.
Bays, Gwendolyn. "Balzac as Seer." *Yale French Studies*, no. 14, 1954, pp. 83–92.
Beau, Rémi, and Catherine Larrère. *Penser l'Anthropocène*. Presses de Sciences Po, 2018.
Beaulé, Sophie. "Tropes Crossing: On Some Québec SF Writers from the Mainstream." *Canadian Science Fiction, Fantasy, and Horror: Bridging the Solitudes*, edited by A.J. Ransom and D. Grace, Palgrave Macmillan, 2019, pp. 311–326.
Beauvoir, Simone de. *Le deuxième sexe*. Gallimard, 1949. 2 vols.
Becker, L.F. *Pierre Boulle*. Twayne, 1996.
Beckett, Samuel. *Oh les beaux jours*. Éditions de Minuit, 1963.
Bénac, Henri. *Vocabulaire de la dissertation*. Librairie Hachette, 1949.
Bergerac, Cyrano de. *Voyage aux états et empires de la lune*. Éditions Cyrano, 2012.
Bessard-Banquy, Olivier. *Le Roman ludique*. Presses universitaires du Septentrion, 2003.
Besson, Luc, director. *Angel-A*. EuropaCorp, 2005.
———. *Les Aventures extraordinaires d'Adèle Blanc-Sec*. EuropaCorp, 2010.
———. *La Femme Nikita*. The Samuel Goldwyn Company, 1990.
———. *The Fifth Element*. Columbia Pictures, 1997.
———. *L'Histoire de Léon*. Intervista, 1995.
———. *L'Histoire du Cinquième Élément*. Intervista, 1997.
———. *The Lady*. EuropaCorp, 2011.
———. *Lucy*. Universal Pictures, 2014.
Blakemore, Erin. "Human-Pig Hybrid Created in the Lab – Here Are the Facts." *National Geographic*, 26 Jan. 2017, https://news.nationalgeographic.com/2017/01/human-pig-hybrid-embryo-chimera-organs-health-science/. Accessed 2 Oct. 2018.
Blanc, Bernard. *Pourquoi j'ai tué Jules Verne*. Éditions Stock, 1978.
Blanckeman, Bruno. "Storytelling/Storyfailing? Avatars du personnage dans le récit de fiction contemporain." *L'Esprit créateur*, vol. 54, no. 1, 2014, pp. 8–21.

Boillat, Alain. "Sept rencontres du 9e type entre un médium (la BD) et un genre (la SF)." *ReS Futurae*, vol. 14, 21 Dec. 2019, http://journals.openedition.org/resf/3969; DOI: https://doi.org/10.4000/resf.3969. Accessed 19 Aug. 2022.

Bonneuil, Christophe, and Jean-Baptiste Fressoz. *The Shock of the Anthropocene: The Earth, History, and Us*. Éditions du Seuil, 2016.

Booker, M. Keith. *Monsters, Mushroom Clouds, and the Cold War: American Science Fiction and the Roots of Postmodernism, 1946–1964*. Greenwood Press, 2001.

Borel-Rosny, R. "Notice bibliographique." *Portraits et souvenirs*. Compagnie Française des Arts Graphiques, 1945, pp. 5–28.

Bostrom, Nick. "A History of Transhumanist Thought." *Journal of Evolution and Technology*, vol. 14, no. 1, 2005, pp. 1–25, https://nickbostrom.com/papers/history.pdf. Accessed 7 Apr. 2019.

———. "Human Genetic Enhancements: A Transhumanist Perspective." *The Journal of Value Inquiry*, vol. 37, no. 4, 2003, pp. 493–406.

Boudreau, Douglas L., and Marnie M. Sullivan. "Introduction." *Ecological Approaches to Literature in French*, edited by Douglas L. Boudreau and Marnie M. Sullivan, Lexington Books, 2017, pp. 1–20.

Boulard, Anaïs. "Writing (on) Environmental Catastrophes: The End of the World in Éric Chevillard's *Sans l'orang-outan* and Michel Houellebecq's *La Possibilité d'une île*." *French Ecocriticism: From the Early Modern Period to the Twenty-First Century*, edited by Daniel A. Finch-Race and Stephanie Posthumus, Peter Lang, 2017, pp. 215–230.

Bourin, André. *Entretiens avec Pierre Boulle*. Radio interview. INA, 29 May 1969.

Bousquet, Danielle, et al. "Inégalités entre les femmes et les hommes dans les arts et la culture Acte II: après 10 ans de constats, le temps de l'action." Haut Conseil à l'égalité entre les femmes et les hommes, 22 Jan. 2018, https://www.haut-conseil-egalite.gouv.fr/IMG/pdf/hce_rapport_inegalites_dans_les_arts_et_la_culture_20180216_vlight.pdf. Accessed 22 Aug. 2022.

Bozzetto, Roger, and Arthur B. Evans. "Intercultural Interplay: Science Fiction in France and the United States (As Viewed from the French Shore) (Des liaisons équivoques: la science-fiction en France et aux Etats-Unis (une vue des côtes françaises))." *Science Fiction Studies*, vol. 17, no. 1, 1990, pp. 1–24, http://www.jstor.org/stable/4239968. Accessed 22 Jul. 2022.

Braidotti, Rosi. "Posthuman Feminist Theory." *The Oxford Handbook of Feminist Theory*, edited by Lisa Disch and Mary Hawkesworth, Oxford University Press, 2016, pp. 673–698.

Bréan, Simon. "Fuir l'exotisme: l'"aventure nostalgique' du merveilleux-scientifique français." *Nineteenth-Century French Studies*, vol. 43, nos. 3–4, 2015, pp. 194–208.

———. 'Hanter la machine: reconquêtes de la conscience humaine dans le cyberpunk à la française', *ReS Futurae. Revue d'études sur la science-fiction*, no. 10, 2017, https://doi.org/10.4000/resf.1028. Accessed 1 Feb. 2023.

———. "Histoires du futur et fin de l'Histoire dans la science-fiction française des années 1990." *ReS Futurae*, no. 3, 2013, https://journals.openedition.org/resf/452. Accessed 26 Jul. 2017.

———. 'Le Rapport à l'avenir dans la science-fiction française, 1970–2012 (1/2)', *ReS Futurae*, 8 Dec. 2013, https://resf.hypotheses.org/2139. Accessed 14 Dec. 2021.

———. 'Le Rapport à l'avenir dans la science-fiction française, 1970–2012 (2/2)', *ReS Futurae*, 19 Dec. 2013, https://resf.hypotheses.org/2136. Accessed 10 Dec. 2021.

———. *La Science-fiction en France: théorie et histoire d'une littérature*. Presse universitaire Paris-Sorbonne, 2012.

Br. F., "Haine et mépris." *Le Monde*, 28 Jan. 1985, https://www.lemonde.fr/archives/article/1985/01/28/haine-et-mepris_2762151_1819218.html. Accessed 22 Aug. 2022.

Brière, Jean-François, et al. 2021. *Les Français*. 4th ed., Hackett, 2010.

Brooks, Xan. "The Long Goodbye." *Guardian*, 21 Jul. 2006, https://www.theguardian.com/film/2006/jul/21/2. Accessed 13 Feb. 2018.

Brough, Aaron R., and James E.B. Wilkie. "Is Eco-Friendly Unmanly? The Green-Feminine Stereotype and Its Effect on Sustainable Consumption." *Journal of Consumer Research*, vol. 23, no. 4, Dec. 2016, pp. 567–582.

———. "Men Resist Green Behavior as Unmanly." *Scientific American*, 26 Dec. 2017, www.scientificamerican.com/article/men-resist-green-behavior-as-unmanly/. Accessed 12 Jan. 2018.

Brown, William. "Sabotage or Espionage? Transvergence in the Works of Luc Besson." *Studies in French Cinema*, vol. 7, no. 2, 2007, pp. 93–106.

Bruckner, Pascal. 'Against Environmental Panic', *The Chronicle of Higher Education*, 17 Jun. 2013, https://www.chronicle.com/article/against-environmental-panic/. Accessed 15 Dec. 2021.

Buckland, Warren. "Video Pleasure and Narrative Cinema: Luc Besson's *The Fifth Element* and Video Game Logic." *Moving Images: From Edison to the Webcam*, edited by John Fullerton and Astrid Söderbergh, John Libbey, 2000, pp. 159–164.

Bukatman, Scott. *Terminal Identity*. Duke University Press, 1993.

Butler, Judith. *Gender Trouble: Feminism and the Subversion of Identity*. Routledge, 1990.

———. "Sex and Gender in Simone de Beauvoir's *Second Sex*." *Simone de Beauvoir: A Critical Reader*, edited by Elizabeth Fallaize, Routledge, 1998, pp. 29–42.

Cameron, James, director. *The Terminator*. MGM, 1984.

BIBLIOGRAPHY

Campbell, Kelly Kathleen. *Film, French, and Foie Gras: Examining the French Cultural Exception.* 2010. Ohio State University, PhD dissertation.

Cario, Erwan. "Jacques Testart: 'Le Transhumanisme est une idéologie infantine." *Libération*, 16 Aug. 2018, https://www.liberation.fr/debats/2018/08/16/jacques-testart-le-transhumanisme-est-une-ideologie-infantile_1672976. Accessed 5 Mar. 2019.

Carroll, Jordan S., and Alison Sperling. "Weird Temporalities: An Introduction." *Studies in the Fantastic*, vol. 9, 2020, pp. 1–22.

"Catachresis." *Princeton Encyclopedia of Poetry and Poetics*, edited by Stephen Cushman et al., Princeton University Press, 2012, pp. 209–211.

Célestin, Roger, et al. "Editors' Introduction." *Contemporary French and Francophone Studies*, vol. 12, no. 3, 2008, pp. 317–319.

Chakrabarty, Dipesh. "The Climate of History: Four Theses." *Critical Inquiry*, vol. 35, no. 2, 2009, pp. 206–207.

Chatelain, Danièle, and George Slusser. "Introduction." *J.H. Rosny aîné, Three Science Fiction Novellas: From Prehistory to the End of Mankind.* Translated by Chatelain and Slusser, Wesleyan University Press, 2012, pp. 9–83.

Chazan, David. "France Drops Legal Quota on French Radio Songs as DJs Forced to Play 'Boring Old Ballads'." *Telegraph*, 18 Mar. 2016, https://www.telegraph.co.uk/news/worldnews/europe/france/12197192/France-drops-legal-quota-on-French-radio-songs-as-DJs-forced-to-play-boring-old-ballads.html. Accessed 10 Jul. 2018.

Chevillard, Éric. *Du hérisson.* Éditions de Minuit, 2012.

———. "Épuiser la forme: entretien avec Éric Chevillard." *Europe*, no. 1026, 2014, pp. 8–14.

———. *Explosion de la tortue.* Éditions de Minuit, 2019.

———. *Nébuleuse du crabe.* Éditions de Minuit, 2006.

———. *Palafox.* Éditions de Minuit, 1990.

———. *Portrait craché du romancier en administrateur des affaires courantes.* Éditions Fata Morgana, 2004.

———. *Préhistoire.* Éditions de Minuit, 1994.

———. *QWERTY Invectives.* Translated by Peter Behrman de Sinety, Sylph Editions, 2018.

———. "Questions de préhistoire." Interview by André Benhaïm. *Écrivains de la préhistoire*, edited by André Benhaïm and Michel Lantelme, Presses universitaires du Mirail, 2004, pp. 177–190.

———. *Sans l'orang-outan.* Éditions de Minuit, 2007.

———. *Scalps.* Éditions Fata Morgana, 2004.

Christin, Pierre, and Jean-Claude Mézières. *Valérian. Intégrales.* Dargaud, 2016.

Christman, John. "Autonomy in Moral and Political Philosophy." *The Stanford Encyclopedia of Philosophy*, Spring 2015, edited by Edward N. Zalta, https://plato.stanford.edu/archives/spr2015/entries/autonomy-moral. Accessed 19 Sept. 2017.

Chu, Seo-Young. *Do Metaphors Dream of Literal Sheep? A Science-Fictional Theory of Representation*. Harvard University Press, 2010.

Clark, Timothy. *Ecocriticism on the Edge: The Anthropocene as a Threshold Concept*. Bloomsbury, 2015.

Clarke, Arthur C. *Childhood's End*. Ballantine Books, 1990.

Clarke, Bruce. *Posthuman Metamorphosis: Narrative and Systems*. Fordham University Press, 2008.

Clermont, Philippe. *Darwinisme et Littérature de Science-Fiction*. L'Harmattan, 2011.

Clermont, Philippe et al., editors. *Un seul monde: relectures de Rosny Aîné*. Presses universitaires de Valenciennes, 2010.

Cocca, Carolyn. *Superwomen: Gender, Power, and Representation*. Bloomsbury, 2016.

Colebrook, Claire. *Death of the PostHuman: Essays on Extinction, Vol. 1*. Open Humanities Press, 2014.

Collard, Sue. "The French Exception: Rise and Fall of a Saint-Simonian Discourse." *The End of the French Exception? Decline and Revival of the "French Model"*, edited by Tony Chafer and Emmanuel Godin, Palgrave Macmillan, 2010, pp. 39–54.

Corbey, Raymond. "Ambiguous Apes." *The Great Ape Project: Equality beyond Humanity*, edited by Paola Cavalieri and Peter Singer, St. Martin's Press, 1994, pp. 126–136.

Cornillon, Claire. *Par-delà l'infini. La Spiritualité dans la science-fiction française, anglaise et américaine*. 2012. Université de la Sorbonne nouvelle – Paris III, PhD dissertation.

Cottingham, John. *Cartesian Reflections: Essays on Descartes's Philosophy*. Oxford University Press, 2008.

Cousin de Grainville, Jean-Baptiste. *Le Dernier homme*. Madame Veuve Barthe, 1859, https://gallica.bnf.fr/ark:/12148/bpt6k55307703.texteImage. Accessed 10 Apr. 2019.

Cousins, Jennie. "Flesh and Fabric: The Five Elements of Jean-Paul Gaultier's Costume Design in Luc Besson's *Le cinquième élément* (1997)." *Studies in French Cinema*, vol. 8, no. 1, Apr. 2008, pp. 75–88.

Cronenberg, David, director. *The Fly*. 20th Century Fox, 1986.

Csicsery-Ronay, Istvan. "On the Grotesque in Science Fiction." *Science Fiction Studies*, vol. 29, no. 1, 2002, pp. 71–99.

———. *The Seven Beauties of Science Fiction*. Wesleyan University Press, 2008.

———. "The SF of Theory: Baudrillard and Haraway," *Science Fiction Studies*, vol. 18, no. 3, 1991, pp. 387–404.

———. "Some Things We Know about Aliens." *The Yearbook of English Studies*, vol. 37, no. 2, 2000, pp 1–23.

———. "What Do We Mean When We Say 'Global Science Fiction'? Reflections on a New Nexus." *Science-Fiction Studies*, vol. 39, 2012, pp. 478–493.

Cuboniks, Laboria. *Xenofeminism: A Politics for Alienation*, [2018], https://laboriacuboniks.net/manifesto/xenofeminism-a-politics-for-alienation/. Accessed 1 Feb. 2023.

Curval, Philippe. 'Bernard Blanc: *Pourquoi j'ai tué Jules Verne*: la science-fiction française', *Quarante-Deux*, 1978, https://www.quarante-deux.org/archives/curval/chroniques/le_Monde/Pourquoi_j'ai_tue_Jules_Verne/. Accessed 10 Dec. 2021.

Cusset, François. *French Theory: How Foucault, Derrida, Deleuze, and Co. Transformed the Intellectual Life of the United States*. University of Minnesota Press, 2008.

Daniel, Marc. *Éric Chevillard: l'art de la contre-attaque*. Éditions le Manuscrit, 2014.

"Dark Matter." *CERN*, European Organization for Nuclear Research, https://home.cern/science/physics/dark-matter. Accessed 2 Jun. 2016.

Darwin, Charles. *On the Origin of Species by Means of Natural Selection, or the Preservation of Favoured Races in the Struggle for Life*. John Murray, 1859.

Dehoux, Amaury. *Le Roman du posthumain: parcours dans les littératures anglophones, francophones et hispanophones*. Honoré Champion, 2020.

Deleuze, Gilles, and Félix Guattari. *Mille plateaux*. Éditions de Minuit, 1980.

Derrida, Jacques. "L'Animal que donc je suis (à suivre)." *L'Animal autobiographique*, edited by Marie-Louise Gallet, Galilée, 1999, pp. 251–301.

———. *La Dissémination*. Éditions du Seuil, 1972.

Derrida, Jacques, and David Wills. "The Animal that Therefore I Am (More to Follow)." *Critical Inquiry*, vol. 28, no. 2, 2002, pp. 369–418.

Descartes, René. *Discours de la méthode*. Flammarion, 2000.

———. *Meditations on First Philosophy: With Selections from the Objections and Replies*. Translated by Michael Moriarty, Oxford University Press, 2008.

———. *Les Passions de l'âme*. H. Legras, 1649, https://gallica.bnf.fr/ark:/12148/btv1b8601505n. Accessed 12 Apr. 2019.

Diaz, Brigitte, and Clément Hummel, editors. *J.-H. Rosny aîné*. Presses universitaires de Caen, 2019.

Dinnen, Zara, and Sam McBean. "The Face as Technology." *New Formations: A Journal of Culture/Theory/Politics*, vol. 93, 2018, pp. 122–136, https://muse.jhu.edu/article/699200.

Ducommun, Pascal. "Alien Aliens." *Aliens: The Anthropology of Science Fiction*, edited by Eric S. Rabkin and George Slusser, Southern Illinois University Press, 1989, pp. 37–42.

Dunyach, Jean-Claude. "L'Art est un dialogue avec la mort et avec la mémoire." *Galaxies*, no. 37, 2005, pp. 119–133.

———. *Autoportrait*. Denöel, 1986.
———. *Le Clin d'œil du heron*. L'Atalante, 2016.
———. "Du Space Opera au Nouveau Space Opera: la métamorphose d'un genre." *NooSFere*, 2006, www.noosfere.org/icarus/articles/article.asp?numarticle=584. Accessed 19 Sept. 2017.
———. *Étoiles mortes*. J'ai lu, 2000.
———. *Les Harmoniques célestes*. L'Atalante, 2011.
———. "The Hitch-Hiker's Guide to French Science Fiction." *Inter Nova*, 2004, https://www.scribd.com/document/354429572/The-Hitch-Hikers-Guide-to-French-Science-Fiction. Accessed 17 Mar. 2017.
———. *The Night Orchid: Conan Doyle in Toulouse*. Translated by Sheryl Curtis, Black Coat Press, 2004.
———. "Science-fiction et ordinateurs." *Galaxies*, no. 1, 1996, pp. 93–101.
———. *The Thieves of Silence*. Translated by Sheryl Curtis et al., Black Coat Press, 2009.
———. *Voleurs de Silence*. Fleuve Noir Anticipation, 1992.
Dunyach, Jean-Claude, and Annaïg Houesnard. "An Interview with Jean-Claude Dunyach from Utopiales 2010," sffportal.net/2011/06/an-interview-with-jean-claude-dunyach-from-utopiales-2010/. Accessed 5 Jul. 2017.
Dupree, Tom, et al., editors. *Full Spectrum 5*, Bantom Books, 1995.
Ebiri, Bilge. "Luc Besson on *Lucy* and Knowing the Limits of the Human Brain." *Vulture*, 25 Jul. 2014, http://www.vulture.com/2014/07/luc-besson-director-lucy-chat.html. Accessed 7 May 2018.
Eco, Umberto. *A Theory of Semiotics*. Indiana University Press, 1976.
Edwards, Malcolm, Brian M. Stableford, and David Langford. "Terraforming." *The Encyclopedia of Science Fiction*, edited by John Clute and David Langford, SFE Ltd/Ansible Editions, 2020. https://sf-encyclopedia.com/entry/terraforming. Accessed 17 Jan. 2023.
Ellis, Cristin. *Antebellum Posthuman: Race and Materiality in the Mid-Nineteenth Century*. Fordham University Press, 2018.
Esslin, Martin. *An Anatomy of Drama*. Temple Smith, 1976.
———. *The Theatre of the Absurd*. Penguin, 1987.
Evans, Arthur B. "Science Fiction." *Handbook of French Popular Culture*, Greenwood Press, 1991, pp. 229–265.
———. "Science Fiction vs. Scientific Fiction in France: From Jules Verne to J.-H. Rosny Aîné." *Vintage Visions: Essays on Early Science Fiction*, edited by Arthur B. Evans, Wesleyan University Press, 2014, pp. 82–95.
Evernden, Neil. "Beyond Ecology: Self, Place, and the Pathetic Fallacy." *The Ecocriticism Reader*, edited by Cheryll Glotfelty and Harold Fromm, University of Georgia Press, 1996, pp. 92–104.
Fagerholm, Matt. "A Very Deep Place: Claire Denis on High Life." 15 Apr. 2019, https://www.rogerebert.com/interviews/a-very-deep-place-claire-denis-on-high-life. Accessed 15 Dec. 2021.

Fay, Jennifer, and Justus Neiland. *Film Noir: Hard-Boiled Modernity and the Cultures of Globalization*. Routledge, 2010.

Feder, Helena. "Ecocriticism, Posthumanism, and the Biological Idea of Culture." *The Oxford Handbook of Ecocriticism*, edited by Greg Garrard, Oxford University Press, 2014, pp. 225–240.

Ferone, Geneviève, and Jean-Didier Vincent. *Bienvenue en transhumanie: sur l'homme de demain*. Bernard Grasset, 2011.

Ferrando, Francesca. "Posthumanism, Transhumanism, Antihumanism, Metahumanism, and New Materialisms: Differences and Relations." *Existenz*, vol. 8, no. 2, Fall 2013, pp. 26–32.

Ferry, Luc. *Le nouvel ordre écologique*. Bernard Grasset, 1992.

———. *La Révolution transhumaniste: comment la technomédecine et l'uberisation du monde vont bouleverser nos vies*. Éditions Plon, 2016.

Fioretti, Daniele. *Utopia and Dystopia in Postwar Italian Literature: Pasolini, Calvino, Sanguineti, Volponi*. Palgrave Macmillan, 2017.

Flammarion, Camille. *La Fin du monde*. Wikisource, 17 Dec. 2017, https://fr.wikisource.org/wiki/La_Fin_du_monde. Accessed 10 Apr. 2019.

———. *Lumen*, https://gallica.bnf.fr/ark:/12148/bpt6k834729. Accessed 8 Apr. 2019.

———. *La Pluralité des mondes habités*. Hachette, 2012.

"Flammarion, Camille (1842–1925)." *Encyclopedia of Occultism and Parapsychology*, 11 Jun. 2018, https://www.encyclopedia.com/people/science-and-technology/astronomy-biographies/nicolas-camille-flammarion. Accessed 9 Jun. 2016.

Flavelle, Christopher, et al. "Climate Change Poses a Widening Threat to National Security." *New York Times*, 21 Oct. 2021, https://www.nytimes.com/2021/10/21/climate/climate-change-national-security.html?searchResultPosition=1. Accessed 10 Dec. 2021.

Forest, Jean-Claude. *Barbarella*. Le Terrain vague, 1964.

Francis, Marc. "Splitting the Difference: On the Queer-Feminist Divide in Scarlett Johansson's Recent Body Politics," *Jump Cut*, no. 57, 2016.

Franck-Dumas, Elisabeth, and Jérémy Piette. "'High Life', vaisseau spécial." *Le Monde*, 6 Nov. 2018, https://www.liberation.fr/cinema/2018/11/06/high-life-vaisseau-special_1690305/. Accessed 15 Dec. 2021.

Francks, Richard. *Descartes' Meditations: A Reader's Guide*. Bloomsbury, 2008.

Freedman, Carl. *Critical Theory and Science Fiction*. Wesleyan University Press, 2000.

Freeman, Hadley. "James Cameron: 'The Downside of Being Attracted to Independent Women Is That They Don't Need You'." *Guardian*, 24 Aug. 2017, https://www.theguardian.com/film/2017/aug/24/james-cameron-well-never-be-able-to-reproduce-the-shock-of-terminator-2. Accessed 23 Feb. 2018.

Freud, Sigmund. *Civilization and Its Discontents*. Translated and edited by James Strachey, Norton, 1989.

———. *The Uncanny*. Translated by David McLintock, Penguin, 2003.
Freund, Karl, director. *The Mummy*. Universal Studios, 1932.
Friedman, Joseph H. "Ten Percent Brain Function: Fact or Fantasy?" *Rhode Island Medical Journal*, vol. 98, no. 9, 2015, pp. 8–9.
Fromm, Harold. "From Transcendence to Obsolescence." *The Ecocriticism Reader: Landmarks in Literary Ecology*, edited by Fromm and Cheryll Glotfelty, University of Georgia Press, 1996, pp. 30–39.
Fry, Paul H. *Theory of Literature*. Yale University Press, 2012.
Fuchs, Cynthia J. "'Death Is Irrelevant': Cyborgs, Reproduction, and the Future of Male Hysteria." *The Cyborg Handbook*, edited by Chris Hables Gray et al., Routledge, 1995, pp. 281–300.
Gardner, Colin, and Patricia MacCormack. "Introduction." *Deleuze and the Animal*, edited by Gardner and MacCormack, Edinburgh University Press, 2017, pp. 1–21.
Garland, Alex, director. *Ex Machina*. Universal Pictures, 2014.
Garrard, Greg. "Introduction." *The Oxford Handbook of Ecocriticism*, edited by Garrard, Oxford University Press, 2014, pp. 1–10.
Gaudreault, Marc Ross. "Anticiper le premier contact: la posture de l'exobiologiste chez J.-H. Rosny aîné." *Le Roman des possibles: l'anticipation dans l'espace médiatique francophone (1860–1940)*, Presses de l'Université de Montréal, 2019, pp. 137–152.
Geroulanos, Stefanos. *An Atheism That Is Not Humanist Emerges in French Thought*. Stanford University Press, 2010.
Gittell, Noah. "Scarlett Johansson's Vanishing Act." *The Atlantic*, 28 Jul. 2014, https://www.theatlantic.com/entertainment/archive/2014/07/what-in-the-world-is-scarlett-johansson-up-to-lucy-under-the-skin-her-a-feminist-disappearing-act/375141/. Accessed 7 May 2018.
Gladwin, Derek. "Ecocriticism." *Oxford Bibliographies*, 26 Jul. 2017, http://www.oxfordbibliographies.com/view/document/obo-9780190221911/obo-9780190221911-0014.xml#obo-9780190221911-0014-bibItem-0115. Accessed 20 Sept. 2018.
Glazer, Jonathan, director. *Under the Skin*. A24, 2013.
Glotfelty, Cheryll. "Introduction: Literary Studies in the Age of Environmental Crisis." *The Ecocriticism Reader: Landmarks in Literary Ecology*, edited by Cheryll Glotfelty and Harold Fromm, University of Georgia Press, 1996, pp. xv–xxxvii.
Godard, Jean-Luc, director. *Alphaville: une étrange aventure de Lemmy Caution*. Athos Film, 1965.
Godfrey, Alex. "Luc Besson: 'You Can't Imagine How Many People Ask Me for a *Léon* Sequel.'" *Guardian*, 15 Aug. 2014, https://www.theguardian.com/film/2014/aug/15/luc-besson-lucy-scarlett-johannson. Accessed 7 May 2018.
Goemare, Pierre. "Rosny, ce méconnu." *Revue Générale Belge*, Feb. 1962, pp. 49–55.

Goffette, Jérôme. "L'espace en résonance: corps, ville et monde dans *Étoiles mourantes* d'Ayerdhal et J.-C. Dunyach." *Poétique(s) de l'espace dans les œuvres fantastiques et de science-fiction*, Michel Houdiard, 2007, pp. 33–52.

Gomel, Elana. *Science Fiction, Alien Encounters, and the Ethics of Posthumanism: Beyond the Golden Rule*. Palgrave Macmillan, 2014.

Gormley, Michael J. *The End of the Anthropocene: Ecocriticism, the Universal Ecosystem, and the Astropocene*. Lexington Books, 2021.

Gouanvic, Jean-Marc. *La Science-fiction française au XXe siècle (1900–1968)*. Rodopi, 1994.

Gourdet, Anna. "Altérités alternatives: les extraterrestres électriques." *Cahiers naturalistes*, no. 80, 2006, pp. 177–192.

Graham, Elaine L. *Representations of the Post/Human: Monsters, Aliens and Others in Popular Culture*. Rutgers University Press, 2002.

Gratton, Johnnie. "Postmodern French Fiction." *The Cambridge Companion to the French Novel: From 1800 to the Present*, edited by Timothy Unwin, Cambridge University Press, 1997, pp. 242–260.

Gunn, James. *The Listeners*. BenBella Books, 2004.

———. "Science Fiction Around the World." *World Literature Today*, vol. 84, no. 3, 2010, pp. 27–29.

———. "Toward a Definition of Science Fiction." *Speculations on Speculation*, edited by Gunn and Matthew Candelaria, Scarecrow Press, 2005, pp. 5–12.

Halliwell, S. "Mimesis." *The Princeton Encyclopedia of Poetry and Poetics*, edited by Stephen Cushman et al., 4th ed., Princeton University Press, 2012, pp. 884–886.

Hantke, Steffen. *Monsters in the Machine: Science Fiction Film and the Militarization of America after World War II*. University Press of Mississippi, 2016.

Haraway, Donna. "A Cyborg Manifesto: Science, Technology, and Socialist Feminism in the Late Twentieth Century." *The Cybercultures Reader*, edited by David Bell and Barbara M. Kennedy, Routledge, 2000, pp. 291–324.

———. "Tentacular Thinking: Anthropocene, Capitalocene, Chthulucene." *e-flux*, no. 75, Sept. 2016, https://www.e-flux.com/journal/75/67125/tentacular-thinking-anthropocene-capitalocene-chthulucene. Accessed 15 Sept. 2020.

Harrison, Albert A. "Fear, Pandemonium, Equanimity and Delight: Human Responses to Extra-Terrestrial Life." *Philosophical Transactions of the Royal Society of London*, no. 369, 2011, pp. 656–668.

Hayat, Pierre. "Introduction." Emmanuel Levinas, *Alterity and Transcendence*. Translated by Michael B. Smith, Columbia University Press, 1999, pp. i–xxiv.

Hayles, N. Katherine. *How We Became Posthuman: Virtual Bodies in Cybernetics, Literature, and Informatics*. University of Chicago Press, 1999.

———. *Unthought: The Power of the Cognitive Unconscious*. University of Chicago Press, 2017.

Hayward, Susan. "Besson's 'Mission Elastoplast': *Le Cinquième Élément* (1997)." *French Cinema in the 1990s: Continuity and Difference*, edited by P. Powrie, Oxford University Press, 1999, pp. 246–257.

———. "From Rags to Riches: *Le Dernier Combat* and *Le Cinquième Elément*." *The Films of Luc Besson: Master of Spectacle*, edited by Susan Hayward and Phil Powrie, Manchester University Press, 2006, pp. 91–108.

———. *Luc Besson*. St. Martin's Press, 1998.

———. "Luc Besson: Bard and Filmmaker." *Fifty Contemporary Filmmakers*, Routledge, 2002, pp. 51–58.

———. "Luc Besson's *Cinquième Élément* (1997) and the Spectacular: The City-Body and the Sci-Fi Movie." *The Seeing Century: Film, Vision, and Identity*, edited by Wendy Everett, Rodopi, 2000, pp. 136–146.

———. *Nikita: French Film Guide*. I.B. Tauris, 2010.

———. "Recycled Woman and the Postmodern Aesthetic: Luc Besson's Nikita (1990)." *French Film: Texts and Contexts*, edited by Susan Hayward and Ginette Vincendeau, Routledge, 2000, pp. 297–309.

Hecht, Gabrielle. *The Radiance of France: Nuclear Power and National Identity after World War II*, MIT Press, 2009.

Heinlein, Robert. *Puppet Masters*. Doubleday, 1980.

Heise, Ursula. *Imagining Extinction: The Cultural Meanings of Endangered Species*. University of Chicago Press, 2016.

———. "Science Fiction and the Time Scales of the Anthropocene." *ELH*, vol. 86, no. 2, 2019, pp. 275–304, *Project MUSE*, doi:10.1353/elh.2019.0015.

Heise-von der Lippe, Anya. "Introduction: Post/Human/Gothic." *Posthuman Gothic*, edited by Heise-von der Lippe, University of Wales Press, 2017, pp. 1–16.

Held, Jacob M. "Introduction: 'In and For a World of Ordinary Mortals'." *Wonder Woman and Philosophy*, edited by Jacob M. Held, Wiley, 2017, pp. 20–21.

Henderson, Randy, and Rose O'Keefe. "Bizarro Fiction 101: Not Just Weird for Weird's Sake." *Fantasy Magazine*, n.d., http://www.fantasy-magazine.com/non-fiction/bizarro-fiction-101-not-just-weird-for-weirds-sake/. Accessed 3 Apr. 2019

"Henri Michaux." *Poetry Foundation*, n.d., https://www.poetryfoundation.org/poets/henri-michaux. Accessed 27 Aug. 2022.

Hippolyte, Jean-Louis. *Fuzzy Fiction*. University of Nebraska Press, 2006.

Hoby, Hermione. "Wonder Woman Director Patty Jenkins: 'People Really Thought That Only Men Loved Action Movies'." *Guardian*, 26 May 2017, https://www.theguardian.com/film/2017/may/26/wonder-woman-director-patty-jenkins-people-really-thought-that-only-men-loved-action-movies. Accessed 23 Feb. 2018.

Hollister, Lucas. *Beyond Return: Genre and Cultural Politics in Contemporary French Fiction*. Liverpool University Press, 2019.
Hoquet, Thierry. *Cyborg philosophie: penser contre les dualismes*. Éditions du Seuil, 2011.
Hottois, Gilbert, et al., editors. *Encyclopédie du transhumanisme et du posthumanisme*. J. Vrin, 2015.
Houellebecq, Michel. "Michel Houellebecq: The Art of Fiction No. 206." Interview by Susannah Hunnewell. *The Paris Review*, no. 194, Fall 2010, https://www.theparisreview.org/interviews/6040/michel-houellebecq-the-art-of-fiction-no-206-michel-houellebecq. Accessed 10 Aug. 2018.
Houppermans, Sjef. "Beckett and Contemporary French Literature." *Edinburgh Companion to Samuel Beckett and the Arts*, edited by S.E. Gontarski, Edinburgh University Press, 2014, pp. 185–198.
Hubbard, Timothy L. "The Inner Meaning of Outer Space: Human Nature and the Celestial Realm." *Avances en Psicología Latinoamericana*, vol. 26, no. 1, 2008, p. 52.
Hughes, Mark. "*Wonder Woman* Is Officially the Highest-Grossing Superhero Origin Film." *Forbes*, 2 Nov. 2017, https://www.forbes.com/sites/markhughes/2017/11/02/wonder-woman-is-officially-the-highest-grossing-superhero-origin-film/#168ea10bebd9. Accessed 23 Feb. 2018.
Hummel, Clémont. "Replonger dans l'inconnu pour y retrouver du connu." *J.H. Rosny aîné*, Presses universitaires de Caen, 2019, pp. 7–16.
Huret, Jules. *Enquête sur l'évolution littéraire*. Charpentier, 1891.
"International Association for the Fantastic in the Arts." *International Association for the Fantastic in the Arts*, https://iaftfita.wildapricot.org/resources/Documents/IAFA%20Global%20Fantastic%20CFP%202022.pdf. Accessed 31 Jan. 2023.
Ionesco, Eugène. "Dans les armes de la ville." *Cahiers de la Compagnie Madeleine Renaud-Jean-Louis Barrault*, no. 20, Oct. 1957.
Jenkins, Patty, director. *Wonder Woman*. Warner Bros. Pictures, 2017.
Johnson, Barbara. "Introduction." Jacques Derrida, *Dissemination*. Translated by Barbara Johnson, University of Chicago Press, 1981, pp. i–xxxiii.
Jouanne, Emmanuel. "How 'Dickian' Is the New French Science Fiction? (La nouvelle science-fiction française: est-elle dickienne?)." Translated by Danièle Chatelain and George Slusser. *Science-Fiction Studies*, vol. 15, no. 2, 1988, pp. 226–231.
Joy, Lisa, and Jonathan Nola, creators. *Westworld*. HBO Entertainment and Warner Bros. Television, 2016.
Kelly, James Patrick. "Slipstream." *Speculations on Speculation: Theories of Science Fiction*, edited by Gunn and Matthew Candelaria, Scarecrow Press, 2005, pp. 343–351.
Kelly, James Patrick, and John Kessel. "Introduction: Hacking Cyberpunk." *Rewired: The Post-Cyberpunk Anthology*, Tachyon, 2007, pp. vii–xvi.

Kempley, Rita. "*The Fifth Element*: A Spacey Odyssey." *The Washington Post*, 9 May 1997, p. D1.

Kent, Laurence. "Becoming-Flashdrive: The Cinematic Intelligence of *Lucy*." *Film-Philosophy*, vol. 24, no. 3, 2020, pp. 284–303.

Kerslake, Patricia. *Science Fiction and Empire*. Liverpool University Press, 2007.

Knight, Damon. *A Century of Science Fiction*. Simon & Schuster, 1962.

Kolbert, Elizabeth, "The Lost World." *New Yorker*, 16 Dec. 2013, https://www.newyorker.com/magazine/2013/12/16/the-lost-world-2. Accessed 14 Dec. 2020.

Kroker, Arthur. *Body Drift*. University of Minnesota Press, 2012.

Kubrick, Stanley, director. *2001: A Space Odyssey*. Metro-Goldwyn-Meyer, 1968.

Kuisel, Richard F. *The French Way: How France Embraced and Rejected American Values and Power*. Princeton University Press, 2012.

Kurtzman, Alex, director. *The Mummy*. Universal Pictures, 2017.

Kurzweil, Ray. *The Age of Spiritual Machines*. Penguin, 1999.

Lamarre, Thomas. "Seeing through the Car: The Automobile as Cosmopolitical Proposition in *The Fifth Element*." *Cinemas*, vol. 21, no. 1, 2010, pp. 105–128.

Lambert, Molly, and Wesley Morris. "Blockbuster Talk: Scarlett Johansson is All-Powerful, but 'Lucy' Still Has Some 'Splainin to Do." *Grantland*, 28 Jul. 2014, https://grantland.com/hollywood-prospectus/blockbuster-talk-scarlett-johansson-is-all-powerful-but-lucy-still-has-some-splainin-to-do/. Accessed 25 Aug. 2022.

Lang, Fritz, director. *Metropolis*. Kino Lorber Edu, 1927.

Langford, David, and Peter Nicholls. "Steampunk." *The Encyclopedia of Science Fiction*, 15 Mar. 2016, www.sf-encyclopedia.com/entry/steampunk. Accessed 5 Jul. 2017.

Langlet, Irène. "Étudier la science-fiction en France aujourd'hui." *ReS Futurae*, no. 1, 2012, https://doi.org/10.4000/resf.181. Accessed 1 Feb. 2023.

———. *La Science-fiction: lecture et poétique d'un genre littéraire*. A. Colin, 2006.

Lanuque, Jean-Guillaume. "La Science-fiction française face au 'grand cauchemar des années 1980': une lecture politique, 1981–1993." *ReS Futurae*, no. 3, 2013, resf.revues.org/430. Accessed 26 Jul. 2017.

Lanzoni, Rémi Fournier. *French Cinema: From Its Beginnings to the Present*. Continuum, 2002.

Lavender III, Isiah. "Contemporary Science Fiction and Afrofuturism." *The Cambridge History of Science Fiction*, edited by Gerry Canavan and Eric Carl Link, Cambridge University Press, 2018, pp. 565–579.

Lavery, Carl, and Clare Finburgh. "Introduction: Greening the Absurd." *Rethinking the Theatre of the Absurd: Ecology, the Environment and the Greening of the Modern Stage*, edited by Carl Lavery and Clare Finburgh, Bloomsbury, 2015, pp. 1–57.

Lecourt, Dominique. *Humain, posthumain: la technique et la vie.* Presses universitaires de Paris, 2011.

Ledit, Guillaume. "Philippe Curval: 'On assiste à une renaissance de la science-fiction française'." *Usbek & Rica*, 9 Dec. 2018, https://usbeketrica.com/fr/article/on-assiste-a-une-renaissance-de-la-science-fiction-francaise. Accessed 10 Dec. 2021.

Ledzinski, Catie. "Les Rêveries biologiques de Rosny aîné." *Écofictions et cli-fi: l'environnement dans les fictions de l'imaginaire*, edited by Christian Chelebourg, Presses universitaires de Nancy, 2019, pp. 103–110.

Le Guin, Ursula. "The Carrier Bag Theory of Fiction." *The Ecocriticism Reader: Landmarks in Literary Ecology*, edited by Cheryll Glotfelty and Harold Fromm, University of Georgia Press, 1996, pp. 149–154.

Lehman, Serge. "Les Mondes perdus de l'anticipation française." *Le Monde Diplomatique*, Jul. 1999, https://www.monde-diplomatique.fr/1999/07/LEHMAN/3112. Accessed 15 Nov. 2021.

———. "Note liminaire." *La Guerre des règnes de J.H. Rosny aîné*, Bragelonne, 2011, pp. 7–8.

Levinas, Emmanuel. *Humanisme de l'autre homme.* Éditions Fata Morgana, 1972.

———. "Liberté et commandement." *Revue de métaphysique et de morale*, vol. 58, no. 3, 1953, pp. 264–272.

———. *Le Temps et l'autre.* Fata Morgana, 1979.

———. *Totalité et infini.* Martinus Nijhoff, 1968.

Leyris, Raphaëlle. "Hervé Le Tellier démultiplié." *Le Monde*, 18 Oct. 2020, https://www.lemonde.fr/livres/article/2020/10/18/herve-le-tellier-demultiplie_6056475_3260.html. Accessed 15 Dec. 2021.

Lillvis, Kristen. *Posthuman Blackness and the Black Female Imagination.* University of Georgia Press, 2017.

Lord, Christina. "The Tragic Comedy of Humanity: Life After Species Extinction in Éric Chevillard's *Sans l'orang-outan.*" *Fiction and the Sixth Mass Extinction*, Lexington Books, 2020, pp. 133–150.

Loreck, J., et al., editors. *Screening Scarlett Johansson: Gender, Genre, Stardom.* Palgrave Macmillan, 2019.

Lucas, George, director. *Star Wars.* 20th Century Fox, 1977.

Lundblad, Michael. "Introduction: The End of the Animal – Literary and Cultural Animalities." *Animalities: Literary and Cultural Studies beyond the Human*, Edinburgh University Press, 2017, pp. 1–21.

Luscombe, Belinda. "12 Questions with Patty Jenkins, Director of *Wonder Woman.*" *Time*, 15 Jun. 2017, http://time.com/4819569/patty-jenkins-wonder-woman-director-interview/. Accessed 9 Apr. 2019.

Lyau, Bradford. *The Anticipation Novelists of French Science Fiction: Stepchildren of Voltaire.* McFarland, 2011.

Lyle, Louise. "Reading Environmental Apocalypse in J.H. Rosny Aîné's Terrestrial Texts." *Histoires de la Terre: Earth Science and French Culture 1740–1940*, edited by Louise Lyle and David McCallam, Rodopi, 2008, pp. 219–234.

Lynes, Krista Geneviève, and Katerina Symes. "Cyborgs and Virtual Bodies." *The Oxford Handbook of Feminist Theory*, edited by Lisa Disch and Mary Hawkesworth, Oxford University Press, 2016, pp. 122–142.

Lyotard, Jean-François. *La Condition postmoderne: rapport sur le savoir*. Éditions de Minuit, 1979.

Magerstädt, Sylvie. "Love Thy Extra-Terrestrial Neighbour: Charity and Compassion in Luc Besson's Space Operas *The Fifth Element* (1997) and *Valerian and the City of a Thousand Planets* (2017)." *Religions*, vol. 9, no. 10, 2018.

Mandelbaum, Jacques. "'High Life': Claire Denis sonde le désir en apesanteur." *Le Monde*, 6 Nov. 2018, https://www.lemonde.fr/cinema/article/2018/11/06/high-life-claire-denis-sonde-le-desir-en-apesanteur_5379326_3476.html. Accessed 15 Dec. 2021.

Mather, Philippe, and Sylvain Rheault, editors. *Rediscovering French Science-Fiction in Literature, Film, and Comics: From Cyrano to Barbarella*. Cambridge Scholars, 2015.

Mattei, Jean-François. *Questions de la conscience: de la génétique au posthumanisme*. Éditions Les Liens qui libèrent, 2017.

Maule, Rosanna. *Beyond Auteurism: New Directions in Authorial Film Practices in France, Italy and Spain Since the 1980s*. Intellect, 2008.

Maupassant, Guy de. *Le Horla et d'autres contes d'angoisse*. Flammarion, 1984.

Max, D.T. "Beyond Human." *National Geographic*, vol. 231, no. 4, Apr. 2017, pp. 40–63.

Mazgaj, Paul. "America through the Prism of French National Identity Debates: Review of Richard F. Kuisel, *The French Way: How France Embraced and Rejected American Values and Power*. Princeton University Press, 2012." *French Politics*, vol. 10, no. 3, 2012, pp. 306–322.

McFarlane, A., et al., editors. *The Routledge Companion to Cyberpunk Culture*. Routledge, 2019.

McKibben, Bill, *Eaarth: Making a Life on a Tough New Planet*. New York: St. Martin's, 2011.

McQuillen, Colleen, and Julia Vaingurt, editors. *The Human Reimagined: Posthumanism in Russia*. Academic Studies Press, 2018.

McTiernan, John, director. *Die Hard*. 20th Century Fox, 1988.

Meeker, Joseph W. "The Comic Mode." *The Ecocriticism Reader: Landmarks in Literary Ecology*, edited by Cheryll Glotfelty and Harold Fromm, University of Georgia Press, 1996, pp. 155–169.

Menely, Tobias, and Jesse Oak Taylor. "Introduction." *Anthropocene Reading: Literary History in Geologic Times*, edited by Tobias and Taylor, Penn State University Press, pp. 1–10.

Miah, Andy. "A Critical History of Posthumanism." *Medical Enhancement and Posthumanity*, edited by Bert Gordijn and Ruth Chadwick, Springer, 2008, pp. 71–94.

Miéville, China. Interview by Mark Bould. *Paradoxa*, vol. 28, 2016, pp. 15–40.

Migraine-Georges, Thérèse. *From Francophonie to World Literature in French: Ethics, Poetics, and Politics*. University of Nebraska Press, 2013.

Miller, Ann. *Reading* Bande Dessinée: *Critical Approaches to French-Language Comic Strip*. Intellect Books Ltd, 2007.

Milner, Andrew. *Locating Science Fiction*. Liverpool University Press, 2012.

"Minifeste." *Le Collectif Zanzibar*, n.d., http://www.zanzibar.zone/. Accessed 15 Dec. 2021.

Montellier, Chantal. *Social Fiction*. Vertige Graphic, 2003.

Moore, Jason W., editor. *Anthropocene or Capitalocene? Nature, History, and the Crisis of Capitalism*. PM Press, 2016.

Morgan, Michael L. *The Cambridge Introduction to Emmanuel Levinas*. Cambridge University Press, 2011.

Morrow, James, and Kathryn Morrow, editors. *The SFWA European Hall of Fame: Sixteen Contemporary Masterpieces of Science Fiction from the Continent*. Tor, 2007.

Mortimer-Sandilands, Catriona. "Melancholy Natures, Queer Ecologies." *Queer Ecologies: Sex, Nature, Politics, Desire*, edited by Mortimer-Sandilands and Bruce Erickson, Indiana University Press, 2010, pp. 331–358.

Morton, Timothy, and Dominic Boyer. *Hyposubjects*. Open Humanities Press, 2021, http://openhumanitiespress.org/books/download/Morton_Boyer_2021-hyposubjects.pdf. Accessed 1 Feb. 2023.

Mulvey, Laura. "Visual Pleasure and Narrative Cinema." *Media and Cultural Studies*, edited by Meenakshi Gigi Durham and Douglas M. Kellner, Blackwell, 2006, pp. 342–352.

Nagel, Thomas. "What Is It Like to Be a Bat?" *The Philosophical Review*, vol. 83, no. 4, 1974, pp. 435–450.

"Nature." *Dictionnaire de l'Académie française, Huitième édition, Tome 2*, 1932, Dictionnaires d'autrefois, The ARTFL Project, https://artflsrv04.uchicago.edu/philologic4.7/publicdicos/navigate/19/5550. Accessed 20 Sept. 2017.

"Nature." *Dictionnaire de la langue française (Littré), Tome 3*, 1873, Dictionnaires d'autrefois, The ARTFL Project, https://artflsrv04.uchicago.edu/philologic4.7/publicdicos/navigate/16/11291. Accessed 20 Sept. 2017.

"Navrant." *Le Monde*, 28 Jan. 1985, https://www.lemonde.fr/archives/article/1985/01/28/navrant_2762227_1819218.html. Accessed 22 Aug. 2022.

Nayar, Pramod. *Posthumanism*. Polity Press, 2014.

Nehamas, Alexander. "Foreword." Alain Renaut, *The Era of the Individual: A Contribution to a History of Subjectivity*. Translated by M.B. DeBevoise and Franklin Philip, Princeton University Press, 1997, pp. vii–xviii.

Neupert, Richard John. *A History of the French New Wave Cinema*. University of Wisconsin Press, 2010.

Newman, Kim. "The Fifth Element." *Sight and Sound*, vol. 7, no. 7, 1997, pp. 39–40.

Nguyen, Sophia. "The Posthuman Scar-Jo." *Los Angeles Review of Books*, 12 Sept. 2014, https://lareviewofbooks.org/article/posthuman-scar-jo/. Accessed 27 Aug. 2022.

Nicholls, Peter. "Hard SF." *The Encyclopedia of Science Fiction*, 19 Mar. 2019, http://www.sf-encyclopedia.com/entry/hard_sf. Accessed 11 Apr. 2019.

Nicholls, Peter, and John Clute. "Horror in SF." *The Encyclopedia of Science Fiction*, 3 Feb. 2019, http://www.sf-encyclopedia.com/entry/horror_in_sf. Accessed 3 Apr. 2019.

Nicholls, Peter, and Nick Lowe. "Blade Runner." *The Encyclopedia of Science Fiction*, 16 Oct. 2017, http://www.sf-encyclopedia.com/entry/blade_runner. Accessed 23 Feb. 2018.

Nicot, Stéphanie. "Détails de l'artiste exposé." *Galaxies*, no. 37, Summer 2005, pp. 108–113.

Orbaugh, Sharalyn. "Sex and the Single Cyborg: Japanese Popular Culture Experiments in Subjectivity." *Science Fiction Studies*, vol. 29, no. 3, 2002, pp. 436–452.

———. "Who Does the Feeling When the Body Is Not There? Critical Feminism Meets Cyborg Affect in Oshii Mamoru's *Innocence*." *Simultaneous Worlds: Global Science Fiction Cinema*, edited by Jennifer L. Feeley and Sarah Ann Wells, University of Minnesota Press, 2015, pp. 191–209.

Orr, Christopher. "With *Wonder Woman*, DC Comics Finally Gets It Right." *The Atlantic*, 2 Jun. 2017, https://www.theatlantic.com/entertainment/archive/2017/06/wonder-woman-review/528816/. Accessed 25 Feb. 2018.

Oshii, Mamoru, director. *Ghost in the Shell*. Manga Entertainment, 1995.

Osterweil, Ara. "*Under the Skin*: The Perils of Becoming Female." *Film Quarterly*, vol. 67, no. 4, Summer 2014, pp. 44–51.

Ott, Brian L. "Counter-Imagination as Interpretative Practice: Futuristic Fantasy and *The Fifth Element*." *Women's Studies in Communication*, vol. 27, no. 2, 2004, pp. 149–176.

Ousselin, Edward. *La France: histoire, société, culture*. Canadian Scholars, 2018.

Ovid. *Metamorphoses*. Wikisource, 8 Apr. 2019, https://en.wikisource.org/wiki/Translation:Metamorphoses. Accessed 9 Apr. 2019.

Oz, Frank, director. *The Stepford Wives*. Paramount Pictures, 2004.

Pastourmatzi, Domna. "Science Fiction Literature." *Post- and Transhumanism: An Introduction*, edited by Robert Ranisch and Stefan Loran Sorgner, Peter Lang, 2014, pp. 271–286.

Perrin, Jean. *La Science et l'espérance*. Presses Universitaires de France, 1948.

Philbeck, Thomas D. "Ontology." *Post- and Transhumanism: An Introduction*, edited by Robert Ranisch and Stefan Loran Sorgner, Peter Lang, 2014, pp. 173–184.

Place, Janey. "Women in Film Noir" (1978). *Women in Film Noir*, edited by Elizabeth Ann Kaplan, British Film Institute, 2005, pp. 47–68.

Pomeau, René. "Notes sur *Micromégas*." Voltaire, *Romans et contes*, Flammarion, 1966, pp. 123–129.

Posthumus, Stephanie. *French Écocritique: Reading Contemporary French Theory and Fiction Ecologically*. University of Toronto Press, 2017.

———. "Vers une écocritique française: le contrat naturel de Michel Serres." *Mosaic*, vol. 44, no. 2, 2011, pp. 85–100.

Pottier, Jean-Michel. "Reparler de J.H. Rosny." *Les Cahiers Naturalistes*, vol. 42, no. 70, 1996, pp. 181–209.

Powrie, Phil. "Nikita." *The Cinema of France*, Wallflower, 2006, pp. 197–206.

Quillien, Christophe. "Interview Luc Besson, Jean-Claude Mézières and Pierre Christin (Part 1)." *Valerian: The Complete Collection Volume One*, Cinebook Ltd, 2016, pp. 5–10.

———. "Interview Luc Besson, Jean-Claude Mézières and Pierre Christin (Part 2)." *Valerian: The Complete Collection Volume Two*, Cinebook Ltd, 2016, pp. 5–10.

Rabadi, Isabelle. "Palafox & Cie ... l'animal dans l'écriture romanesque d'Éric Chevillard." *Écrire l'animal aujourd'hui*, edited by Lucile Desblache, Presses Universitaires Blaise Pascal, 2006, pp. 103–112.

Rabin, Nathan. "Follywood: How Valerian Earns Its Place among Film's Strangest Big-Budget Flops." *Guardian*, 4 Aug. 2017, https://www.theguardian.com/film/2017/aug/04/valerian-jupiter-ascending-science-fiction-film-flops. Accessed 19 Aug. 2022.

Rabkin, Eric S., and George E. Slusser. "Introduction." *Aliens: The Anthropology of Science Fiction*, edited by Eric S. Rabkin and George E. Slusser, Southern Illinois University Press, 1987, pp. vii–xxi.

Ransom, Amy J. "The First Last Man: Cousin de Grainville's *Le dernier homme*." *Science Fiction Studies*, vol. 41, no. 2, 2014, pp. 314–340.

———. "The New French SF: The Imaginary Worlds of Jean-Claude Dunyach." *The New York Review of Science Fiction*, 2 Jun. 2014, www.nyrsf.com/2014/06/amy-j-ransom-the-new-french-sf-the-imaginary-worlds-of-jean-claude-dunyach.html. Accessed 17 Mar. 2017.

———. "Will the Real Rosny ainé Please Step Forward?" *Extrapolation*, vol. 54, no. 3, 2013, pp. 291–333.

Raup, D.M., and Sepkoski, J.J., Jr., "Mass Extinctions in the Marine Fossil Record, " *Science*, no. 215, 1982, pp. 1501–1503.

Regnier, Isabelle. "'Valérian', un défilé de cartes postales intergalactiques." *Le Monde*, 26 Jul. 2017, https://www.lemonde.fr/cinema/article/2017/07/26/valerian-et-la-cite-des-mille-planetes-un-defile-de-cartes-postales-intergalactiques_5164968_3476.html. Accessed 19 Aug. 2022.

Renard, Maurice. "On the Scientific-Marvelous and Its Influence on the Understanding of Progress." Edited and translated by Arthur B. Evans. *Science Fiction Studies*, vol. 21, no. 3, 1994, pp. 397–405.

Rérolle, Raphaëlle. 2021. "Quand l'armée engage des auteurs de science-fiction pour imaginer les menaces du futur." *Le Monde*, 7 Jul. 2021, https://www.lemonde.fr/culture/article/2021/07/07/quand-l-armee-engage-des-auteurs-de-science-fiction-pour-imaginer-les-menaces-du-futur_6087366_3246.html. Accessed 15 Dec. 2021.

Richard, Olive. "Our Women Are Our Future." *Family Circle*, 14 Aug. 1942, https://www.castlekeys.com/Pages/wonder.html. Accessed 26 Jul. 2022.

Rieder, John. *Colonialism and the Emergence of Science Fiction*. Wesleyan University Press, 2008.

Riendeau, Pascal. "Des leurres ou des hommes de paille." Interview with Eric Chevillard. *Société roman*, no. 46, 2008, pp. 11–22.

Riesman, Abraham. "Luc Besson, Utopian, Spaceman." *Vulture*, 9 Jul. 2017, http://www.vulture.com/2017/07/luc-besson-valerian-interview.html. Accessed 23 Feb. 2018.

Rifkin, Glenn. "Marvin Minsky, Pioneer in Artificial Intelligence, Dies at 88." *New York Times*, 25 Jan. 2016, www.nytimes.com/2016/01/26/business/marvin-minsky-pioneer-in-artificial-intelligence-dies-at-88.html?_r=0. Accessed 10 Mar. 2017.

Roberts, Elizabeth. "UN Drops Wonder Woman as Honorary Ambassador." *CNN*, 13 Dec. 2016, https://www.cnn.com/2016/12/13/health/wonder-woman-un-ambassador-trnd/index.html. Accessed 25 Feb. 2018.

Robles, Fanny. "Of Cavemen, 'Struggleforlifeurs' and Deep Ecology: J.-H. Rosny Aîné's Literary Response to Darwin and Human Evolution." *The Literary and Cultural Reception to Charles Darwin in Europe*, edited by Thomas F. Glick and Elinor Shaffer, Bloomsbury, 2014, pp. 458–479.

Robson, David. "Frye, Derrida, Pynchon, and the Apocalyptic Space of Postmodern Fiction." *Postmodern Apocalypse*, edited by Richard Dellamora, University of Pennsylvania Press, 1995, pp. 61–78.

Rogers, Adam. "Luc Besson's Outer Limits." *Wired*, 6 Jul. 2017, https://www.wired.com/2017/07/luc-besson-valerian/. Accessed 19 Aug. 2022.

Rolls, Alistair. "Fatal(e) Crossings: Figures of the Feminine in French and American Film Noir." *French and American Noir: Dark Crossings*, edited by Rolls and Deborah Walker-Morrison, Palgrave Macmillan, 2009, pp. 132–148.

Rose, Mark. *Alien Encounters: Anatomy of Science Fiction*. Harvard University Press, 1981.

Rose, Steve. "*Ex Machina* and Sci-Fi's Obsession with Sexy Robots." *Guardian*, 15 Jan. 2015, www.theguardian.com/film/2015/jan/15/ex-machina-sexy-female-robots-scifi-film-obsession. Accessed 26 Sept. 2017.

———. "Valerian: Why Luc Besson Is the Unsung Hero of World Cinema." *Guardian*, 31 Jul. 2017, https://www.theguardian.com/film/2017/jul/31/valerian-why-luc-besson-is-unsung-hero-world-cinema. Accessed 19 Aug. 2022.

Rosny aîné, J.H. *La Force mystérieuse, suivi de Les Xipéhuz*. Bibliothèque Marabout, 1972.

———. "La Mort de la Terre." *La Guerre des règnes de J.H. Rosny aîné*, Bragelonne, 2011, pp. 687-755.

———. *L'Immolation*. Albert Savine, 1887, https://gallica.bnf.fr/ark:/12148/bpt6k81125g/f15.item. Accessed 9 Nov. 2016.

———. *Three Science Fiction Novellas: From Prehistory to the End of Mankind*. Translated by Danièle Chatelain and George Slusser, Wesleyan University Press, 2012.

———. *Les Navigateurs de l'infini*. 4th ed., La Nouvelle revue critique, 1927, https://gallica.bnf.fr/ark:/12148/bpt6k80700j?rk=21459;2. Accessed 8 Apr. 2019.

———. Notes and drafts of *Le Manifeste des Cinq*. Box number 6: "Œuvre littéraire: manuscrits autographes." Legs Borel-Rosny, La Médiathèque Municipale de Bayeux, Bayeux, France.

———. *Torches et lumignons: souvenirs de la vie littéraire*. La Force française, 1921.

———. "Vers le quatrième univers." *Mercure de France*, 15 Feb. 1931, pp. 5–41, https://gallica.bnf.fr/ark:/12148/bpt6k202110k.item. Accessed 11 Apr. 2019.

———. *Les Xipéhuz*. Albert Savine, 1888, https://fr.wikisource.org/wiki/Les_Xip%C3%A9huz/%C3%89dition_Albert_Savine_1888. Accessed 10 Jul. 2016.

Rosny aîné, J.H., and Jean Baptiste Baronian. *Récits de science-fiction*. Éditions Gérard, 1973.

Rousseau, Jean-Jacques. *Discourse on Inequality: On the Origin and Basis of Inequality among Men*. The Floating Press, 2009.

———. *Discours sur l'origine et les fondements de l'inégalité parmi les hommes*. Flammarion, 1992.

Rueckert, William. "Literature and Ecology: An Experiment in Ecocriticism." *The Ecocriticism Reader: Landmarks in Literary Ecology*, edited by Cheryll Glotfelty and Harold Fromm, University of Georgia Press, 1996, pp. 105–123.

Sagan, Carl. *Contact*. Simon & Schuster, 1985.

Samoyault, Tiphaine. "Rendre bête." *Pour Éric Chevillard*, edited by Bruno Blanckeman, Éditions de Minuit, 2014, pp. 37–58.

Sanders, Rupert, director. *Ghost in the Shell*. Paramount Pictures, 2017.
Schaefer, Stephen. "Luc Besson: So Not Hollywood." *Boston Herald*, 16 Jul. 2017, https://www.bostonherald.com/2017/07/16/luc-besson-so-not-hollywood/. Accessed 25 Aug. 2022.
Schaeffer, Jean-Marie. *La Fin de l'exception humaine*. Gallimard, 2007.
Scott, Paul. "Aliens and Alienation in Pierre Boulle's *La Planète des singes*." *Romance Studies*, vol. 38. no. 1, 2020, pp. 26-37, DOI:10.1080/02639904.2020.1766858.
———. "Interplanetary Intimacy: Alien-Human Love in J.-H. Rosny Aîné's Martian Novels." *Neophilologus*, vol. 105, no. 3, 2021, pp. 349–364.
Scott, Ridley, director. *Alien*. 20th Century Fox, 1979.
———. *Blade Runner*. Warner Bros., 1982.
Seed, David. "Introduction." *Imagining Apocalypse: Studies in Cultural Crisis*, St. Martin's Press, 2000, pp. 1–14.
Senior, Matthew, et al. "Editors' Preface: *Ecce animot:* Postanimality from Cave to Screen." *Yale French Studies*, no. 127, 2015, pp. 1–18.
Sermet, Tessa. "Comment vivre sans lui? Anthropocentrisme et posthumanisme dans *Sans l'orang-outan* d'Éric Chevillard." *La Science-fiction en langue française*, special issue of *Œuvres et Critiques*, vol. 44, no. 2, 2019, pp. 135–151.
Serres, Michel. *Le Contrat naturel*. Éditions F. Bourin, 1990.
———. *Le Parasite*. Éditions Grasset et Fasquelle, 1980.
Servigne, Pablo, and Raphaël Stevens. *Comment tout peut s'effondrer*. Éditions du Seuil, 2015.
Shelley, Mary. *Frankenstein*. Liveright, 2017.
Shetley, Vernon. "Performing the Inhuman: Scarlett Johansson and SF Film." *Science Fiction Film and Television*, vol. 11, no. 1, 2018, pp. 13–19.
Shklovsky, Viktor. "Art, as Device." *Poetics Today*, vol. 36, no. 3, 2015, pp. 151–174.
Sims, David. "How *The Fifth Element* Subverted Sci-Fi Movies." *The Atlantic*, 19 Jul. 2017, https://www.theatlantic.com/entertainment/archive/2017/07/how-the-fifth-element-subverted-sci-fi-movies/534108/. Accessed 23 Feb. 2018.
Slusser, George. "Rosny's Mars." *Visions of Mars: Essays on the Red Planet in Fiction and Science*, edited by Howard V. Hendrix et al., McFarland, 2011, pp. 36–48.
———. "Why They Kill Jules Verne: SF and Cartesian Culture." *Science Fiction Studies*, vol. 32, no. 1, 2005, pp. 61–79.
Sojcher, Frédéric. "Luc Besson, ou les contradictions du cinéma français." *Quelle diversité face à Hollywood?*, edited by Thomas Paris, Arte, 2002, pp. 142–156.
Sommers, Stephen, director. *The Mummy*. Universal Pictures, 1999.
Spicer, Andrew. "Introduction." *A Companion to Film Noir*, edited by Andrew Spicer and Helen Hanson, Wiley, 2013, pp. 1–14.

Spielberg, Steven, director. *Indiana Jones and the Raiders of the Lost Ark.* Paramount Pictures, 1981.

Springer, Claudia. *Electronic Eros: Bodies and Desire in the Postindustrial Age.* University of Texas Press, 1996.

Stableford, Brian M. "End of the World." *The Encyclopedia of Science Fiction*, 11 Aug. 2018, http://www.sf-encyclopedia.com/entry/end_of_the_world. Accessed 13 Aug. 2018.

———. "Introduction." Camille Flammarion, *Lumen*. Translated by Brian Stableford, Wesleyan University Press, 2002, pp. ix–xxxv.

———. "Introduction." J.H. Rosny aîné, *The Navigators of Space and Other Alien Encounters*. Translated by Brian Stableford, Black Coat Press, 2010, pp. 7–60.

———. "The Paradoxical Career of J.H. Rosny the Elder." *New York Review of Science Fiction*, vol. 22, no. 12, 2010, pp. 15–23.

Stableford, Brian M., and John Clute. "Dick, Philip K." *The Encyclopedia of Science Fiction*, 3 Nov. 2018, http://www.sf-encyclopedia.com/entry/dick_philip_k. Accessed 5 Mar. 2019.

———. "Flammarion, Camille." *The Encyclopedia of Science Fiction*, 25 Aug. 2015. http://www.sf-encyclopedia.com/entry/flammarion_camille. Accessed 8 Nov. 2016.

———. "Rosny aîné, J-H." *The Encyclopedia of Science Fiction*, 31 Aug. 2018, http://www.sf-encyclopedia.com/entry/rosny_aine_j_h. Accessed 11 Apr. 2019.

———. "Wells, H.G." *The Encyclopedia of Science Fiction*, 21 Oct. 2017, www.sf-encyclopedia.com/entry/wells_h_g. Accessed 28 Nov. 2017.

Stableford, Brian M., and David Langford. "Parallel Worlds." *The Encyclopedia of Science Fiction*, 23 Apr. 2016, http://www.sf-encyclopedia.com/entry/parallel_worlds. Accessed 19 Jul. 2016.

Stableford, Brian M., and Peter Nicholls. "Technology." *The Encyclopedia of Science Fiction*, 2 Apr. 2015, www.sf-encyclopedia.com/entry/technology. Accessed 17 Mar. 2017.

Stableford, Brian M., et al. "Terraforming." *The Encyclopedia of Science Fiction*, 19 Mar. 2018. http://www.sf-encyclopedia.com/entry/terraforming. Accessed 18 Mar. 2020.

Steinkopf-Frank, Hannah. 'Solarpunk Is Not About Pretty Aesthetics. It's About the End of Capitalism', *Vice*, 2 Sept. 2021, https://www.vice.com/en/article/wx5aym/solarpunk-is-not-about-pretty-aesthetics-its-about-the-end-of-capitalism. Accessed 16 Dec. 2021.

Stevens, Kirsten. "Between Attraction and Anxiety: Scarlett Johansson, Female Knowledge and the Mind-Body Split." *Science Fiction Film and Television*, vol. 11, no. 1, 2018, pp. 21–28.

Stevens, Kirsten, et al. "Why Scarlett Johansson?" *Screening Scarlett Johansson: Gender, Genre, Stardom*. ed. Janice Loreck et al., Palgrave Macmillan, 2019, pp. 1–22.

Stromberg, Joseph. "What Is the Anthropocene and Are We in it?" *Smithsonian Magazine*, Jan. 2013, https://www.smithsonianmag.com/science-nature/what-is-the-anthropocene-and-are-we-in-it-164801414/. Accessed 5 Mar. 2019.

Suvin, Darko. "Estrangement and Cognition." *Speculations on Speculation: Theories of Science Fiction*, edited by Gunn and Matthew Candelaria, Scarecrow Press, 2005, pp. 23–35.

———. *Metamorphoses of Science Fiction: On the Poetics and History of a Literary Genre*. Yale University Press, 1979.

Tasker, Yvonne. "Women in Film Noir." *A Companion to Film Noir*, edited by Andrew Spicer and Helen Hanson, Wiley, 2013, pp. 353–368.

Tello, Carlos. "Les multiples visages du posthumanisme au cinéma." *Usbek et Rica*, 30 May 2017, https://usbeketrica.com/article/les-multiples-visages-du-posthumanisme-au-cinema. Accessed 5 Mar. 2019.

Thacker, Eugene. *After Life*. University of Chicago Press, 2010.

Thévenet, Elisa. "Quand la science-fiction abandonne les récits de fin du monde pour un optimisme subversif." *Le Monde*, 36 Jun. 2020, https://www.lemonde.fr/livres/article/2020/06/25/quand-la-science-fiction-abandonne-les-recits-de-fin-du-monde-pour-un-optimisme-subversif_6044201_3260.html. Accessed 15 Dec. 2021.

Thomas, Paul. "The Current State of Science Fiction in France (L'État actuel de la science-fiction en France)." *Science-Fiction Studies*, vol. 16, no. 3, 1989, pp. 298–306.

Todorov, Tzvetan. *Imperfect Garden: The Legacy of Humanism*. Translated by Carol Cosman, Princeton University Press, 2002.

Toffoletti, Kim. *Cyborgs and Barbie Dolls: Feminism, Popular Culture and the Posthuman Body*. I.B. Tauris, 2007.

Traisnel, Antoine. 'No, American Academe Is Not Corrupting France', *The Chronicle of Higher Education*, 1 Apr. 2021, https://www.chronicle.com/article/no-american-academe-is-not-corrupting-france. Accessed 6 Dec. 2021.

"Transhumanist Declaration." *Humanity+*, https://www.humanityplus.org/the-transhumanist-declaration. Accessed 5 Mar. 2019.

Tremblay, Anne. "France Breeds a New Crop of Auteurs." *International New York Times*, 21 Jul. 1985, http://www.nytimes.com/1985/07/21/movies/france-breeds-a-new-crop-of-auteurs.html. Accessed 20 Oct. 2017.

Tunbridge, Laura. "Scarlett Johansson's Body and the Materialization of Voice." *Twentieth-Century Music*, vol. 13, no. 1, 2016, pp. 139–152.

Turcanu, Radu. "'Le Horla' et 'l'effet de réel'." *Nineteenth-Century French Studies*, vol. 26, nos. 3–4, Spring–Summer 1998, pp. 387–397.

Utterson, Andrew. "Tarzan vs. IBM: Humans and Computers in Jean-Luc Godard's *Alphaville*." *Film Criticism*, vol. 33, no. 1, 2008, pp. 45–63.

Vance, Ashlee. "Merely Human? That's So Yesterday." *New York Times*, 12 Jun. 2010, https://www.nytimes.com/2010/06/13/business/13sing.html. Accessed 5 Mar. 2019.

VanderMeer, Jeff. "Hauntings in the Anthropocene." *Environmental Critique*, 7 July 2016, environmentalcritique.wordpress.com/2016/07/07/hauntings-in-the-anthropocene. Accessed 17 Jan. 2023.

VanderMeer, Jeff, and Ann VanderMeer, editors. *The Big Book of Science Fiction*. Vintage Books, 2016.

Van Herp, Jacques. "Introduction." J.H. Rosny aîné, *Les Récits de science-fiction*, edited by Jean Baptiste Baronian, Bibliothèque Marabout, 1975, pp. 9–12.

Vas-Deyres, Natacha. "Les Animaux-villes de Jean-Claude Dunyach, lieux de rencontre entre l'univers et l'humanité." *Les Lieux de passage en science-fiction*, University of La Rochelle, La Rochelle, France, Apr. 2013, pp. 11–13, https://www.academia.edu/8738149/_Les_Animaux-villes_de_Jean-Claude_Dunyach_lieux_de_rencontre_entre_lunivers_et_lhumanit%C3%A9. Accessed 11 Apr. 2019.

———. *Ces Français qui ont écrit demain: utopie, anticipation et science-fiction au XXe siècle*. Honoré Champion, 2012.

———. "De l'exosquelette au cyberpunk: imaginaire des rapports entre l'homme et la machine dans la science-fiction." *Transverses 2011 "Des Hommes et des machines,"* Université Michel de Montaigne-Bordeaux 3, https://www.academia.edu/8024000/De_lexosquelette_au_cyberpunk_imaginaire_des_rapports_entre_lhomme_et_la_machine_dans_la_science-fiction. Accessed 11 Apr. 2019.

———. "Jean-Claude Dunyach, Poet of the Flesh." *Lingua Cosmica: Science Fiction from around the World*, edited by Dale Knickerbocker, University of Illinois Press, 2018, pp. 46–55.

Vas-Deyres, Natacha, et al., editors. *C'était demain: anticiper la science-fiction en France et au Québec (1880–1950)*. Presses universitaires de Bordeaux, 2018.

Verhoeven, Paul, director. *Robocop*. Orion Pictures, 1987.

Vermeulen, Pieter. *Literature and the Anthropocene*. Taylor & Francis, 2020.

Versins, Pierre. "J.H. Rosny aîné." *Encyclopédie de l'utopie, des voyages extraordinaires et de la science-fiction*, L'Âge d'Homme, 1972, pp. 775–778.

Vial, Éric. "Éric Chevillard: *Sans l'orang-outan*." *Quarante-Deux: Keep Watching the Skies!*, nos. 62–63, Jul. 2009, http://q-d.fr/4vt. Accessed 27 Aug. 2022.

Viart, Dominique. "Littérature spéculative." *Pour Éric Chevillard*, edited by Bruno Blanckeman, Éditions de Minuit, 2014, pp. 59–92.

Viennet, Denis. "Animal, animalité, devenir-animal." *Le Portique*, nos. 23–24, 2009, pp. 1–11, http://journals.openedition.org/leportique/2454. Accessed 2 Aug. 2018.

Villeneuve, Denis, director. *Blade Runner 2049*. Warner Bros., 2017.

Villiers de l'Isle-Adam, Auguste. *L'Ève future*. Gallimard, 1993.

Vint, Sheryl. *Bodies of Tomorrow: Technology, Subjectivity, Science Fiction*. University of Toronto Press, 2006.

———. "Simians, Subjectivity and Sociality: *2001: A Space Odyssey* and Two Versions of *Planet of the Apes*." *Science Fiction Film and Television*, vol. 2, no. 2, 2009, pp. 225–250.

Voltaire. "Micromégas." *Romans et contes*, Flammarion, 1966, pp. 131–147.

Wakefield, Stephanie. *Anthropocene Back Loop*. Open Humanities Press, 2020.

Warczinski, Anne. *Luc Besson: entre exception culturelle et Hollywood*. 2013. Universität Leipzig, PhD dissertation.

Warren, Karen J. "Feminist Environmental Philosophy." *Stanford Encyclopedia of Philosophy*, 27 Apr. 2015, https://plato.stanford.edu/entries/feminism-environmental/. Accessed 23 Feb. 2018.

Waters, Alyson. "A Conversation with Éric Chevillard." *Music & Literature*, 26 Oct. 2017, https://www.musicandliterature.org/features/2017/10/26/a-conversation-with-eric-chevillard. Accessed 31 May 2021.

Welles, Orson, director. *The Lady from Shanghai*. Columbia Pictures, 1947.

Wells, H.G. *The Time Machine; The Invisible Man; The War of the Worlds*. Alfred A. Knopf, 2010.

"What Are Genome-Editing and CRISPR-Cas9?" National Institute of Health, MedlinePlus, National Library of Medicine (US), updated 22 Mar. 2022, https://medlineplus.gov/genetics/understanding/genomicresearch/genomeediting/. Accessed 20 Jan. 2023.

White, Nicholas. 2011. "Naturalism." *The Cambridge History of French Literature*, edited by William Burgwinkle et al., Cambridge University Press 2011, pp. 522–530.

Wilder, Billy, director. *Double Indemnity*. Paramount Pictures, 1944.

Witmer, Mark C., and Anthony S. Cheke. "The Dodo and the Tambalacoque Tree: An Obligate Mutualism Reconsidered." *Oikos*, vol. 61, no. 1, 1991, pp. 133–137.

Woerner, Meredith. "Why I Cried through the Fight Scenes in *Wonder Woman*." *Los Angeles Times*, 5 Jun. 2017, http://www.latimes.com/entertainment/herocomplex/la-et-hc-wonder-woman-crying-20170605-htmlstory.html. Accessed 23 Feb. 2018.

Wolfe, Cary. *Animal Rites: American Culture, the Discourse of Species, and Posthumanist Theory*. University of Chicago Press, 2014.

———. *What Is Posthumanism?* University of Minnesota Press, 2009.

Wolfreys, Julian, et al. *Key Concepts in Literary Theory*. Edinburgh University Press, 2006.

Wosk, Julie. *My Fair Ladies: Female Robots, Androids, and Other Artificial Eves*. Rutgers University Press, 2015.
Zeitz, Christian David. "Dreaming of Electric Femmes Fatales: Ridley Scott's *Blade Runner: Final Cut* (2007) and Images of Women in Film Noir." *Gender Forum*, no. 60, 2016, pp. 1–10.
Zola, Émile. Letter to J.H. Rosny aîné, 4 Nov. 1886. Box number 26: "Correspondance: dossiers classés alphabétiquement par signataire (R–Z et varia)." *Legs Borel-Rosny*.

Index

2001: A Space Odyssey (Kubrick) 87, 135, 151

the Absurd 18, 67–69, 75–76, 80–81
Académie Goncourt 24, 27
action films 124, 129, 133
adaptation 52–55, 84
Afrofuturism 155, 155–56n5, 159
AI *see* artificial intelligence
alien encounters 23–64, 82
Alien film series 80–81, 129, 135
alien Other
 body 44
 coexistence with 56–57
 confrontational encounters 32–33
 facelessness 26, 41
 fear of 34–41
 humans as 43
 love for 48
 posthumanist understanding 34, 51
 scientific observation 36–41
 seeing the face of 18, 41, 47–48, 61
aliens, cognitive estrangement 3
alternative realities 28–29n11
American "cultural penetration" 129–30
American science fiction 12–13, 14
 Golden Age of 33, 45
 scientific progress 99
 techno-optimism 153–54
 technology 103
Anglo-American science fiction
 hegemony of 12, 13
 human–alien contact 28–33
 posthumanist influence 7–8, 155–56
 shift away from 100–101
 techno-optimism 153–54
 translations 99
animal encounters 65–90
animal extinctions 54, 70, 73–82, 83–87
animal rights movements 7, 8
animals, human dependence on 54–55
animistic view, alien Other 35, 36
animot 72–73
Anthropocene 2, 4, 44, 46
 the Absurd 69
 alien Other and 47
 animal extinctions 75, 79, 88
 body and 54
 deep geological time 57
 ecology of 52
 evolution and 17, 27–28, 57, 60
 gender and 19–20
 humanist model 7
 identity and 137
 ideological perspectives 5
 language and 89

189

scaling up 136, 148
utopian outlook 154
Anthropocene back loop 82
anthropomorphization, alien Other 37–40
anti-humanist activists 7, 8
apes
  evolution 70, 73, 84
  medieval imagery 70
apocalypse 74, 75
art
  human extinction relationship 114
  mortality/immortality and 115
  technology as 114
artificial intelligence (AI) 94–95, 104–6, 108, 113–14, 116, 128
Asimov, Isaac 45
astronomy 31–32
"Astropocene" 44n26
atomic energy 52–53
auteurism 124, 135
autobiography genre 132n5
Ayerdhal 14, 16, 93–122, 153–54
  Demain, une oasis 97
  Étoiles mourantes 5, 19, 94–96, 103–22
  Mytale 97

B-movies 129
Badiou, Alain 11
Bakhtin, Mikhail, *Gargantua* 48
Balzacian realism 68, 69
"Ban" 105n15
bandes dessinées (BD) 17, 124, 131–35, 138
Barbarella film 132
Bardot, Brigitte 132
Barjavel, René, *Ravage* 98
Baudelaire, Charles 65
  Fleurs du mal 65
BD *see bandes dessinées*
Beauvoir, Simone de 19, 125, 127, 134, 142, 147, 159
  Le deuxième sexe 127, 137
Beckett, Samuel 68, 80, 101
  Happy Days 81
behavioral experiments 83–87
behavioral modification 67
Beineix, Jean-Jacques, *Diva* 143n15
Besson, Luc 14–15, 17, 123–50, 154
  Le dernier combat 150
  La Femme Nikita 124–26, 131n3, 136, 140
  The Fifth Element 5, 17, 19, 123–26, 131, 134–44, 153
  Lucy 5, 17, 19, 123, 125–26, 131, 135–37, 142, 144–48
  The Professional 133
  Valerian 131, 135
Bezos, Jeff 1, 93
Bilal, Enki, *Nikopol* trilogy 138n14
biohorror 80–81, 114, 117–18
biological enhancements 6
biotechnological experiments 67, 87–89
black bodies 8
Blade Runner film 128, 129
Blanc, Bernard 14, 15
  Pourquoi j'ai tué Jules Verne 1–2
bodily difference, fear of 117
bodily dysmorphias 80
bodily modification 10
body 48–51, 145
  animal extinctions and 75–76, 83–84, 86
  climate change and 54
  cybernetic enhancement 97, 140–44
  memory and 108–9
  space exploration 43–44
  transcendence 110, 147
  transhumanist manipulation of 145–47
  vulnerability 112
body–mind interface 94–122
Bostrom, Nick 6, 9
Boulard, Anaïs 67, 79

INDEX

Boulle, Pierre 73
   La Planète des singes 71–72
Boyer, Dominic 95, 128
Bréan, Simon 8, 15–16, 102, 119, 153
British colonial expansion 45n28
Bruckner, Pascal 156
Burroughs, Edgar Rice, *A Princess of Mars* 43, 137
Butler, Judith 147
butterfly effect 77–79, 82, 83

"Carrier Bag Theory" 151, 152n2
chaos theory 78n20
Charpentier, Emmanuelle 3n4
Chatelain, Danièle 27, 52, 58–59, 82
   Three Science Fiction Novellas 25
Chevillard, Éric 14, 16, 58, 65–90, 101
   Du hérisson 69
   L'Explosion de la tortue 69
   Palafox 69
   Préhistoire 69
   QWERTY Invectives 69
   Sans l'orang-outan 5, 18, 66–90, 93, 152–53
Chiva, Emmanuel 157
Christianity 32, 33, 127
Christin, Pierre 133
cinéma de qualité 131
cinéma du look 131n3, 143n15
cinematic male gaze 123
cinematic traditions 17
civilization 71, 84
Cixous, Hélène 7
Clark, Timothy 2, 4, 69
Clarke, Arthur C. 101n6
   Childhood's End 35
   The Sands of Mars 46n32
Clement, Hal, *Mission of Gravity* 101n6
climate change 53–54
Climent, Michel 130

Clustered Regularly Interspaced Short Palindromic Repeats (CRISPR) 3–4n4
Cocteau, Jean
   La Belle et la bête 129
   Orphée 129
cognitive estrangement 3, 66
Cold War 32
Colebrook, Claire 114
collapsology 156
Le collectif Zanzabar 155
colonial conquests 35
colonial expansion 45n28
comic forms 81, 85
comics 17, 124, 131–34, 145
commodification of culture 130
communicative alien encounters 29, 33
confrontational alien encounters 29, 32–33, 40
Connery, Sean 145
consciousness 73
contes philosophiques 11, 30, 71–72, 98
cosmic force, human as 44–47
countercultural movement 115
countergaze 123, 126, 139–40, 146
Cousin de Grainville, Jean-Baptiste, *Le Dernier homme* 74
creation stories 51, 127
CRISPR *see* Clustered Regularly Interspaced Short Palindromic Repeats
Crutzen, Paul 2
cultural containers 152
"cultural exception" 130
cultural mores, relativity 33
culture, commodification of 130
Curtis, Sheryl 97
Cuvier, Georges 60n62
cyberpunk SF 95, 97, 103
cyborg
   feminist criticism 136, 148
   Self and 142

theory of 125
  woman as 127–37, 139
cyborg bodies 19, 140–44
cyborg encounters 93–122
cyborg Other, facing 96, 116–21
cyborg societies 19
Cyrano de Bergerac 26, 29
  L'Histoire comique des États et Émpires de la Lune 29

dark humor 81
Darrieussecq, Marie
  Notre vie dans les forêts 158
  Truismes 80
Darwin, Charles 25, 40, 42, 54, 70
Daudet, Léon 98
'deconstruction' 9
deep geological time 52, 57–61
Deleuze, Gilles 7, 11, 69, 72n9, 87, 89, 96
Delevigne, Cara 133
Denis, Claire 159
  High Life 135–36
Derrida, Jacques 7, 9, 72–73
Descartes, René 6–7, 9
  Discourse on Method 73
desert imagery 137–38
devenir-animal 83
Dick, Philip K. 101
Diderot, Denis 11
"distributed cognition" 104–5
divinity
  aliens 35
  universe 42
dodo extinction 77–78
Doudna, Jennifer 3n4
Downey, Robert Jr. 145
"dream" device 59–60
Druillet, Philippe 132
Dunyach, Jean-Claude 14, 16, 93–122, 153–54
  Étoiles mortes 94
  Étoiles mourantes 5, 19, 94–96, 103–22

Earth, possessing 55
Ebiri, Bilge 144
ecological forces 85
ecological horror 80
ecological real 67
ecology
  Anthropocene 52
  of Mars 46n32, 47
Edison, Thomas 128
Éditions de Minuit publisher 68
Egyptian culture 138
Einstein, Albert 31
elegiac forms 75, 77
Éluard, Paul, *Capitale de la douleur* 100
embedded embodiment 96, 119, 149–50
"end of History" proposition 102
Enlightenment humanism 6–7
ethics, posthumanist 41–42, 122
eugenics 4n4
European Union enlargement 115
Evans, Arthur 15
evolution 17–18, 24, 28, 40, 42, 152
  animal–human link 85
  Anthropocene and 17, 27–28, 57, 60
  ape-human link 70, 73, 84
  of the body 48
  regression of 87
  scale effect 84
evolutionary ecology 27, 52
evolutionary science 25
evolutionary time 57–61
exceptionalism 33, 110
extinctions
  animals 54, 70, 73–82, 83–87
  humanity 55, 85, 114
  mass extinctions 59–60

face
  of the alien Other 18, 41, 47–48, 61
  ethical framework of 49
  humans 50

of the Other 18–19, 26, 28, 39–40, 47–48, 96, 107, 118
'fantasy' 101
fear
    of alien Other 34–41
    of bodily difference 117
female posthumans 123–50, 159
feminism 136, 148
femmes fatale trope 127–37, 146
Fermi, Enrico 53
Ferry, Luc 8–10, 154, 156
film noir 128
Finburgh, Clare 80
Fisher, Elizabeth, *Women's Creation* 152n2
"flagship species" 78
Flammarion, Camille 31, 74
    La Fin du monde 32, 74
    Lumen 31
    La Pluralité des mondes habités 31
Fleuve Noir Anticipation publishing house 68n6
The Fly film (Cronenberg) 80
Fontenay, Élisabeth de 72n9
Fontenelle, Bernard Le Bovier de, *Entretiens sur la pluralité des mondes* 28–29n11
Ford, Harrison 138
Forest, Jean-Claude, *Barbarella* 132
Foucault, Michel 7, 9, 72n9
fourth universe (*quatrième univers*) 42, 106
France
    countercultural movement 115
    modernization 99–100
Freeman, Morgan 146
French language 11–12, 27
"French Theory" 7, 8
"Frenchness" 129, 154
Freud, Sigmund 35, 71, 72, 84
Fukuyama, Francis 102–3

Gallic cyberpunk 103
Gaudreault, Marc Ross 43
Gaultier, Jean-Paul 124, 140
gender 19–20

gender transgressions 147
gendered archetypes 125, 128, 137
gene-editing tools 3–4n4
Genefort, Laurent 156–57
geological forces 44
geological time 52, 57–61
germline editing 4n4
Gernsback, Hugo 13
    Amazing Stories 12
Gide, André 66n3
Gittell, Noah 147
global view, SF 158
global warming 58n58
Glotfelty, Cheryll 157
Godard, Jean-Luc 124, 131n3
    Alphaville 100, 129, 144
God's existence 29–30
Gomel, Elana 28–29, 38–39
Goncourt, Edmond de 23–24
Goodall, Jane 71
Gormley, Michael J., *The End of the Anthropocene* 44n26
Gothic aesthetic 80
Graham, Elaine 3, 17
grotesque bodies 48
Guattari, Félix 69, 87
Gunn, James 12–13
    The Listeners 35

Haraway, Donna 19, 125, 127, 142, 148
    "A Cyborg Manifesto" 137
hard SF 24, 25n5, 31–32, 65, 98, 101
Hayles, Katherine 19, 96, 104, 117
Hayward, Susan 126
Heinlein, Robert 32–33, 45
    The Puppet Masters 32
Heise, Ursula 47, 57, 69, 75, 78, 158
Her (Jonze) 147
Herbert, Frank, *Dune* 137
heroic narrative 90, 151–52
Hexagonal SF 99, 129
history in SF 102

Hollywood film 124, 129–31, 134n10, 138n14, 141, 143, 145
Hoquet, Thierry, *Cyborg philosophie* 9n10
horror stories 80–81, 114, 117–18
Hottois, Gilbert, *Encyclopédie du transhumanisme et du posthumanisme* 9
Houellebecq, Michel 67
 La Soumission 158
human–alien contact 28–33
human–animal encounters 70–73
human animality 70–71, 72n9
human augmentation 9–10
human–machine interface 93–122
human–nonhuman–posthuman encounters 17–20
humanism 6–7, 9, 10–11, 149
Hummel, Clément 65
Huret, Jules, *Enquête sur l'évolution littéraire* 23
"hyperobjects" 58n58

identity, posthuman women 137
identity-based studies 7–8
immortality 93, 94, 109–11, 114–15
Indiana Jones film 124, 138
informational patterns 111
involution 87
Ionesco, Eugène 68
irony 82, 85, 88

Jenkins, Patty 134n10, 143
Jeunet, Jean-Pierre 135
Johansson, Scarlett 126, 133–34, 144, 147–48
Jovovich, Milla 133–34, 141
Jurassic Park (Spielberg) 129

Kafka, Franz 80, 101
Kelly, James Patrick 95n2
Kessel, John 95n2
killer story 151–52
King Kong film 70–71

Kipling, Rudyard, "The White Man's Burden" 45n28
Klein, Gérard 11
Kurzweil, Ray 5–6, 9, 111
 The Age of Spiritual Machines 6

The Lady from Shanghai (Welles) 128
Laloux, René, *La Planète sauvage* 129
Lamarck, Jean-Baptiste 25
Lang, Jack 130
Langlet, Irène 27
language 11–12, 72–73, 81–82, 89, 101
Lanuque, Jean-Guillaume 102
last man narratives 74
Lavery, Carl 80
Le Clézio, J.M.G., *Désert* 137
Le Guin, Ursula 69, 151, 152
Le Tellier, Hervé 158
 L'Anomalie 157
Lehman, Serge 16, 26
Levinas, Emmanuel 19, 28, 39–40, 41, 47–49, 148
life story 152, 155
Limite collective 101–2
literature, disappearance 81–82
littérature conjécturale rationnelle 66
Lorenz, Edward 78n20
love 48, 100, 107, 118–19, 125–26, 142–44, 146
Lovecraft, H.P. 80
Lucas, George 156
Lucy, *Under the Skin* (Glazer) 147
Lyotard, Jean-François 151

machine–human interface 93–122
machinisme 100
McKibben, Bill, *Eaarth* 47
Magerstädt, Sylvie 144
magnetism 31
male gaze 123, 125, 132, 134, 139
male objectivity 19
malleable human 5–11
man-made female 127, 129

INDEX

Mars 43, 46n32, 47
Marston, William 125, 143
mass species extinctions 59–60
The Matrix (Wackowskis) 111
Méliès, Georges, *Un voyage dans la lune* 129
memory 86, 108–9, 114, 118
le merveilleux-scientifique 15–16, 65
Mesmer, Franz 31
mesmerism 31
Messac, Régis 98
Métal hurlant comic series 132
metanarrative of technology 151, 153
metaphysical experiences 32, 33
Mézières, Jean-Claude 124, 133, 135
Miano, Léonara, *Rouge impératrice* 159
Michaux, Henri 66, 66–67n3, 68
microbes 54
Miéville, China 4
military applications 156–57
Milner, Andrew 13n17
mind–body interface 94–122
mind over body 145
Minsky, Martin 93, 111
Missa, Jean-Noel, *Encyclopédie du transhumanisme et du posthumanisme* 9
modernization 99–100
Moebius 124, 132, 135
Montaigne, Michel de 6, 9
Montellier, Chantal 132, 159
Moravec, Hans 10, 93
Mortimer-Sandilands, Catriona 75
Morton, Timothy 58n58, 95–96, 128
multiverse (multiple universes) 28n11
Mulvey, Laura 19, 123, 133
The Mummy (Freund) 138n14

narrative perspective 52, 58–59
natural history 32
Naturalism 23–24

Nature
  dominance over 33, 84
  technology and 153
neo-auteurism 124, 126, 131, 135, 145, 147
neo-noir thrillers 126
New Wave filmmakers 124, 130–31
Newton, Isaac 30, 55
Nguyen, Sophia 146
nouveau roman 68

observational alien encounters 29, 33, 36–41
origin stories 137–40
the Other
  face of 18–19, 26, 28, 39–41, 47–48, 96, 107, 118
  fear of 34, 36, 117
  humanism and 10–11
  Self and 36, 39–40, 41–42, 51, 118
  woman as 123
  see also alien Other; cyborg Other
Otherness
  feminism and 136
  human/nonhuman dichotomy 17
  of woman 143–44
Oulipo group 158
Ovid, *Metamorphoses* 127

Panique (Duvivier) 128
parallel dimensions 28n11
Perbal, Laurence, *Encyclopédie du transhumanisme et du posthumanisme* 9
'perfectibility' 7
Perrin, Jean 53
personae, AI 94, 108
"personality," alien Other 37
phenomenological realism 68
philosophy and literature 11–12
Pilote magazine 131–32

Planet of the Apes film franchise 71–72
Plato, *Timaeus* 28n11
Platonic-Christian thought 33
pluralism 28
Poetic Realists 130
poetic writing 49, 51, 65–66, 77, 100
political storytelling 100
Pomeau, René 30
Portman, Natalie 133
positivist science 33
possession 55
posthuman, definition 111
posthuman women 123–50, 159
posthumanism 5–11, 27–28, 34, 38, 158–59
   Anglo-American influence 155–56
   animal encounters 69–70, 74–75, 77, 84
   Anthropocene and 4
   body in 48, 50–51
   definition 10
   ethics of 41–42
   feminism and 136
   mind–body connection 94–122
   scale 57
   transhumanist synergy 19, 44, 52, 88, 148
Posthumus, Stephanie 4, 11
poststructuralism 7–8
prehistory 33, 56, 65, 69, 89, 151–52
psychological realism 68
psychological storytelling 100–101
punk aspects, cyborgs 95–96
Pygmalion impulses 127, 147

qualité française 131n4
quasi-divine alien encounters 29
quatrième univers (fourth universe) 42, 106
Queneau, Raymond 99

"radioactive era" 52, 53
Raiders of the Lost Ark film 138
Ransom, Amy 74
rationalism 6
realism 68, 69
reason 33, 148
"La Red Team" 156–57
relativity 33, 61
religion 41, 74, 75–76
Renard, Maurice 15–16, 65
Reno, Jean 133
ReS Futurae journal 27
Resident Evil film franchise 141–42
rhizomatic relationship, animal–human 83, 85
Richard, Olive 125
ritual 77
Rivalland, Mireille 154
Robinson, Kim Stanley 46n32
robot archetypes 128
Rogers, Adam 131
roman d'hypothèse 98
roman scientifique 65
Rose, Steve 131
Rosny aîné, J.H. 14–16, 65, 68, 74, 106, 115, 119
   alien encounters 23–64
   La Mort de la Terre 5, 18, 25–26, 28, 51–61, 74, 79, 152, 156
   Les Navigateurs de l'infini 5, 26, 28, 43–51, 80
   Nell Horn 23, 24, 65
   Les Xipéhuz 5, 16–18, 24–26, 28, 33–43, 48, 56, 60–61, 82, 85, 137, 148, 152–53
Rosny jeune, J.H. 23n1
Rousseau, Jean-Jacques 6–7, 9, 11
   Discourse on the Origins of Inequality 6

sacrifice 146
Sagan, Carl, *Contact* 35
Sartre, Jean-Paul 7
   Les Chemins de la liberté 11
   La Nausée 11
satire 90

INDEX

scale effect 58–59, 79, 84, 142, 148
scaled narrative perspective 52
scaling up 57, 124, 133, 136, 148
Schwarzenegger, Arnold 141
science, negative view of 98
science fiction (SF)
  devices 66
  first use of term 15
  as language 101
  shift from scientific fiction 16
  speculative nature of 3
scientific extrapolation 24–25, 27, 65–66
scientific fiction 16
scientific gaze 139–40
scientific method 33, 37
scientific observation 36–41
Self
  AI dissolving 116
  cyborg and 107, 142
  the Other and 36, 39–42, 51, 118
self-identity, female posthumans 125
sensorial experiences 103–4
Serres, Michel
  Le Contrat naturel 72n9
  Le Parasite 72n9
Servigne, Pablo 156
SF *see* science fiction
"SF awareness" 125
Shelley, Mary, *The Last Man* 74
Slusser, George 27, 44, 47, 52, 58–59, 82
  Three Science Fiction Novellas 25
social media 111
solarpunk 155
somatic gene editing 4n4
space exploration 43–44
space opera narrative 102–3
space-time
  fabric of 95, 105–6
  scale effect 142
special relativity theory 31
speculative mode 3, 78

speculative thinking 67, 157–59
Spitz, Jacques 98
Stableford, Brian 27
Stapledon, Olaf, *Last and First Men* 46n32
Star Wars films 124, 138, 140
Star Wars US strategy 156
steampunk 97
The Stepford Wives film 128
Stevens, Raphaël 147
storytelling and ideas 72
sublime 48, 49
subscendence 95–96, 123
superhero trope 131, 134n10, 140, 142–45
superiority logic 8, 33, 60
superstition 34–35
Surrealism 99, 100, 129
Suvin, Darko 3
Swendenborg, Emmanuel 31

tambalacoque tree extinction 78
techno-bodies 140–44
techno-optimism 1–2, 153–54
techno-pessimism 154
technological progress 87
technology
  as art 114
  biohorror and 80
  changing Earth 52
  Gallic cyberpunk 103
  hard SF 98
  human–animal rift 87–88
  machine–human encounters 93
  metanarrative of 151, 153
  the Other and 96
  transhumanist beliefs 5–7, 46
  women and 128
terraforming 46n32
"textual thickness" 97
Theater of the Absurd 18
Theory of Mind 39
thought experiments 3, 66, 158
time 32, 52, 57–61, 114, 134
  see also space-time
time travel 31

Todorov, Tzvetan 6
Tournay, Virginie 157
tragic forms 75, 81
transcendence 95–96, 108, 110, 147
transhumanism 5–11
   animal encounters 69–70
   Anthropocene and 4
   atomic energy creation 53
   body in 48, 145–47
   definition 9
   human–machine interface 95
   immortality quest 93, 109–11
   nature, overcoming 84
   posthumanist synergy 19, 44, 52, 88, 148
   power of humans 46
   Rosny's works 27–28
   universalism and 154
Trudel, Jean-Louis 97
Truffaut, François 124, 131n4
Tunbridge, Laura 147

universalism 154
universe
   divine manifestation of 42
   dynamic nature of 28, 42, 62, 63n65
   liminal pockets 63
utopian outlook 115, 154

Valérian et Laureline comics 133, 145
VanderMeer, Jeff 58n58
Varlet, Théo 98
Vas-Deyres, Natacha 115

Verne, Jules 1–2, 13–14, 24–25, 65–66, 93, 97
   De la Terre à la Lune 1, 14, 129
Versins, Pierre 66
Vian, Boris 99
Viart, Dominique 67
Villeneuve, Denis 137
Villiers de l'Isle-Adam, *L'Ève future* 127, 139
Vint, Sherryl 87
"violent projects" 136
Volodine, Antoine 158
Voltaire 26, 29, 72
   contes philosophiques 11, 30
   Micromégas 30
Vonarburg, Elisabeth 13
vulnerability of the body 112

Waked, Amr 145
Wakefield, Stephanie 82
Wells, H.G. 1, 15, 25–26, 32–33
   War of the Worlds 32, 34
Westworld series 128
Wiener, Norbert 10
"wokeness" 8–9n8
women
   in Besson's films 123–50
   as "containers"/"tools" 159
   Otherness of 143–44
Wonder Woman film 125, 134n10, 143
Wul, Stefan, *Oms en série* 129

Zola, Émile 23, 68
   La Terre 24
zoonotic diseases 54n48, 79